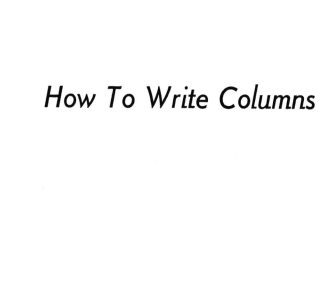

*How To Write Columns*

# How To Write
# *Columns*

Illustrated by

**Harry E. Walsh**

GREENWOOD PRESS, PUBLISHERS
NEW YORK

To the late J. J. Taylor, "State Press" of *The Dallas Morning News*. His memory endures as a benediction on the small-town press which he loved.

—O. E. H.

To Leon N. Flint of the University of Kansas, who guided me into columns.

—J. M. H.

# Foreword

THE ART OF COLUMN WRITING could be presented as a highly technical craft. Its trenchant tools of finesse might be analyzed: *Anachronism, synecdoche, onomatopoeia, hyperbole, alliteration, prolixity, pleonasm, periphrases* — these are some of the tools which might be illustrated and discussed.

These authors have chosen a less technical approach — and wisely. The result is a more readable and a more natural presentation. Their down-to-earth style is more interesting to the initiated and more helpful to the beginner. It is likewise more appropriate to the craft they are discussing.

Critics of the community newspaper are distressed about the declining vitality of the editorial page. A newspaper without vigorous editorials is likened to a man without a soul.

The growing popularity of the local column has helped to rejuvenate that soul and, more importantly, it has given many a community newspaper a heart. The authors explain in forthright manner how writers conceive, name, nourish and manipulate these periodical cardiograms of their communities. It is a book for and about columnists. It is a recognition of a thriving instrument of expression. It is a tribute to a growing army of some 8,000 philosophers who are attune to hinterland Americana. These community columnists are providing articulation for the philosophy of millions of readers. And they are having fun doing it.

Few people have studied columns and column writing as the authors of this book have. Their product is an entertaining and informative contribution to the journalist's bookshelf.

K. R. MARVIN
*Head*
*Technical Journalism Department*
*Iowa State College*

# Preface

THIS IS A "HOW TO" BOOK on the writing of personal columns for the newspapers of the towns and smaller cities of America.

The authors have drawn upon their backgrounds as former columnists and as readers and collectors of column materials. They have tried to catch the spirit and transmit some of the methods of the non-metropolitan writers in ways which shall, it is hoped, prove helpful to columnists now active and others who yet shall discover the effectiveness and fascination of this lively journalism.

The authors have blended, too, an enthusiasm for the columning art which they readily admit. They have watched small-town editors, too hard-pressed for time to do extensive research, find in personal columns a flexible instrument of comment, reader amusement, and promotion peculiarly suited to their daily routines. They have noted a growing resurgence of personal journalism and of editorial influence at the grass roots of America.

Column writing is a subject of obvious values but elusive details. Many niceties of style and concept are more often derived from example than taught. But this volume has been written in the belief that columnists of the smaller papers would welcome a guide-book prepared especially for them. This is it — a report to these columnists, with ideas and examples chosen not because they are "best" but because they are representative of the better practices.

The authors gratefully acknowledge their indebtedness to the many columnists who have permitted examples of their work to be used, and to others who have answered questionnaires and have written letters which enhance the value of this book.

For permission to use excerpts from copyrighted material, they wish to express their appreciation to the following:

Louisiana State University Press, publishers of *The Rural Press and the New South,* by Thomas D. Clark; the Curtis Publishing Company, publishers of the *Saturday Evening Post* articles, "Detroit's Sharpest Wit," by Robert M. Yoder, and "Panhandle Puck," by Jack Alexander; the Macmillan Company, publishers of *American Journalism,* by Frank L. Mott; Rinehart & Company, Inc., publishers of *Forty Years on Main Street,* by William Allen White; Alfred A. Knopf, Inc., publishers of *The Column,* by Hallam Walker Davis; Dodd, Mead & Company, publishers of *Plain People,* by E. W. Howe; the Department of Journalism Press, University of Kansas, publishers of *The Paragrapher's Sprightly Art,* by L. N. Flint; Iowa State College Press, publishers of *How to Write for Homemakers,* by Lou Richardson and Genevieve Callahan; also *The National Publisher, The American Press, Publishers' Auxiliary,* and *The Quill.*

OLIN E. HINKLE
*University of Texas*

JOHN M. HENRY
Des Moines *Register and Tribune*

January, 1952

# Table of Contents

*How To Write Columns*

# 1.

# Background of the Newspaper Column

IN A SMALL TOWN in Georgia an editor remarks that "Good fences make good neighbors comfortable while they gossip."[1] In Mississippi, another writer says "To me, a child is the only way of looking at the world of tomorrow and seeing what it will be."[2] A Kansas paper writes an amusing essay on what it means to mothers to have the kids back in school. A California editor is moved to verse by early fall. A Texas editor is eloquent in reminiscences of old cattle drives. In the Midwest, an editor lashes an errant city commission accused of neglecting the people's business.

These writings are entertaining components in the personal columns of the weeklies and small dailies of America. Preparation of these columns involves reaching a certain state of mind; an adjusted approach to living in the small-town manner

[1] By Raymond Duncan in "Sunrise Paragraphs," Ellaville (Ga.) *Sun,* April 19, 1951.

[2] By Carolyn DeCell in "Trimmed in Lace," Rolling Fork (Miss.) *Pilot,* February 2, 1951.

Socrates might have been the Lippmann of the Grecian press . . .

Last week we discovered a very satisfactory juke-box. It was busted.—Revere (Mass.) **Budget-News.**

— friendly, responsible, and as refreshing as a glass of cool lemonade handed a neighbor cutting his lawn on a sultry afternoon. Readers appreciate localized philosophy at the grass roots.

And the readership of these unpredictable collections of this, and that, and the other is terrific; up to 95 per cent, say the surveys.

"Everyone is a paragrapher; that is to say, everybody likes to make concise and pointed comments on the news of the day," wrote Professor L. N. Flint of the University of Kansas back in 1920.[3]

By the same reasoning, it may be demonstrated today that most persons are columnists, with or without benefit of printing presses. For columnists express subjective reactions to the news and circumstances of the day. People pick their targets as they will and use familiar column devices — humor, criticism, wisecracks, judgments, observations, philosophies, apologies. As a form of composition, the variety column is as natural as conversation, which it most resembles. Some one-subject columns are comparable to the declarations of a father, or teacher, or preacher.

A newspaper columnist has tenure; he supplies a certain amount of copy at agreed intervals. Before 1920, this material usually was humorous or semi-humorous. Today it includes anecdotes, short essays, reviews, editorials, reader contributions, comments on news, announcements, and promotions. Such a column may be general or specialized, staff written or contributed. It may express the policy of the paper or constitute an independent voice. It therefore takes rank as one of the newspaper's most flexible departments.

The scope of this book is largely limited to colum-

---

[3] L. N. Flint, *The Paragrapher's Sprightly Art,* p. 5. Copyright 1920 by Department of Journalism Press, University of Kansas.

ning in non-metropolitan newspapers. Writers in towns and small cities are not full-time columnists. Usually they are busy editors, reporters, housewives, and other people who write columns for the love of it, rather than for money. Moreover, the column content and writing style are determined by local conditions and the inclinations of the writers. They do not attempt to match sensations and subject matter with syndicate columnists — and this is not said in disparagement of small-town writers. Many of them are sharp writers, with keen insight. As a class they are improving steadily as they realize the literary possibilities in twenty inches of twelve-pica type, or even less. And the best of the small-town paragraphers take rank with any now writing in this country.

A pocket dictionary definition of a column was paraphrased by Leo Aikman of the Marietta (Ga.) *Cobb County Times* when he wrote in *Publishers' Auxiliary* that it was "any body pressing vertically upon a cut-off rule, with enough basic appeal to stand up." If printing had been invented earlier, he added, Socrates might have been the Lippmann of the Grecian press and Diogenes the Pegler of the Peloponnesus, on his search for an honest man.

If the beginnings of small-city columns could be traced in the literary forms which comprise them, a researcher would have to mention the sayings of wise men from earliest recorded times. He could not overlook the proverbs, parables, mottoes, and the poetic comments of every century. He would give close attention to the wits of the coffee houses and the anecdotes of wandering bards. As some have done, he would attach much importance in this regard to the works of Daniel Defoe, who was much quoted in the American Colonies and whose *Religious Courtship* is believed to have been the first

Someone has said that it is love that makes the world go round. Maybe that's so, but it is the little white lies that keep it in balance.—Eugene L'Hote, Milford (Ill.) **Herald-News.**

**COLUMN GRIST**

From colonial days to now, small-town readers have shown a lively interest in the unusual — the opposite of their quiet lives. Newspapers have obliged with news of oddities, freaks, unusual weather, s t r a n g e people, and remarkable lands. For decades, small papers clipped and reprinted such material, with credit or without. If by-lines were used on the longer features, they often were pen-names.

**BEN FRANKLIN**

Benjamin Franklin has been called the first American columnist of note. But first or not, or columnist or not, he had the style, the genius, the philosophy, and the productive capacity which the art requires. Interest in his writing has endured. He had a keen news sense and a flair for the unusual in subject and expression.

serial story in an American newspaper.[4] He would note the paragraph humor and philosophizing of Benjamin Franklin and other editors and reader-contributors of his time.

Frank Luther Mott says the first syndicated column in this country probably was the "Journal of Occurrences" edited by Boston patriots and distributed in the Colonies and in England in 1768–69. Containing news events of Boston, it emphasized suffering under British military rule. It lasted about ten months.[5]

But there is little reason to examine times and writings so remote. In the Colonial period of pamphleteering, editors did not embrace comment and controversy as legitimate and desirable newspaper content. Later periods of political controversy were to develop the ideas that editors are intellectual leaders and that a newspaper is hardly worthy of the name without an editorial page. However, the editorial essay as a form was firmly established by 1800 and some papers had regular departments, but not pages. The rural and frontier press had little space, few advertisements, and no dependable source of news. Still to be conceived was the idea that a small paper should confine its news mainly to local affairs.

The nineteenth century established most of the patterns familiar to newspaper readers today. The War of 1812–14 and the Mexican War starting in 1846 built up tremendous demands for news. It was the period, too, of the sweeping westward movements, expansion of the rural press, beginning of railroads, extension of telegraph lines, rapid growth of cities and improvement of printing methods. Then the Civil War and its violent controversies, followed

---

[4] Frank Luther Mott, *American Journalism*, rev. ed., p. 27. Used by permission of The Macmillan Company. Copyright 1950.
[5] *Ibid.*, p. 99.

by Reconstruction, made expression of opinion mandatory and profitable. Abundance of news whetted readers' curiosity and provided ample sources of subjects for comment. Upon this scene stepped the "great personal-editors" who were to profoundly influence public thinking for the rest of the century.

Meanwhile, weekly newspapers were increasing rapidly in numbers and in influence. But lacking news, they used much filler material, including ready-print sheets, serial articles, and shorts clipped from exchanges. Reprinting of filler material became so widespread that some names became known to millions. Of these, Mark Twain is best remembered. But in many cities newspaper men wrote popular satire, light essays, verse, and comments on the news. They created clownish characters, usually semi-illiterate, transparently hypocritical, and full of bragadoccio. Among these were Artemus Ward (Charles Farrar Browne of the Cleveland *Plain Dealer*), Petroleum V. Nasby (David Ross Locke of the Toledo *Blade*), Bill Arp (Charles Henry Smith of the Rome (Ga.) *Southern Confederacy*), and M. Quad (Charles B. Lewis of the Detroit *Free Press*).

"Most of these men capitalized their newspaper popularity on the lecture platform and books," said Frank Luther Mott. "They were the forerunners of the later columnists."[6]

In his studies of newspapering in the South, Professor Thomas D. Clark of the University of Kentucky found in yellowing files "many intimate explanations of why southerners have always behaved like they do." He added:

There is almost no end to the stories of a purely personal and local nature which were printed in the southern country papers. Somewhat unconsciously editors were contemporary historians serving faithfully the

---

[6] *Ibid.*, p. 394.

ends of posterity. . . . Through the magic door of their pages these editors made it possible to reveal the past in perhaps its most adequate form to a quizzical constituency of remote generations to come.

Concisely the southern rural paper has lived up, historically at least, to Bill Nye's declaration that it is an encyclopedia, a timetable, a poem, a history, a guide to politics, and a grand plan to a newly civilized world. A low-priced *multum in parvo*, it is a sermon, a song, a circus, an obituary, a shipwreck, a symphony in solid measure, a medley of man's glory and his shame. It is, in short, a bird's-eye view of all the magnanimity and meanness, the joys and sorrows, the births and deaths, the pride and poverty of the world, all for a few cents.[7]

Professor Clark wrote that in the reconstruction period fantastic stories, column-like in form, were used as filler material while real news was in short supply.

The southerner was fond of the unusual, the jocular, and most of all the everyday wisdom expressed in a continuous stream of editorial observations. . . . Bored with a solitary existence, the rural patron welcomed accounts of the unusual. Living close to the soil, the country man had a ready appreciation of freaks of nature which made periodic appearances. . . . One of the easiest ways for a constituent to get his name into the news, aside from getting married or shooting someone, was to discover and deliver to a newspaper office a freak of nature.[8]

Comparable patterns of editorial comment and jocularity were also developing in other sections of this country. As news became more plentiful, humor and light comment were drawn into regular departments as continuing features.

Professor Clark noted that "many of the editorials, special-feature articles, and news stories were written in a friendly vein, couched in the simple semi-illiterate vernacular of the backwoods community, and highly flavored with dashes of folk humor." Concerning Bill Arp, he wrote:

---

**BIG-NAME WRITING**

In building full-page editorial layouts, many city papers depended mainly upon syndicated writers. These "name" writers stabilized big morning-paper circulations, particularly in the Southwest and West. For example, the Fort Worth (Texas) **Star-Telegram** in 1926 carried these editorial page columns and features: "New York Day by Day," by O. O. McIntyre; "Punkinville Paragraphs," by George Bingham; "Uncommon Sense," by John Blake; "Your Folks and Mine," by Claude Callan; "My Favorite Stories," by Carolyn Wells; "Just Folks," by Edgar A. Guest; "Daily Editorial," by Glenn Frank; "Abe Martin," with sketch; "Little Benny's Notebook," by Lee Pape; "The Worst Story I have Heard Today," by Will Rogers; and "More Truth Than Poetry," by James J. Montague.

---

[7] *The Rural Press and the New South*, pp. 15–16. Used by permission of the Louisiana State University Press. Copyright 1948.
[8] *Ibid.*, pp. 40-41.

Arp's columns were dialetic, humorous, opinionated, and extremely influential. He was a master at interpreting the prejudices of readers all over the South, and of expressing them with exactness in the language of the semi-illiterate so as to mold the reader's thinking into a definitely limited provincial thought pattern which precluded any other explanation of an issue. . . . To understand the philosophy and methodology of Bill Arp is to grasp a fundamental knowledge of the intellectual development of much of the New South.[9]

Writing of column-like material developed gradually in the smaller papers but the larger, with their higher salaries and potentialities of fame, attracted the most outstanding humorists. A standout among these was Eugene Field, whose "Sharps and Flats" column was printed in the Chicago *Daily News* in the 1880's. Field had worked on St. Louis, St. Joseph, Kansas City, and Denver papers before Melville E. Stone hired him for the *News* in 1883. For twelve years, Field set a pace for wit, satire, and light verse which has never been excelled. He established a vogue and gave it weight because of his standing as a literary personality. Imitators were not long delayed.

The discovery that feature and filler material might be as saleable as news led to increasing syndication. Magazines sold material to small papers. Large papers syndicated their name-writers. Women's columns appeared. Sunday papers increased the demand for continuing features. Many of the best writers of the day saw their output distributed to small papers for a few dollars a week.

Syndication brought fame to still other columnists. Bill Nye founded the *Boomerang* in Laramie, Wyoming, and his humorous column got him a job with the New York *Sunday World.* J. Armory Knox and Alex E. Sweet

[9] *Ibid.,* pp. 32–33.

. . . higher salaries attracted outstanding humorists . . .

It's not how much you know but how little of it you tell that is important.—Kemmerer (Wyo.) **Gazette.**

went to the New York scene after running a humorous sheet in Austin, Texas. In Burlington, Iowa, the *Hawk-Eye* was made prominent by the humorous sketches and essays of Robert J. Burdette. A book of his essays, *The Rise and Fall of the Mustache,* was printed in 1878. Opie Read wrote homespun articles in the Little Rock (Ark.) *Traveler.* Joel Chandler Harris wrote his features, editorials, and Uncle Remus stories for the Atlanta *Constitution.* Soon came the period, too, of George Ade of the Chicago *Record* and *Daily News.* Finley Peter Dunne of the Chicago *Times,* and *Peck's Bad Boy.* Regular contributors were given special positions by many papers to facilitate make-up and to let readers know where the features would be found. Called "colyums," they were firmly established by 1890 and new departments were appearing every year.

Bert Leston Taylor of the Duluth (Mich.) *News-Tribune* became so well know for his wit that the Chicago *Journal* hired him, only to lose him to the Chicago *Tribune.* His "A Line o' Type or Two," signed B. L. T., made him one of the best known column conductors of his day. Taylor was followed on the *Journal* by Franklin P. Adams, who went on to great fame in New York with his "The Conning Tower" on the *Tribune.* Don Marquis established the "Sun Dial" in the New York *Sun.* Verse poured from the typewriters of Wilbur D. Nesbit, Walt Mason, and Edgar A. Guest. New York flowered as a center of columning.

Meanwhile, part-time contemporaries and predecessors of these professional columnists had strong followings in the smaller cities. Notable among these was E. W. Howe, publisher of the Atchison (Kans.) *Globe,* Ambrose Bierce of the San Francisco *News-Letter,* Louis T. Stone of the Winsted (Conn.) *Evening Citizen,* and James M. Bailey of the Danbury (Conn.) *News.*

What this country needs is a stork with a housing bill.—R. B. Lockhart, Pittsburg (Tex.) Gazette.

Many people think it unlucky to postpone a wedding. The superstition has no foundation as long as you keep on postponing it.—Cumberland (Wis.) Advocate.

The 1920's brought some changes in columns but no lessening of the popularity of established forms. In Chicago, B.L.T. died and Richard Henry Little took over "A Line o' Type or Two." H. I. Phillips shone on the New York *Herald Tribune* and Keith Preston won distinction on the Chicago *Daily News*. Richard Atwater was an outstanding by-line in the Chicago *Post*. Will Rogers was idolized by millions until his death in an airplane accident in 1935. Arthur Brisbane, who introduced his page one column "Today," in 1917, climaxed his long experience in building Hearst editorial pages by gaining even greater influence and earning more money than presidents.

Columns also took a sharper turn toward politics and other specialization, such as life in Washington, New York, and Hollywood, in the writings of Heywood Broun, Raymond Clapper, Walter Winchell, Dorothy Thompson, Westbrook Pegler, O. O. McIntyre, and others. Sports, music, drama, and literature were written up by other circles of columnists. Finally, columning became a popular avocation for the famous, including General Hugh S. Johnson, Dr. Frank Crane, and Mrs. Eleanor Roosevelt. Topflight writers also took to the radio, becoming commentators. Humor in newspapers declined, comics tended to become adventure strips, and cleverness in phrase-making became a commodity saleable to movies and radio. Columnists found it easier to ride the crest of the news, hire assistants, talk and write as if specially endowed, and predict the future. Bigname writers thundered in every metropolitan paper, echoed in syndicate form in smaller dailies, and reechoed in the "patent insides" of very small weeklies.

After 1920, column writing as an added duty became common on small dailies as well as large, and some weeklies date columns from that year, or before. The small-town press had long preferred the

To keep young, associate with young people. To get old in a hurry, try keeping up with them.—Moose Lake (Minn.) **Star-Gazette.**

A chrysanthemum by any other name would be a helluva lot easier spelled.—Wade Guenther, Sabula (Iowa) **Gazette.**

The modern husband doesn't ask, "What's cooking?" He leans on the deep freeze and inquires, "What's thawing?" — Overbrook (Kans.) **Citizen.**

The modern woman's place is in the home, working out a slogan for soap, soup, or baking powder.—Fairfield (Ohio) **Courier.**

barbed paragraph and the humorous editorial or sketch. Paragraphing reached an all-time popularity while the old *Literary Digest* was running a page of the briefs in every issue. Editors got a thrill out of seeing a paragraph in the *Digest,* and won local distinction and some national reputation by having many reproduced.

Jay E. House wrote in the *Saturday Evening Post* in 1925 that "the present day columnist is at once an evolution and a response to a simple human need. Biologically speaking, he is the get of the old-school humorist and the oldtime paragrapher. Curiously enough, the foal has few of the characteristics of either sire or dam."

Few of the paragraphers were given by-lines. The paragraphs were as impersonal as they were universal in application of their truths. And when the "great" editors disappeared from the American scene a pall of anonymity settled over the big-city press — now so big, so rich, so institutionalized. Still, people liked the human touch. Columnists of a new school stepped in gaily to fill the void, first with fun and then with "inside" information, gossip, and a great show of infallibility.

The personal column caught on slowly outside the big cities in the 1920's and 1930's. Busy newspaper executives did not think of themselves as humorists, nor did they relish the thought of baring their souls and philosophies to readers. Small-town printer-editors were conservative and while there were notable exceptions, many found ample outlets in short, biting editorials and paragraphs. News writing forms had jelled on big newspapers and in wires services and journalism classes. The idea prevailed that a newspaper worthy of the name should have formal editorials, some paragraphs, perhaps a political

"... few characteristics of either sire or dam."

cartoon, possibly a serial story and several syndicate features. The World War I impact was not as great as it would have been had not people thought victory meant a permanent return to peace and normalcy.

A depression and World War II brought significant evolution of the column, as will be described in the next chapter. Today newspaper men debate whether local columns, with their high readership and popularity, are detracting from effectiveness of editorials and institutional policy. At a time when significant changes are coming rapidly in communications, a closer examination of the column form of the printed word seems appropriate.

If the world laughs at you, laugh right back at it. It's as funny as you are.—Leonard Sekavec, Holyrood (Kans.) Gazette.

. . . a closer examination seems appropriate.

# 2.

# Significance of the Personal Column

It's the little things that make life sweet,
Like going to bed with uncold feet.
—Catherine M. Sheire,
Fairfax (Minn.) **Standard**

THE UNITED NATIONS, GUADAL, THE BULGE, and the plunging neckline were not the only significant milestones marking the middle of the century. Significant changes appeared throughout the decade; the old civilization would never be the same again.

Not the least among the things that came and made a difference were some 6,000 smaller-town newspaper personal columns. Six thousand, maybe more; no one's ever been able to count them. They kept coming; few disappeared. They came and were significant; significant not only to newspapers, but in public affairs, which influenced all of us. Significant also to education, because some of the columns were nothing less than literature.

In the bustling about of getting that war won, the smaller-town personal newspaper column got itself born without a birth announcement in the columns of the newspaper most concerned. It grew up in about the same casual way. Its birth was like that of Minerva, who sprang full grown and swinging from the brow of Jove.

The modern cautious lover checks into how steady she is in her job.—Gene D. Robinson, Loudon (Tenn.) **Herald.**

[ 14 ]

Readers adjusted themselves to postwar habits. They found themselves anticipating this wonderfully efficient, very personable newspaper column. Publishers noted, with maybe a little apprehension stratifying their pride in it, that the column was getting a lot of things done about the journalism house that they had been intending to do all these decades. Apprehensively they wondered if, in its efficiency, the column might elbow out of the way the old symbolic editorial column which may have been gathering more moss than readers.

Summing up: during the 1940's some 6,000 small-town American newspaper began using personal columns. Probably 2,000 already had them, so the total probably has grown to around 8,000.

These columns are significant in public affairs, because they are popular and because the columnist frequently is saying what the editor would say in an editorial column if he had one. So, these well-read columns contain comment by an editor or other writer who is in touch with what is going on and is qualified to comment.

These new columns are not all editorial comment, however. They are mostly entertaining or interesting. The editorializing is carried along with the entertaining or startling comment. They are like the radio program that entertains you and then slips across a commercial; or like the engaging conversationalist who enthralls you with his talk and then, without resentment or lessened interest by you, passes across a plug for this or that idea. Result: new millions of people read columns, including the editorial messages in them.

Readership surveys list the per-

**NOT SO LIGHT**

It is our studied belief that from no other source may one so clearly list to the speaking voice of the heart and soul of democratic America as by harking to the so-seemingly-lightly-written comments of the small-city editor or of the big-city columnist. Here is the voice of a free people unhampered by the restrictions of a predetermined editorial policy geared to meet business and political considerations. — Ray Murray in Buffalo Center (Iowa) Tribune.

. . . entertains you and slips across the commercial.

sonal column of today right at the top in popularity, with the possible exception of local news in which appears a wealth of names.

Since the very existence of the paper is based on popularity with readers, it is readily evident why the column is important. It is one more reason why people subscribe to the paper, and why they renew their subscriptions when they have expired.

Subscriptions enable the publisher to sell his advertising, pay his bills, keep publishing the paper. That is a very bread-and-butter, discount-your-bills reason for the growth of columns.

Another is the fact that the publisher likes to be influential, for the good it does his community, state, and nation, and for the benefit to his own ego.

Also columns contribute to education. They afford a pleasing and frequent contact with the public. That means a lot both in support of general school matters and more directly in adult education.

As to the column's significance in literature, evidence is there. Probably many professors — the purists among them at least — will insist that nothing written as hurriedly as a column, about such rural topics as a small-town columnist would note, could possibly be literature. But, if they could read, month after month, the hundreds of columns in the country press, they would know that the successors to Mark Twain are among the men and women who shove back the live ad copy once a week, push the exchanges off the desk, elevate their elbows, frown and grin, and peck out columns.

Many of the periodical creations contain immortal gems of narration, exposition, and description. Examples are found regularly in the writings of such columnists as Bernice Mc-

> Just because he was nice yesterday, women and dogs expect a man to be nice today.— Lebanon (Ohio) **Star.**

> A lot of people too polite to talk with full mouths will go around talking with empty heads. — Coloma (Mich.) **Courier.**

**As to columns' significance in literature . . .**

Cullar of Georgia; Earl Tucker of Alabama; Duke
Norberg, LaVerne Hull, Kay Metz, and Duane
Dewel of Iowa; Giles French, Oregon; Florence Stone
and Clarke Sanford, New York; two dozen Kansans
("every Kansas editor fancies he is a columnist");
Mrs. Gene Davis and Opal Melton, Missouri; Hazel
Murphy Sullivan, Wisconsin; and Nelson Brown of
Michigan.

> It's an awful feeling, when
> you attempt to kid somebody
> and discover he is taking you
> seriously.—Ralph S h a n n o n,
> Washington (Iowa) **Journal.**

Yes, columns sprang full-grown as from Jove's
brow; or better, if from Mars Minerva did her spring-
ing, because it was in war that so many new personal
columns had their origins.

Dozens on dozens of the columns had the same
birth and early case histories. Because of the shortage of help, the editor or pro tem editor was getting
along as best he or she could. This meant taking
every shortcut possible. There were numerous war
projects he wanted to help along, bond sales, Red
Cross, and such. The publicity material about these
he put together with some personal comment in a
column to which he gave a title while swallowing a
fourth cup of coffee. As time went on, he added
comment on this and that. The column was a very
handy place to dump the things he didn't have time
to arrange for publication elsewhere. This made the
column pretty much of a hodge-podge, but no one
seemed to worry about that.

When the war ended and help became more
plentiful, the editor tried to liquidate the column.
But the readers wouldn't let him.

The wartime experience of Earl Tucker is indicative of the popularity of columns. Earl is like most
other small-town editors; he's a printer. When most
all his help left during the war he became a fulltime
printer. And all, absolutely all, the local news, comment, anything that appeared in his Thomasville, Alabama, *Times,* was in his "Ram-

**The column was a very handy place to
dump things . . .**

**PAGE OPPOSITE**

Big newspapers have developed the "page opposite editorial page" as the location of feature articles, big-name writers, and background material. Columns found there are of personal opinion, specialized comment, and entertainment values. Small newspapers usually must disperse such material or omit it altogether. Yet some small-city papers give space to many columnists, mostly local. These column personalities include the thinkers, the boosters, the humorists, the spice-and-variety boys, the hobbyists, the sports commentators, the farm agents, etc. Each regularly turns out a more-or-less fixed amount of space-filling, reader-p l e a si n g material. The best of the output is worth wide reprinting.

bling Roses and Flying Brickbats" column. Five daily papers circulated in the town, two of them with local correspondents. Despite that competition, and with no solicitation by Mr. Tucker, his circulation total at the end of the war was even with that at the start.

After the war, many people expected the columns to fold up. But when they survived, the analysts began to examine them. A new recognition of their worth became evident. Many of the columns were intimate, personalized chats with readers, like gossiping over the back fence with a neighbor. They were varied. They offered more emotional release than the cold news columns and editorials. They throbbed with life of the community. Readers anticipated what the home town columnist would say about an event. They frequently turned to the column first when the paper came. They noted and quoted. Advertisers asked to have their messages run alongside the column. When the columnist left on vacation readers asked, "Who will write the column?" and "When will he be back?" In many a small-town newspaper "the column" became as stable a community insignia as the clock in the court house tower — and more intimate even though less predictable.

The state press associations began giving awards for the best columns in dailies and weeklies. Some associations made the division as between columns written on one topic and several topics — a division used in the first-place award of the National Editorial Association contest.

The metropolitan papers are quoting the smaller-town press columns as never before. Several have begun putting such quotations over in the literati and arty parts of their magazine sections.

At about the same time the metropolitan papers began quoting the smaller press more liberally, the national magazines started using small-town quotes at the bottom of back pages. A little later some of them boxed the quotes in the middle of a page, offering an earned prominence.

Perhaps the most significant recognition of the small-town columns came in 1949 when *Cosmopolitan,* certainly not a publication given to ruralities as such, instituted a page devoted to the small-town sayings. This was given even billing with quotes from the metropolitan columns.

Now there's scarcely a national magazine of general appeal that does not use some small-town column material.

So the war baby with the neglected adolescence now becomes a candidate for newspapering's Miss America.

**THRILLING EXPERIENCE**

We rate being a columnist on a little country weekly newspaper in Iowa as being one of the most satisfying, outstanding, and thrilling experiences of our life.—Florence Laffer in Correctionville (Iowa) News.

# 3.

# *Naming a Personal Column*

**"Words are things . . ."**
—BYRON

MORE THAN ONE COLUMNIST, one of these authors included, has fashioned a column heading around this Byron quotation. One column was "Words" in large hand-drawn letters, boxed, with the quotation above inserted in small italics.

To think of a clever heading is to wish to write a column. Conversely, many a column is aborted because the would-be writer has thought of no suitable heading. Of course one can call upon the public, which names everything from gasoline to movie actors. But there is satisfaction in choosing one's title after days of toying with ideas. Type and rule can be used in the heading, or commercial artists can supply hand-drawn art titles.

One could emulate the columnist who launched his department without a name. "Don't Name It"

Of course, one can call upon the public . . .

was the temporary heading. Several years later the same heading was still in use. This was no worse, perhaps — and no better, either — than the no-name cafes frequently seen on transcontinental highways.

Standing headings quickly win acceptance by readers, who then characteristically resist change. One of the several conductors of "Random Thoughts" columns was elected county surveyor and asked readers to vote on the old name versus "Surveying the Situation." The old title won, 1,040 votes to seven.

Column headings are seldom duplicated in the same region, but titles are seen in scores of papers which have no overlapping of circulation. Doubtless some of this duplication is accidental rather than imitative.

Titles initially attract readers by their newness and sometimes by their uniqueness. They also identify the writers, suggest the type or content, or associate content with places. Some suggest that the writers are modest to a fault. These titles include "Chatter," "Idle Talk," and similar vagaries. Yet some very sound prose is written under titles which seem to promise only trivia.

Requisites of a good column name include:

1. Brevity, so it will fit in one or two columns.

2. Exclusiveness, at least in a circulation area.

3. Aptness, in that the heading suits the content, the personality of the writer, the locale, etc.

4. Appropriateness. It is not enough to be merely clever and original. Columns must wear well.

Some headings suggest a design. Examples are "Circling the Square," with a circle inside a rectangle; "Circling Around," "Milling Around," "Short Shavings," and many others not necessary to mention. Points of view are indicated by "From the Crow's Nest," "From the Top of the Windmill," and "Getting Out on a Limb."

**COINCIDENCE**

A couple of Nebraska columnists had the same idea in naming their columns. Jack Lough, editor of the Albion **News,** named his column 'The Loughdown.' Jack Lowe of the Sidney Telegraph then called his 'The Lowe Down.' Remarkable coincidence, eh! We suggest one of them change. Ideas we have to offer include: How Lowe Can You Get, Swing Lough, Lowe'n Ranger, Un-Lough-ded, Lowe Cowe, and Lough Man on the Totem Pole. —Bill Greenless, Garden City **News.** Oshkosh, Nebraska.

I like wrinkles in people's faces. Nearly always they were put there by work or by laughter, or both, and each necessary to genuine neighborliness. — Willcox (Ariz.) **News.**

IT SEEMS TO ME:

Settin Front The Fire by Cliff Pither

About
ENNIS
With Weldon
THE ENNIS DAILY NEWS

AROUND
TOWN
SIGHTS, FACES
SEEN

a shot of SCOTCH
by L.S. Mc.

Talk
of the
TECHE

Deck's
DIDACTICS

GETTING OUT
On The
LIMB
By
EDDIE the EDITOR

Down by the
SYCAMORE

TUMBLEWEEDS
By Jean

The
Editor's
Say-
So

The Century Expressed
(Or 50 down & 50 to go)

These
Things
We
Note

Dear Readers:

THE
BREWERY
GULCH
PHILOSOPHER
SAYS —

Simple Stuff
By THE EDITOR

"DIRTY
DIGS"
BY
W.G. EUBANKS

Under headings like the above, 8,000 columnists write every week with verve and wit.

Columns also call attention to the writers' names or pen names. The "Tactless Texan" becomes Old Tack. "Annegrams" identifies the writer, Ann England. Others are "Aunt Lou's Scrapbook," "Billbored," "Claud's Comments," and "From A to Izzard." "The Woman in the Shoe" is appropriate; she has six children.

Place identification appears in "Bull Creek Philosopher," "About Ennis," "Dillon Doodlings," "Homer Hometown," and "Paducah Prattle." "Don Pedro Says" suggests a Latin environment.

Some of these names are indicative of little high concentration at midnight. Columns often have the casual nature of their headings. We see "Huntin' and Peckin,'" "Things 'n Stuff," "Of This, That, and the Other," and "Simple Stuff." We read "Toonerville Toots," "Pi-Lines," and "Sunshine and Shadows."

We also catch the thought of a busy but contemplative editor taking the time to write a letter to his people. We find "The Editor's Corner," "The Editor's Column," "The Editor's Desk," and many others. We see "Hastings Thinks," "So We Think," and just plain "Think." And there are "Deck's Didactics," "Brain Storms," and "It Seems to Me."

A literary tone is suggested by "Trail Dust," "The Spectator," "Sand Dunes," "Musings," and "A Style of My Own." Chamber of commerce influence in "Going Forward With Eastland." A built-in apology is provided by "Maybe We're Wrong," "You Might Doubt It," and "Slicing It Thin." Farm life situations are promised in "Mrs. Poke Bonnett." There are no inhibitions in "Rips and Tears." And the English language is typically reversible in "On the Record" and "Off the Record"; also in "On the Cuff" and "Off the Cuff."

Name-values and the intimate exchange of small

---

**COLUMN NAMES**

Some additional column titles seen recently:
"That's My Q."
"I Could Be Wrong."
"FYI—for Your Information."
". . . Son-of-a-Gun."
"WAGGING of a Loose Tongue in an Empty Head."
"Type Ticks."
"Swabbing the Deck."
"Old Inky Sez."

Inflation is an economic condition which enables two 5c cigars to go up in 25c worth of smoke.—Chilton (Wis.) **Times-Journal.**

This is the season when you can't tell whether the lady has a chigger bite or a crawly girdle.—St. John (Kans.) **News**.

talk are implied in "About People You Know," "Around the Coffee Table," "Between You and Me," "Dear Folks," and "Mostly About People." "The Gay Philosopher" is a bit gayer than most columns. There's complete candor in "Fact and Fancy — Let the Wise Man Make the Distinction." You have to read the columns to catch the spirit of "Getting Out on a Limb" and "Not Kidding." A few columns are "Offhand" and we find some readers "Following the Sheriff's Trail."

"Generally Speaking," however, a column title doesn't indicate accurately the content. Here are some unique titles chosen from a much greater number of availables:

Here are more titles . . .

| | |
|---|---|
| Sideswipe and Scramble | HYN? |
| Snooter Knows | Sass and Bull |
| Why? | Dirty Digs |
| Column One | The Brewery Gulch |
| Pot-Pourri | A Shot of SCOTCH |
| Eighter From Decatur | Flicks and Flips |
| Girl of the Gumbo | Static |
| Grumblings | Chips and Slivers |
| Etaoin and Shrdlu | Caught in the Web |
| The Eagle's Eye | Around the Edges |
| The Hell-Box | Read 'Em and Weep |
| Hereford Bull | Reflections in a Star |
| In the Dog House | Sek's Appeal |
| PATter | Tom and Pete—the Home Towners |
| Polk Street Professor | 12th Street Rag |
| Rambling Roses and Flying Bricks | The Grin Reaper |
| 'awkins Talkin' | Shinglediggins |
| | The Horse Fly |

Even stranger titles come to hand. One is "Fool Column." Another, picturing a balding editor at his typewriter, shows a number of cartoonist's balloons filled with "Why?" But the most unusual of all ran for a time in the Lexington (Ky.) *Herald*:

### BLUEGRASS AND HORSE FEATHERS
#### "The Bluegrass Isn't Blue and the Horse Has No Feathers, but Half You Know 'Ain't So'"

# 4.

# Typography and Position

MOST NEWSPAPER COLUMNS are easy to read, and their appeal is broader than that of most other journalistic offerings. Readers approach them in a spirit of relaxation, often before they have seen any other part of a paper. Yet these readers are alert for novel ideas, chuckles, arguments, and barbed comment.

The columnist's style and his message should not be impeded by the typography of the material. Readers should "hear" his characteristic tones and get his ideas without being aware of type faces as such. They should be aware of his emphatic phrases without noting his indentions, bold-face type, and other mechanical factors. There should be no squinting at type which is too small, too dim, or over-inked. And typographical errors put a proud columnist in an undignified position.

Typography is not of first importance in column conducting, but it is worth some study. Readability is a timely subject in this age of radio, television, facsimile, colorful magazines, and other rivals for readers' attention. Recent studies have shown that

**TYPE**

Old-style Roman type is still preferred for straight matter in columns. It is a part of the heritage of everyone who attended the public schools. It carries the columnist's message without ostentation and with maximum readability. Type for column headings must be selected for character count and size, or it can be hand-drawn and sized by the engraver's camera. Such type, however, can be chosen from contemporary families which suggest the personal message of handwriting — from delicately feminine to rugged masculine. However, column names sometimes demand typography which illustrates a clever idea. Again, it is best to call in a competent artist.

**Roamin' the Range**

# Farmer Peck's Wife
Down on the Farm of
Mrs. Ray W. Peck

# TRAIL DUST
By
DOUGLAS MEADOR

Sketchbook . . .

*Circling* THE SQUARE

SHORT *and* TALL tales
By FRED KORTE

Baker's Dozen

~Girl Of The Gumbo~

IN OUR VALLEY

**Just About** *Anything*
•
By Bob Crompton

"Our Town"
*by*
J. B. WHITE

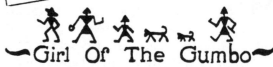
DOWN in COCHISE COUNTY

*Around* OUR HOUSE
by Kathryn Tucker Windham

Looking 'Em Over
FROM WEEK TO WEEK
WITH W. H. C.

"CLIMBIN' FENCES"
•
By BOB GREGG

Typical column headings

readers use almost any excuse — even a subhead or a bold-face paragraph — to leave a story in which their interest lags. But, on the other hand, gray body type is a monotone not very well suited to a column's change of pace.

Column typography involves the headings, body type, illustrations, spacing and width, dashes, by-lines and signatures, position, and various other factors. Usually it is letterpress printing which is involved. Columnists of offset papers could, however, achieve unusual effects — sketches, marginal notes, etc. — at little added cost.

Columns are not likely to be better printed than other parts of a paper, although at their inception special art work may have been bought for the headings. These standing heads are too often neglected. Zincs may be damaged and casts may be worn and not replaced. Engraved lines may be so fine that they quickly become clogged with lint, dirt, and ink. Yet there are many well maintained headings which are bright and clean year after year. Some state press associations have instituted campaigns to clean up nameplates, mastheads, ears, signature cuts, and standing heads.

Enthusiasm for a column heading is usually high in the beginning. However, some clever headings, like some gaudy store fronts, do not retain their appeal. Like a catchy song, a heading may offend by too much attention to its devices. A less original heading may prove easier to live with.

Long headings may be workable in two columns, but not in twelve picas. Very short ones may be difficult to set in foundry type, although they are quite useable in art work. Of several hundred column headings within the view of this writer at the moment, fewer than half are constructed of machine set slugs or foundry type. The type headings usually

A Kentucky school superintendent fired five times at a burglar, but missed him every time. The professor needs to do some reviewing on trigonometry. — Thomaston (Ga.) Times.

Applause is about the best interruption we know. — Napoleon (Ohio) Signal.

Think twice before you speak—especially if you intend to say what you think. — Rothsay (Minn.) Argus.

## The SPECTATOR
* * *
SCOUTS PLAN TRIP
* * *
STARTS NEW FEATURE
* * *
SCHEDULE GIVEN
* * *
ROTARY OBSERVES XMAS

'awkins Talkin'

"I know not what the truth may be,
I only tell it as it's told to me." Anon

Most columns are twelve picas wide.

have full or partial rule borders. The tendency is away from full borders.

Most columns are twelve picas wide. Not many words can be used in this width. Yet the column frequently must, in make-up patterns, have the strength of a top-of-column headline. Heading combinations in type include:

1. A single word, centered. If a long word, it usually is in caps and lower case; if short, it likely will be in all-caps. For contrast, this type should differ from the faces of the headline schedule if the units are to be positioned together.

2. Two lines, centered or flush left. One of these may carry only the word *the*. The second may be in all-caps to even it with the two sides or the top line if full.

3. Odd effects, such as setting the first and last letter of a word in caps larger than the rest of the word. The appearance usually is artificial.

4. A similar effect, with one large capital standing as the first letter of two words.

5. Ordinary type, but jumbled or otherwise twisted into irregular shapes.

6. Cursive type, to suggest the personal touch of hand-written words.

7. Combinations with halftones or art work. In some of these the type is foundry or machine; in others it is in hand-drawn imitation of foundry type. Reversed cuts give a harsh look, but reversed type in halftone shades is currently popular.

Caricatures of columnists, done in line cuts, are fairly common. They print well, and last longer than small halftones. Some have large heads and small bodies.

Artist-made headings are flexible and may better suggest the tone of a column. However, in too many cases some free-lance letterer has only the words of

**VARIATIONS**

Column headings need not always look the same. If the columnist's picture is in the heading, or his caricature, the people will not expect a change of face. Why not surprise them by running a smiling face when news is good — very good — and a wry face when news is bad; a brow-mopping face when it is hot, a steam-blowing face when it is cold. . . . A few papers have lately introduced changes in nameplates, reflecting the weather, and some have run raindrops across Page One after a long awaited downpour.

Educated is that which if a school teacher isn't he is sure gonna be when the students get done learnin' him. — St. John (Kans.) **News.**

### ILLUSTRATIONS

Type masses in columns can be broken up by pictures, but halftones seldom are effective in small size. Full-width cuts interrupt reading of the type, while sliver cuts reduce detail too much, with the single exception of a large head. Of all illustrations, the line cut prints best in most newspapers. But even here the lines must not be reduced too much.

The shortest perceptible unit of time is that between the traffic light's change and the honk from the driver behind you.— Niagara Falls (N. Y.) **Review.**

the column before him and no appreciation of the make-up of the paper as a whole. In his inexperience he may make the lines too thin, or too black, and the sketch too deep. A heading designed for two columns in width may not be appropriate in one-column reduction. The artist should know all the facts. These include a knowledge of the headline schedule and of the position in which the column will be run.

Columns run on Page 1, or alone elsewhere, can stand out sharply and still be in good taste. But on an editorial page it may be desirable to achieve a common motif in the standing heads. Cuts drawn from stock and from advertising services may be lacking in harmony with a paper's basic typography. Small line cuts surrounded by white space appear amateurish. Boxing them may be necessary.

In many line drawings one finds a chamber of commerce influence. In one are palm trees, citrus fruits, cotton, oil wells, and three types of transportation. That columnist is proud of his valley. In another a line cut of a cowboy and horse has an up-thrown lariat which ropes the type of the word "Round-up."

Column headings of type and rule can be made up in small print shops, but typography of distinction or unusual effects can be done better in specialized composition shops. The added cost of a heading done by people who serve advertisers and advertising agencies is an investment in appearance, satisfaction, and sustained readership.

Printers who fashion heads in small shops should bow to the requirements for harmony or harmonious contrast. Both in type and in rules, weight harmony and design harmony are important. One sees too many black rules combined with delicate scripts and too many thin rules with heavy type. Similarly, straight borders which may harmonize with the sans serif and square serif types may appear stiff and out of place when used with scripts and cursives. Although headings are not bound to the close harmonies of a headline schedule, they do not have the freedom of advertising blocks, which may be isolated in white space.

Rhythm is a desirable quality in standing heads running on the same page. This may be carried out through repetition of a type, a wavy rule, a black dot, a thumbnail cut, or other typographical device.

Perhaps it should be added here that column headings are subject to the laws and rules of English and headline structure. Split phrases, dangling modifiers and prepositional endings usually are avoided. Nevertheless, contractions and coined words are sometimes used.

Newspapers having more than one edition sometimes use column headings in more than one width. If it appears on Page 1 daily or at mid-week in twelve picas, it may change to two-column width on Sundays. Sometimes the change is accompanied by variations in content. Features are favored in the wider width, although sometimes the type is raised to ten-point and set two columns wide. A rather rare innovation is the reduction of a column heading to about six picas so that it may be used as an inset byline on special features by the same author. A highly popular columnist no doubt could pull much of his following with any printing of his headings, but some discretion is advisable. Reprinting of column headings and some body type in advertising is noted, especially when a columnist interviews a merchant on his trip to market.

### FEW DEVICES NEEDED IN BODY TYPE

An ordinary conversational tone is represented by body type. It is good enough for the folksy style of most columnists, providing paragraphs are short. A

Trying to talk to farmers nowadays is like trying to rope a yearling in a five-section pasture on foot. They are as busy as a bobtail mule in fly time, trying to get in their wheat between thunder showers. — Amarillo (Tex.) **Globe.**

Another thing about being poor is that your kids in your old age don't break your heart by asking a court to declare you incompetent. — Lawrenceburg (Tenn.) **Democrat-Union.**

minimum of odd effects makes reading easier. Tricks are poor substitutes for clever words. However, printing of an animated conversation, talk, or argument requires some evidence of spirit. Type is flexibly suited to these distinctions of tone. Some standard devices of the typographer include:

1. *Indentions.* Indenting an occasional paragraph provides a break in the regularity of typography, but readers will attach more importance to indentions if the subject matter is varied. To give unusual treatment to an ordinary statement is another version of crying "Wolf!"

**2. Bold-face. Emphatic statements, key paragraphs, and certain types of recurring material are more effective in bold-face type, usually indented. But blackened type is lower in readability and should not be used lavishly. Variations are use of bold-face in single words, names, top lines, and phrases the columnist wishes to emphasize.**

*3. Italics. Italic type is unavailable in body type size in many small shops. Effective for emphasis on single words or phrases, it is hard to read in full paragraphs.*

4. *All-caps.* Used occasionally, these may be quite effective in either light or bold faces. BUT ALL-CAP LINES ARE HARD TO READ AND IN GENERAL SHOULD BE AVOIDED.

5. *Initial letters.* These take more time to set, and time is not as plentiful in small shops as many people imagine. A single initial may dress up the first paragraph of an essay-type column. It usually is followed by two or three words in all-caps. (See the initial letters used in this book at the opening of each chapter.) Sometimes an initial letter is used whenever the

Yes, Mrs. Gildersleeve, our girdles come in five sizes . . . small, medium, large, WOW, and YE GODS! — Craig (Colo.) Empire-Courier.

. . . Time is not as plentiful in small shops as many people imagine.

subject changes. Use of such a letter in every paragraph destroys the effect.

6. *Leading.* Most columns are set in body type with normal leading. Seven or eight-point type leaded one point is most often found. Ten-point type, set in 18-pica or 24½-pica width, can take two points of leading. Nine-point type on a ten-point base is seen. Body type set solid gives a crowded effect.

7. *Dashes.* Some publishers have dropped all dashes; others would as soon leave off their neckties at church. Some columnists devise ornamental dashes — names, initials, slogans, etc., centered in agate type. One paper uses five "z"s centered. The connotation seems dubious. In lieu of dashes, some printers substitute ornamental dots, paragraph signs, stars, short lengths of Oxford rule, and combinations of dashes and "o"s. An effect which calls attention to itself may be good promotion, but bad typography.

8. *Numbering.* One columnist runs thirteen numbered items each week. The reason is found in his title, "Baker's Dozen." Similar are "Six Bits."

The over-all typography of a column should be suggestive of its contents. If paragraphs are short and subject changes frequent, some indenting or other use of contrast may be desirable. Sparkling prose, however, needs only the eye relief of short paragraphs to be well read. A variety column offers more opportunity for innovations within the spirit of the subject matter. Use of a short poem or several one-sentence pithy paragraphs has much to recommend it. Cluttering a column with typographic oddities wins no applause from an average reader, especially after the newness wears off.

In most small papers, use of line and halftone cuts in columns and editorials is rare, although the sepa-

Dachshunds are not to be recommended as pets this time of year. They keep the door open too long, going in and out, thereby letting in flies.— O. C. Kelley, Onawa (Iowa) Sentinel.

A man, getting his first peek through the Palomar telescope, exclaimed, "God!" A professor turned to him and said, "Pretty good telescope, isn't it?" — J. O. Jewett, Fairfield (Calif.) Republican.

To live longer and healthier and get ahead in the world, stop thinking so much, a British surgeon advises. That's something to think about.—Wellington (Tex.) **Leader.**

Just as I swore I d quit using puns, a Texas judge sends a girdle thief up for a stretch.—Al Hinds, Paducah (Tex). **Post.**

Some men are known by their deeds, others by their mortgages.—Berkeley (Calif.) **Courier.**

rate editorial cartoon — usually syndicate — is not hard to find. And the readership of news photos is everywhere recognized. People who do no more than glance at the title of editorials might be persuaded to stop and read if pictures made the subject more challenging. Columnists sometimes use small line cuts from advertising services. Stock cuts are offered by engravers in great abundance. These are topical, but not timely in the usual sense.

You're writing about dogs? Why not insert a small cut of a dachshund, fox terrier, or some other pooch? And hats? Cuts are available to suggest most any shade of opinion — yours — about hats. You also will find assortments of stars, dots, flags, mistletoe, and ornamental borders. These are for the special occasions when the ads are colorful in seasonal illustrations.

Inquiring photographers have long made use of thumbnail cuts. Alone, they cost as much as a twelve-pica cut. An economy procedure is to mount a row of pictures of uniform size, order one cut, then have your tinsmith snip the cuts apart. Or you can order a mat, make a cast, and saw the cuts out in the composing room. A one-column cut may be inserted in a column, but some writers object to its bulk as compared to the heading. However, such cuts can be run alongside a column and reference made to them.

When columnists turn promoters they need the punch of graphic presentations. A map may be demanded. When a campaign lags, a "thermometer" of progress may be made of type-high rule. A resourceful columnist can think of many devices. And when it is time to extend Christmas Greetings, he may fill an entire column with a 72-point "MERRY CHRIST-MAS" with the word spelled vertically. But a year later he will have an entirely different typographical device.

The typography of by-lines reveals no standard practice. Most columnists are well-known. They may use an ordinary by-line, but popular substitutes are "Mac's Musings," "Snooter Knows," "The Old Professor," and others which cause the writer to be called, on the street, by his pseudonym. A few columns are followed by names in light caps or by cut signatures.

Although clowning is still a part of columning, the fad has weakened in recent years. It is fortunate that typographic high jinks is not very common. For type, said Beatrice Warde, noted English typographer, "should be invisible." Readers should see the message, not the letters and the design. But even this "invisible" type is capable of style, and change of pace, and minor niceties of design which attract readers.

### TOP OF COLUMN POSITIONS PREFERRED

The typical small-city column starts at the top of a newspaper page and runs down beyond the half-way point. Some are shorter, however, while others fill a column, or even more. Since Brisbane, many columns have taken Column 1, Page 1. When publishers are the columnists, the Page 1 position seems appropriate; otherwise, the influential position might appear to out-weigh an inside editorial page. There are exceptions, of course. Many news editors and a few reporters are given Page 1 space. No pulpit in town is of greater potential influence.

Inside page columns also normally take top-of-column positions. But some begin under cartoons or other features. A position preferred by some writers is just inside the paper — at the top of Page 2 in the first two columns. A two-column heading is strong

A local man has a new way to moisten stamps. With several thousand liquor stamps to affix to bottles, he rubs them on an ice cube.—John E. Hoffbauer, Brainerd (Minn.) **Journal-Press.**

A man who saves for a rainy day gets a lot of bad weather reports from his relatives. — Raymond Duncan, Ellaville (Ga.) **Sun.**

The more alert jewelers are limiting the installment sales on engagement rings to get the money collected before alimony payments start. — L a n g d o n (N. D.) **Republican.**

enough to hold its appeal against cuts and spread headlines on the same page.

On the editorial page, the personal column usually is complementary to double-column editorials, on the opposite side of the page — or sometimes 18-point width is used — but when used side by side one should be in sharp contrast to the other. If the editorials are set double column in width, the personal column can be twelve picas wide. Occasionally editorials are set in twelve ems and the column is widened. Short columns and groups of paragraphs are spotted on the page as make-up demands.

A column is what the name implies — a vertical stack of type lines. It is true to its name when the column is full and unbroken. Running the type out from under its head, into an adjoining column, is frowned upon. Fitting copy to a given space is not usually a problem. But some writers do have the requirement of a certain number of words. It is easy to kill out, or set aside, a few short paragraphs. A reserve of timeless bits is kept on hand. Small-city columnists have so much freedom in choice of subjects that filling a space is not the problem. Time, if it can be had, quickly converts ideas and observations into copy. Yet in the absence of a systematic way of producing a column, the floor men are likely to gaze at an empty strip in the chase until near press time.

Since a column is a continuing feature, its location in the paper should be consistent. Readers don't like to hunt for favorite features. The personal column is likely to run in the same place each week — a place on Page 1 or the editorial page where it won't be bumped by advertising.

# *5.*

# *Column Content and Structure*

COLUMNS have drawn nearly every literary device known to writers. Subject matter has been combined in diverse ways, making classification rather difficult. One can say that some columns are humorous in tone, some are serious, and some run the scale of human emotions. Some are on a single subject. Others have as many topics as there are paragraphs.

Comment predominates in some, news items and anecdotes in others. Length varies, too. When is a department six inches long, or eight, or ten, a column? The answer isn't important.

### FIVE GENERAL TYPES IN SMALL PAPERS

Open to challenge but useful in discussing small-town columns are these five classifications:

1. *Variety.* This type also is called the catch-all, the about-town, the hodge-podge, and the miscellaneous. There is a parallel between the

variety of the offerings and the diversity of contacts in an editor's day.

2. *Personal essay.* The essay column may have one subject, or several, but the distinguishing fact is that the writer takes a topic and proceeds to kick it about with whatever skill he possesses. The result may be hilarious or it may be as dry as the dour personality behind it. Words may flow from a personal philosophy set vibrating by a remark heard somewhere. Again, the latest news, accident, election, or flood may bring problems which need clarification.

Some columns actually are lay sermons. A few columnists have written Bible stories in news style on Sundays. And hard put for time and ideas, a writer may select a few facts from an encyclopedia and expand them and localize them in words reaching from chin to toe — and filling a column.

3. *Humor* This classification may be used when the writer is trying to amuse and entertain. He may devise or refurbish jokes, humorous essays, or compress his humor into paragraphs of two to five lines. His style depends upon his point of view, his whimsical comments on life, and his ability to twist his philosophizing into sentences which crackle with paragraphs having rhetorical surprises. Some will call his output "corn," but if subtle truths nestle behind his exaggerations and absurdities he will be credited with more sense than he claims. Another variation is the amusing anecdote, tall tale, or "whopper." Such yarns are in the folklore of every region.

4. *Syndicated columns.* These deserve scant mention here. Small papers do not gain in stature by printing the output of a nationally known columnist. Almost invariably, local columns are better read than any outside contributions. Actually, we don't suppose "Baukhage Talking," for example, is any better or worse in a weekly paper than in a big daily, ex-

**FOOTNOTES**

Footnotes are marks of sound scholarship in formal types of research. They round out discussions, invite readers to consult other sources, and carry contrary opinions. In a sense, editor's columns can be footnotes to the local news report. In fact, many stories can hardly be written fully without footnotes. The delicate—or indelicate — handling of human angles in the columns completes reader understanding. Speculation and judgments are denied most reporters in spot news coverage.

A near-hit bolt of lightning can create a lot more Christian thinking than a long-winded sermon.—Algona (Iowa) **Advance.**

cept that the former hasn't the space for it and, in competition with rival papers and radio, needs to develop exclusive local features.

There are, however, some regionally syndicated columns which have large followings. A recent success story is that of Henry B. Fox. Twelve years or so ago he felt an urge to make chiding remarks about his neighbors, the government, and anything else which pleased or annoyed him. His was not the art of the paragrapher; he sees many chuckles in a single subject. In time he shared his column with a fellow publisher, then another, and still others. Eventually fifty papers in half a dozen states were printing the weekly humorous essay of the "————— Philosopher." (Supply name of local creek.) He writes it so editors can insert name of local bankers, preachers, lawyers, and other standard citizens. The Taylor, Texas, man has become nationally known for his contributions in *Cosmopolitan's* "Main Street," *Country Gentleman,* and *Collier's*.

Other writers, too, have achieved regional fame and syndication. In some cases, they have inserted propaganda or promotional material paid for by organizations interested in safety, good roads, economy in government, and other subjects linked with their welfare. Their number is decreasing as newspapers realize that good will is lost when readers recognize hidden propaganda in columns and news stories. The material is not purified by the fact that editors agree with it.

5. *Specialized columns.* These include columns in the departments—sports, society, agriculture, hobbies, business, politics, religion, etc. Add the literary columns, how-to columns, reports from Congressmen, capital city comment, business trend reports, and letters from hometowners traveling in distant lands. Include gossip columns if you must. For additional comment on specialized columns, see Chapter 17.

What this country needs in October is a combination suntan lotion, mosquito ointment, and chilblain remedy.—T. A. Lally, Bridgeport (Nebr.) **News-Blade.**

We are the slaves of fear; courage is scattered rebellion.— Matador (Tex.) **Tribune.**

It will be nice when spring comes and the grass grows up along the roadside and hides the discarded beer cans.—Falls. Church (Va.) **Standard.**

Columns could be classified in other ways, of course. They have tones—angry, quiet, egoistic, bored, inspired. They have attitudes—see no evil, see no good, flattering, bullying, etc. They have styles—terse, rambling, eloquent, flamboyant, poetic, prosy. Some columnists carry the world and its problems on their shoulders and in their words. Not so the cheerful boosters. Not so the flippant wags. Not so the columnists who best reflect the spirit of Main Street. These differences are traceable in the implied intentions of the writers. Some try only to entertain. Some try to show an erudition beyond that of the average reader. Others merely comment on the news of their day, pleasantly yet with a moral tinge, in remarks which are as timely and as briefly considered as repartee of neighbors across an alley fence.

The small-town columnist aims to please, to entertain, and to instruct. He does a lot of kidding. He writes as he feels, usually without any attempt to be literary, or profound, or infallible. He frequently confesses his own weaknesses. His method is to mix the light and lively with serious implications and inferred civic duties. A bit of whimsy increases his circle of readers. Columnists dwell in that enjoyable no-man's land between fact and fiction. And one columnist uses the title, "FACT AND FANCY—Let the Wise Man Make the Distinction."

It is characteristic of these columns that in content they are warmly personal, occasionally witty, and always clean. Some are entirely philosophical; others are based on the old maxim that "names make news." But not everything printed in column form is a true column. Some very dull editorial essays are run under standing headings.

It is typical of columnists that they know their readers and their environment. More than

Something should be done about the dogs in our fair city. They are...

**He writes as he feels . . .**

editorial writers, they speak the language of the people about them. For this reason future historians will give columns close study. What is popular in one region may be unacceptable in another. Paragraphs, characteristic of the crisp talk of New England and some of the middle states, give way to the anecdotes, philosophical essays, and newsy columns of the Southwest. Nostalgic references may bore a very old community, but in the West the old is still new; many persons living remember the last Indian depredations. Moreover, an item may be considered risque in one community yet be tolerated in another. People become conditioned to a columnist's brand of humor.

All regions have had one fault in common: too much material has been reprinted without credit. Truly, as one reads in some paper every few months, "It is a wise crack which knows its own father." In the later years of the *Literary Digest,* papers sometimes picked up whole pages of briefs and set them as fillers, credit lines omitted. Proof of guilt, however, is not always possible to obtain. Coincidences will happen; two columnists may make the same jest from the same raw materials, such as wire stories.

Rewriting of paragraphs is common. A more acceptable practice is printing a credited excerpt, then commenting on it. Certainly neighboring editors can sharpen their wits and entertain readers by exchanging mild insults or bantering comment with each other. These need not lead to the extremes of a column by a pioneer editor who referred to a rival as being "the offspring of a razorback hog sired by a ringneck buzzard."

Reams of miscellany fill the minds of editors and reporters, but these may never reach their typewriters. By the nature of their work they see and hear things which fit nowhere in the paper unless there is a place for jokes, funny stories, random observations,

A regrettable aspect of columning in American newspapers is the widespread piracy of others' ideas. Fillers in editorial columns are so often reprints without source credits that one writer titled his column, "Original — at any rate." Early in 1950, a columnist wrote that a person always called a spade a spade until one fell on his foot. Other writers grabbed the idea, repeated it with or without credit, paraphrased it, and kicked it around in all the ways known to columnists. Finally, in 1951, a popular magazine versified it, with illustration. Originality is rare and coincidences do happen, but every columnist can meet the problem ethically. Syndication complicates the problem when sources are not shown.

If the worms weren't up so early there wouldn't be so many early birds, either.—New Ulm (Minn.) **Journal.**

The height of delicacy was displayed by the flag-pole sitter who, when his wife died, came down half way.—Albany (Ky.) New Era.

The man who invented the eraser had the human race pretty well sized up.—Glenn E. Bunnell. Hartington (N e b r .) News.

If the youngsters like you, there's nothing the matter with you.—Edmore (Mich.) Times.

thank-you's to readers, and other odds and ends. And many a sharp comment, in which a truth occurs to them in crystal clearness, may be lost unless they have a place for it—and with its loss goes much influence never exerted.

Readers, too, contribute column material—both in the mails and in oral offerings. This usually requires some polishing and close editing. It includes doggerel verse, platitudes, expressions of prejudice, verbal bouquets for friends, and potential libel. Satire and irony may seem innocent yet have overtones which will destroy friendships. Parodies and puns usually are discarded unless especially clever. Bits of verse from readers' scrapbooks may be used if credited to the source and if no copyright is involved.

Even in the arrangement of a column there is more skill than most people think. The editor's day, and possibly his mind, are a hodge-podge of unrelated items. The variety column may be a cross-section of his mind, but usually he considers his material long enough to fit it to some habitual pattern. Broadway and Hollywood columnists use a variety of subjects but their organization is repetitious. Arthur Brisbane and O. O. McIntyre were expert arrangers of miscellany.

The variety column appeals, as the name implies, to a wide assortment of reader tastes. It accepts many ideas, many subjects, many names. Using it, the columnist has no need to pursue an idea for more than an appropriate time.

#### READER INTERESTS GUIDE CHOICE OF MATERIALS

Since their efforts are aimed at the same readers as those of other writers in the newspaper, columnists are governed by the same considerations in choice of materials. They write about the topics that are of the greatest interest to the greatest number of people. So, of course, their columns carry much material about the home, family, men, women, kids, teen-agers, and neighbors. People, almost without exception, make up the No. 1 classification in any list of general column content.

Second in rank, the surveys show, are the non-personal topics, such as philosophy, the seasons and weather, nature, pleasant nostalgia, and current public affairs.

In third place are the miscellaneous topics that are as varied as the quirks of nature: Verse, the columnist's hobby, historical and literary allusions, pet hates, travel abroad and in the township, where beauty is found, ugly streets, the mean man who poisons dogs, soil conservation, etc. The list is as long as the sum of the imaginations of more than eight thousand columnists, and so varied that any one writer, seeking ideas, can always find topics on which he has never written if he will dip into his neighbor's writings. For a list of one hundred ideas which columnists have used, see Chapter 13.

Choice of column material hinges somewhat on the basic literary methods of the writers. To get laughs, they use exaggeration, understatement, and incongruity. For pungent observation they coin or adapt an epigram. To drive home a point on which they have intense feelings, they fashion satire.

The examples which follow illustrate typical column materials:

**MEN**

A young man's fumblings and an old man's philanderings are much alike. And are laughed off by the same-age girl.

New Iberia (La.) *Iberian*

**WOMEN**

A foreigner visiting in the United States thought "oakie doakie" was the feminine of "O.K." He was, of course, mistaken. The feminine of "O.K." is "maybe." —Everett M. Remsberg.

"Impressions"
Vista (Calif.) *Press*

It's all right to tell a little boy not to cry because crying won't help. But that's really not honest advice to give a little girl.— Kingsport (Tenn.) **Times.**

The "upper crust" is often made up of a lot of crumbs held together by their own dough.— Wade Guenther, Sabula (Iowa) **Gazette.**

**MAN AND WOMAN**

Our friend has a neighbor who carries so much life insurance that his wife is mad at him every morning when he wakes up.—Edgar Harris.

"The March of Events"
West Point (Miss.)
*Times Leader*

**PEOPLE**

We have been thinking of developing a serum that would make people live forever, but after looking them over we have decided against it until we can develop an applicator that is very specific.—George W. Bowra.

"Rips and Tears"
Aztec (N. M.)
*Independent-Review*

**KIDS**

All these years I have been saving my Tinker toys, my iron soldiers, my wind-up alligator, for the time when I would have children of my own. But in the face of present-day events I keep them concealed with the other antiques in the attic. There isn't any use of bringing out those papier-mache soldiers that were imported from England — they would be shattered to bits by a blast from my little daughter's new supersonic, ultra-powered, jet-propulsed, recoilless, flash-proof six-gun. And God help Santa Claus when he comes down that chimney. —C.A.V.A.

Duncannon (Penn.) *Record*

**CUSTOMS**

One of the causes of high living costs is the fact that a family has to have so much more to have even a little more than the neighbor family.

"At Random"
DePere (Wis.)
*Journal-Democrat*

**AT HOME**

Many's the middle-aged wife and mother who had rather have her tired, aching back rubbed three minutes per night than get three or four kisses.—A. C. Jolly.

"Chuckles"
Cartersville (Ga.) *Herald*

**TEEN-AGERS**

The automobile took the children out of the home, and along about midnight we begin wondering where it put them.—John C. Herr.

"Thar's Gold"
Wickenburg (Ariz.) *Sun*

Have you ever lain awake at night listening to a rat gnaw on something? Have you ever eased out of bed and beat on the wall in the hope that you could go to sleep before he started gnawing again? The rat will stop for about four to five minutes and then, just as you are about to doze off, he will start up again. It is one of the most exasperating things in the world until you figure it out. Simply consider that you are causing the rat a lot of inconvenience too by beating on the wall, and you'll go to sleep plumb satisfied.— Earl L. Tucker, Thomasville (Ala.) **Times**.

**PHILOSOPHY**

The world is divided into three groups, viz: The small group which makes things happen, the larger group which watches things happen, and the multitude which never knows what happens.—Dora Barnard.

"I Heard That"
Harrisonville (Mo.)
*Missourian*

**NATURE**

We have a liking for the lowly sunflowers. They stand up so straight and look you in the eye. And they keep their faces to the sun, so the shadows fall behind.—Jessie L. Duhig.

"Musings"
Thermopolis (Wyo.)
*Independent-Record*

**PUBLIC AFFAIRS**

Now it seems a transparent cellophane mattress is to be developed. We'll reveal those communists, one way or the other.—L. S. McCandless.

"A Shot of Scotch"
Craig (Colo.) *Empire-Courier*

**LIKES AND DISLIKES**

As for this Editor, he refuses to be pushed around by the press agents for these numerous "weeks," or regimented or told to do even the things he wants to do or was going to do anyway. The Editor can't remember what this "week" is, or what he's supposed to be doing, but whatever it is, he isn't going to do it.—Paul F. Watkins.

"In My Opinion"
Ashland (Va.) *Herald-Progress*

**PLEASANT MEMORIES**

A dance program and a bit of ribbon tumble from the diary into your hands. Ah, that was such a happy night! Your little silver-slippered feet danced and danced, your skirts swirled and frothed about your ankles, your cheeks were like roses, your eyes were stars. The night was laughter, music, and romance. It was a man's dark head close to yours. It was his low voice murmuring in your ear. It was the rhythm of your matching steps, the magic attunement of your hearts. At dawn you trailed down the ballroom stairs, arm in arm, hushed before the miracle you had found.—Mrs. Gene Davis.

"Topics in Type"
Boonville (Mo.) *News*

Folks in the country wouldn't argue the point to any great length but one of our rural philosophers took the straw out of his mouth, scored a bullseye on the spittoon, and sagely remarked, "We live in the section of the country where folks in the city save their money all year 'round to spend two weeks in."—Claude Eames, Elkhorn (Wis.) **Independent.**

Ever notice? The man who never made an enemy never made anything. — T. A. Lally, Bridgeport (Nebr.) **News-Blade.**

Have you noticed those dachshunds of low, rambling architecture, two and a half dogs long by half a dog high? They are comparatively inoffensive and a nice thing for one of my Scotch friends who got one so all his six children could pet him at one time.—Wallace Barnes, Gallup (N. M.) **Independent.**

**THEN AND NOW**

When our youngest paused in passing to dry his tears on our pant leg, we were struck by the sudden realization that the lady of the house no longer wears aprons. Since women have discovered the mild, every-day elegance of house dresses, aprons have become a thing of the past. Our children are now deprived of the convenience of having that vast area at hand for the wiping of eyes — or noses.—Wayne D. Allen.
"Sun Beams"
Morning Sun (Iowa)
*News-Herald*

**LOVE**

Whatever the mathematicians may contend, the whole can be greater than the sum of the parts. What you think of her nose, plus what you think of her hair, etc. cannot begin to equal the effect of the girl herself.
Colfax (La.) *Chronicle*

**CHARACTERS**

A lot has been accomplished in this world because some neurotic woman drove her husband nearly nuts.
Bethseda (Md.) *Record*

**MAN AFTER WOMAN**

A jingling sound adds a note of sincerity to the whistle.—Billy Arthur.
"Down East"
Jacksonville (N. C.)
*News and Views*

Commencement address: Be honest with yourself and others, work hard, be prompt, and always be willing to learn something new and useful. — Fred Roble, Granville (N. D.) **Herald.**

The methods of columnists are as varied as their subject matter. To present a picture, they use a metaphor. To preach a little, they find the aphorism or homily a convenient tool. For the bitter comment that "ends that comment," they choose irony. And always, to get the attention which may be difficult otherwise, there is paradox. To spark a reply or enjoy reflected glory, they quote another person and comment on the quotation. Quite often, of course, they raise a hortatory voice and demand, "Hear ye, hear ye!" And when the columnist wants to have fun, just fun, he begins grinning at his typewriter, more or less idiotically, and tossing puns.

Further comment on these methods including ideas

on how to make column items quotable can be found in Chapter 11.

### CONTENT GUIDES ARRANGEMENT OF COLUMNS

Most columns are written to a pattern, or several patterns, because writers form habits just as other people do. Their verbal menu may consist only of a main dish and more of the same. Such writers may merely comment on things which come to mind as they sit down to fill their column space.] Opening sentences may read like these:

"As I was walking to work this morning, I saw . . ."

"President James Brown of the chamber of commerce is to be commended for. . . ."

"Have you noticed how many teen-age drivers have been involved in automobile accidents lately?"

"Joe Smith is a lucky man. . . ."

"Back from market, William Davis of the Davis-Green Hardware tells an interesting yarn he heard last week. . . ."

In an *a la carte* column, however, writers often serve their quips and comments in courses already well known to readers. They may open with a five-paragraph discourse followed by an anecdote, or begin with an anecdote followed by one paragraph. In physical appearance a column is known by the length of its paragraphs, its indentions, and the order of its elements.

To develop a formula for purposes of illustration, it may help to assign letters to units of content one may wish to use. These might include:

A—Current news item, preferably exclusive to the column.

B—An interesting fact, possibly related to the readers.

C—Comment by the columnist.

D—More comment by the columnist.

A railroad passenger on a limited train cannot help feeling vicariously important when the carrier goes whistling through the small towns without stopping. And similarly anyone standing at a railroad station when a fast train goes gliding by without a pause cannot escape the feeling of inferiority. — Dallas E. Wood, Palo Alto (Calif.) **Times.**

It isn't unlucky these days to come into possession of a $2 bill. It comes in handy to buy a dollar's worth of most anything. — Warren C. Nelson, Lebanon (Ohio) **Western Star.**

E—A witty paragraph, two to five lines.
F—An anecdote or funny story.
G—A bit of verse.
H—Brevitorial—a paragraph of opinion.
I—An apology, or some praise.
J—Clipping or excerpt.
K—Local quote or brief item in dialogue form.
L—Half-minute interview, or biographical sketch.
M—Letter or excerpt of letter, from reader.
N—Announcement or request.
O—Name-item or newsy note about local resident.

> Youth ends and manhood begins when you stop studying your face in the mirror to find an excuse to shave and when you start studying your face in the mirror to see if you can possibly put it off until tomorrow.—Glenn E. Bunnell, Hartington (Nebr.) **News.**

Let these and more of your choice be the ingredients of potential columns. Combine them according to the subject matter, but remember that readers like to see favorite items in the same place each time.

With the above letters as keys, it is possible to show in brief form the pattern of a column. Arrangement of a variety column is relatively unimportant compared to content, but it is worth some study. Here are typical column patterns:

1—EEEE-A-C-D-G-F-J-C-N-E-H.
2—N-E-A-C-E-F-E-K-C-F.
3—G-EEEE-F-E-J-D-K-L-E.
4—N-F-M-C-J-C-E-OOOO-H.
5—A-C-DDD-M-C-J-C-EEEEE.

> People still talk about the weather, but now it's because everybody is doing something about it.—Somerset (N. J.) **Messenger-Gazette.**

For greater simplicity and fewer subject changes the following formulas reshuffle the same letter symbols:

1—A-C-DDDD-M-C-D-F-H.
2—EEE-FFF-L-H.
3—N-C-I-C-DDD-J-C.
4—B-C-DDDD-E-K-C.
5—EEEE-F-E-F-E-F.

Choice of subject matter is usually haphazard, yet here, too, certain patterns are kept in mind. Lewis Nordyke, whose column in the Amarillo (Tex.) *News-Globe* had an exceptional response from readers, makes this comment:

The formula for my column is basically inspirational. Each day there is a tear, a chuckle, a touch of nostalgia, bit of mild controversy, maybe a little story about people who seldom are mentioned in a newspaper. Mixed with this is an occasional shot of seriousness on politics and other current topics. In a good many instances, I make myself the goat. This works wonderfully well and brings a tremendous response. Publication of a note bawling me out brings a lot of letters telling the critics to go straight to hell. This formula was worked out on the notion that the average human being on an average day has in his system a tear, a bit of sentiment, a prayer, a touch of nostalgia, some sunshine and some seriousness, and that he likes having them pricked just a little. The column seldom varies from this formula.

It should be remembered that readers cannot change moods as readily as writers who already have the facts in mind. Frequent shifts from the sublime to the ridiculous should be avoided. Columnists who keep notebooks with them constantly may find it advisable to write each item on a half sheet, then to arrange in a logical order before pasting together. Exceptions are those experienced writers who compose and arrange in their heads before committing ideas to paper. To paraphrase an old bit of advice:

"THE BEST COLUMNS ARE NOT WRITTEN: THEY ARE REWRITTEN."

"I make myself the goat . . ."

## 6.

# Well, Let's Get Started

THIS CHAPTER is addressed to the several hundred persons who each year start a column for the first time, and to others who are still feeling their way.

So you would like to write a column!

"Writing a column every week isn't easy," said Earl Tucker, author of "Rambling Roses and Flying Bricks" in the Thomasville (Ala.) *Times.* "Last night I was trying to think up something to write about and all I could do was make little sketches on a piece of paper. I would pick up a newspaper, thinking I might get an idea, but all I saw was something about Korea, and I'm just not going to write about Korea."

In their mischievous manner, columnists attribute their skills to everything from inheritance to being sort of "queer." But beneath their self-conscious "Oh shucks" denial of having any literary secrets, you will find some solid patterns for getting and developing ideas. They are good folks to know. They are friendly, quick to sense a joke and catch a slant, sympathetic, resourceful, unerring in spotting a stuffed-shirt personality and able to make and hold friends at all levels of society. They know the power of the inference and the danger of innuendo. They love to plant an idea and see it flower in the minds of public officials and average citizens.

In a phrase, columnists are moulders of public opinion. They have perspective. They have insight. But like other literary men they sow their philosophies in well-plowed ground; that is, in observations, anecdotes, verse, and other standard forms of reading and entertainment.

In writing a column, one starts from where he is; all he has to do is to come alive. A small-town reporter who has a keen awareness of people and things can find a column of news and gather data for a personal column in the course of circling a single block. Every life is an adventure and every day has meaning for each person. Then there are *things*— the paving one walks upon, the sky above, the state of the growing plants and flowers, the mechanical gadgets which give Americans seven-league boots.

Some extrovert columnists use all of their senses in developing columns. Others prefer leisurely meditation at the end of a busy day. Many combine the two methods. But anything is likely to inspire a column, as Earl Tucker illustrates:

"A horse galloped by and disturbed my unthinking mood. He came back by in a few minutes and disturbed it again. I said to myself, 'I'm called to write about horses.' If preachers can get called on to preach I reckon I can get called on to write. So, I'll tell you all I know about horses. Having owned a horse once, I feel like these few remarks may be worth something to those interested in the study of equestrianism. That's the study of horsemanship, and a right fine word if I did look it up myself.

"I acquired my horse from a friend of mine when I was about 12 years old. . . ."

The column continued through

". . . so I'll tell you all I know about horses . . ."

. . . they keep the column in mind
as they see the people . . .

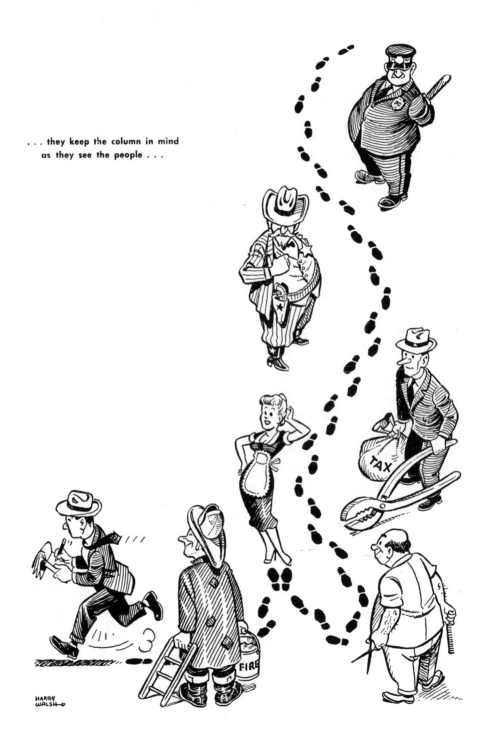

several hundred words to the day when the horse of the writer's boyhood died of sweet potato poisoning. Pathos was combined with talk of how to tell a horse's age, racing, Kentucky derby, hoss trading.

Busy small-town publishers cannot, however, depend on column subjects to come galloping by their windows. Neither do they have the time deliberately to go out looking for column items. If they had a lot of time, they probably would do research for formal editorials and a carefully edited page of editorial features. But lacking this time, they keep the column in mind as they see the people—the police, the sheriff, the tax collectors, the office secretaries, the chamber of commerce staff, their barbers, firemen, janitors, farmers in town, and business men at civic club luncheons. They listen, and they take notes.

"The average small-town editor is not really an editor at all," wrote Hugo K. Frear of the Bedford (Penn.) *Gazette* in *The National Publisher*.[1] "He may be a first-rate managing editor, a good business-man, and a competent reporter; but seldom an editor. He can't afford the time to be. . . . Bear in mind that we refer to the editor who fulfills the larger-city definition of that title—the man described by Roget's *Thesaurus* as 'a commentator, critic, essay-ist, pamphleteer, publicist, reviewer.' The man, that is, who writes editorials."

Frear, winner of a National Editorial Association award for columning, pointed out that bigger-city editorial writers have the time and resources to make small-town writers look bad by comparison. While he does not regard the column as a *cure-all*, he gave this advice:

"Give yourself three hours of free time out of that busy week—Sunday evening is an elegant, trouble-free time. Put a heading on the column. Relax. Forget

---

**SEE BOTH ENDS**

While many columnists accumulate their material and write it as time permits, most of the better columns are planned. The writers have at least a rough idea of the development of the piece, and its ending. The essayists plan even more carefully. Humorists can afford to let their fun develop spontaneously, providing they later edit the stuff carefully. Planned hodge-podge columns can follow a frequently repeated formula. An idea for a column should include both ending and conclusion. What goes between will take some digging. Digging is fun when the end is in sight.

If you can't influence a man any other way, praise him for being the kind of a man who can't be influenced, and you'll have him eating out of your hand.—Odebolt (Iowa) **Chronicle.**

---

[1] February, 1950, pp. 7–8.

That girl on Broadway says it seems like those who get the biggest kick out of life do the least kicking. — Lubbock (Tex.) **Avalanche.**

**BEHIND SCENES**

Speech coverage from manuscripts and from the audience may be quite good and yet the occasion may have ignored news angles. Both reporters and columnists sometimes find the real news in things not done, words not spoken, delegations not present. When editors write columns they may find their regular space ideally suited to elaboration of event-coverage, public business, and politics. There are no towns so small as not to have occasional news of this negative sort. And what people **think** can be news.

your own worries, and the world's worries. Just start writing about the interesting things that happened around town last week. Write to fill the column. And keep writing each week thereafter. Come hell or high water, *write that column!* The column succeeds, of course, because of its versatility. Readers are drawn to it because they can't afford to miss it. There might be a juicy morsel of fun about a neighbor."

Now, let us assume that you wish to write an "about town" column. You wish to report and comment on the lighter side of the news and to record the jokes, anecdotes, gripes, and smart sayings you hear on your rounds. Occasionally you will find a situation which will inspire you to "let yourself go." Then you will write with feeling, some fine phrases, and possibly some indignation over official malfunctioning. Yet you don't expect to be a scold. Mainly, you wish your paper to have a voice, or several. And you wish an outlet for ideas which may not be worth a long editorial but which will express a point of view and gain converts to your way of thinking.

But now, you must begin. You ask some advice and seek some ideas.

First, who are you? The columnist may be himself, writing as he talks and merely delivering a monologue on a few subjects. But as a variety columnist you may wish to strike a pose. Now is the time to decide. You must select a tempo. Will you pose as a clown or a scholar? Will you be a "regular fellow" or will you speak with authority, or as one having inside information? Why not be yourself—your brighter self. Later, with experience, you can develop into a "character" if you wish.

What does a columnist do? He reports . . . gripes . . . praises . . . wisecracks . . . philosophizes . . . apologizes . . . explains . . . worries . . . exults . . . tells stories.

But, you ask, from what pulpit; what is his point of view? Well, you don't need an ivory tower (remember to trade that expression some day). Columnists write from all kinds of places, such as editorial desks, easy chairs, teachers' platforms, doghouses, sidewalks, and—we could almost say—the edges of gutters. They feign many points of view and assume characterizations ranging from dolts to poets. Yet they are consistent.

Your column title, "About Town," is non-committal as to tone. It suggests a reporting job. You can ask readers for contributions—written or oral. You can confess that filling a column requires a lot of items. You will condition your audience gradually to your ideas before you start meddling with neighborhood mores. First, get a following. Develop your column formulas. Gain confidence.

Know your people well. Remember that many of them never went to college. You may unconsciously talk down to readers sometimes, but only because you have information and ideas to report. Do it man-to-man. Don't be afraid to give the impression that you have an idea in which you believe, but always assume that the readers are intelligent and that, given your facts, they will see things as you do. But don't be surprised if they don't, and don't fail to share your space with them.

"Your best columns will be about something you feel very keenly and know thoroughly," wrote Robert K. Beck of the Centerville (Iowa) *Iowegian and Citizen* in *Publishers' Auxiliary.*

Beck's subjects range from baby sitting to Joe Stalin. His most talked-about paragraph was about his 18-month-old son's sticking his blond head in a bucket of blue paint. Mothers live in fear of such happenings.

Don't think it is necessary to be a clown, to use

**LOOKING AHEAD**

Spontaneity is a vital thing in columns, but subject matter is not found without alertness and some planning. An idea book can be kept to remind one he had a swell thought on how to write a column for a special event or holiday. This futures book should be large enough to carry brief notes for later reference.

The coward's meanest trick is to nod agreement with a catty criticism when he doesn't agree with it at all.—Fountain Inn (S. C.) **Tribune.**

trick typography, and to think up asinine spelling. You don't have to use bad manners to get attention. You don't have to shout. You do have to keep on writing week after week. Some of the biggest reader responses have come from appreciation of a modest little paragraph in ordinary body type.

Write as if writing is fun; it is. Write as if you expect readers to have fun in the reading. Put readers' names in your column, but don't repeat the same names or cater overmuch to people who travel in sets and cliques. Be grateful for contributed items. Say that you are. And don't forget your colleagues in the print shop; include them in your mentions, but not often.

Here are two good ideas from Harlan Miller of the Des Moines *Register*:

1. Carry a notebook everywhere.
2. Spend some time facing your typewriter in solitude.

An ever-present notebook is an invitation to see, to ask, to record. A typewriter, however, is an invitation to write—too hastily. Columnists need to see, deeply, then to write in a novel way. They should refrain from expressing ordinary opinions in an expected sort of way. Facts are seldom humdrum; opinions often are. The reader's reward should be your clever phrase, your hidden quip, your subtle statement which permits the reader to draw the conclusion or state the moral. You wouldn't explain the obvious point of a joke; don't force the reader to enunciate a platitude he saw coming several sentences back.

Having a regular place to write is important. Many a columnist is a slave to a place and a time. We knew a gifted paragrapher who wrote his barbed bits in a cubbyhole behind a cut cabinet. He sat beside a huge roll-top desk and wrote on an ancient typewriter. Progress came, with new desks, new partitions, and new typewriters. The columnist never had another

Psay, did you ever psee anything pso funny as the English language? Psuch words as psychology, for example. Psuch pspelling is just too psilly for anything.—D. L. Keith, Windom (Minn.) **Citizen.**

**LITTLE QUESTIONS**

In their request for the unusual and the significant, reporters habitually overlook small news which readers want. A big neon sign is erected. How was it made? How much electricity does it consume? What does it weigh? . . . The cornerstone for a public building arrives. Who carved the names, and with what? Does he ever make a mistake? What would be done if a tiny corner were broken off the cornerstone, ruining its perfection? Sidewalk crowds ask these questions. Who, better than a columnist, can answer them?

happy Sunday morning, which was his regular time for writing his paragraphs.

Some columnists write only after others in their families have retired. Others write at intervals as time permits, and a few have typewriters for the purpose hidden in back shops among stacks of paper and supplies. Charles A. Guy, the "Westerner" of the Lubbock (Tex.) *Journal,* contributes this comment on his methods:

"I write under the worst conditions possible, which means I write both in the office and at home and, when out of town, in hotel rooms, newspaper shops—anywhere and everywhere. Customarily, I do my writing during the working day at the office. Since I have a policy of not closing my office door, I write a paragraph, then talk to a visitor; write another paragraph, then answer the phone; write another paragraph. then talk to a staff member who comes in with a problem. In short, I have written my column in airplanes, on trains, in a mine, in the patio of a Yaqui military garrison—almost everywhere but in a submarine.

"I have tried only once to dictate my column. It was fifteen years ago after a horse fell with me and I came up with a broken arm. Although I had been dictating letters for many years, I simply couldn't dictate the column. It had run out of my fingers for too long. I wrote the column with one hand. You would be surprised how well you could run a typewriter with one hand—if you had to."

Any interest which readers feel in a column arouses their curiosity about the columnist. They wish to know whether he is human, as they feel they are. People are funny. Columnists are people. You can profitably share some of your personal problems. The great and greatly beloved William Allen White of Emporia, Kansas, wrote about shaving "this funny

**DICTATION**

Editors who have stenographers or voice-recorders sometimes dictate their columns. The practice has the merit of encouraging a tell-it-as-you-talk style. But most journalists think better at their typewriters. A few compose at their Linotypes. In any event, good writing habits can be formed, as judged by results.

Anybody could get rich if he could guess the exact moment at which a piece of junk becomes an antique. — Youngstown (Ohio) **Vindicator.**

**DEADLINES**

Newspaper workers produce great volumes of articles under the pressure of deadlines. In turning to free-lance writing, without deadlines, they sometimes flounder miserably, unable to get started. And many professional writers s u ff e r agonies in working themselves into a creative mood. Columnists, too, need the pressure of a definite time and place to finish their stint. This discipline seems to put one in the spirit of columning. Some syndicate writers find they do their best work under the pressure and worry of a narrow margin between them and their deadlines. The thrill of feeling a good column developing is heightened by the knowledge that the deadline will be met, after all.

old face." His editorials had a column-like tone and structure. People knew not only how he thought, but also how he felt.

You, the new columnist, awaken to the raucus buzz of an alarm clock. Thousands have the same experience in your county. There you have it—something in common. All right; report it. Be specific. What was your first thought on awakening? Why? Had you rather be awakened with music? What kind of music? Or can you depend on the noise of the neighbor's lawn mower at 6 a.m.? You recall other ways of being roused: Army bugles, the cacophony of alarm clocks in a dormitory, a fraternity brother's poke in the ribs, a telephone call from a hotel desk clerk. You wonder how Farmer Brown routs the sandman. Or does the modern farmer get up before the sun? You ask a real dirt farmer. He says he has a cow which bawls for her feed at a convenient early hour. You record his remarks in your notebook for later typing.

But, back to clocks; you note that most alarm clocks displayed today are electric. Wonderful thing, this electricity. But who fixes electric clocks? Take it from there. You may get an ad when you look up the repair man.

On another awakening, you notice the wall paper designs and recall that frontier cabins were papered with newspapers. What are the new styles in wall coverings? What about wall coverings through the ages? What about new plastic materials? Take it from there.

In another room, you see a hole in the wall paper. Bad news that; the termites are at work. Why not poison them with arsenic in the paste? But then you would not know the pesky things were eating down the house. Clever things, the termites defy even modern chemistry. They are competent engineers and are masters of camouflage. They are bad news but good column material.

Now in the bathroom, sight of a tube of toothpaste remind you that cake decorating mixtures now come in tubes. What next? You wonder if you can shave with cake filling. Shaving takes water, soft preferred. How many gallons are used in a bathroom every day? With water tables falling, people must give some serious thought to conserving rainfall. Cities are dying for want of water. Will your town ever be short?

Junior has dirt on his hands, but doesn't worry. The farmer loses dirt to drainage ditches and does worry. What is alive in a cubic inch of soil? It's amazing when you know the answer.

Junior balances on his toes on the rim of the bath tub and you think of insurance company ads on household accidents. How can the home, man's castle, be so lethal? Call the roll of hazards in the home and ask readers for ideas.

You haven't far to look about the house to see all the personal mentions you should make in a year. Other column subjects will occur to you on the way to your office. What a beautiful day. Or perhaps not, to a farmer needing rain. Look at that saucy cardinal. He almost moves one to poetry. Back in 1928 when William Allen White saw a similar sight he wrote:

He was singing his heart out in the sun of the early morning today; sitting on the top branch of a brown lilac bush, all burning red was he. His throbbing notes came full and fine. Clothed in the feathery brown lace of the bush the red bird glowed like a drop of blood bursting from a heart full of passionate faith. He sang because he had to sing. His urge was part of the force that moves the stars — mechanical maybe; certainly natural. But we who heard him, we who translated his joy into gratitude, who took his song and made it our own delight, who caught it on our own wavelength and so aspired with the high gods, well, if our thrill was only

A bride out in Purdyville got a whistling tea kettle for a wedding gift. Next morning as she was getting breakfast, clad in an abbreviated nightie, the kettle startled her with a lusty wolf whistle. — Lyons (Kans.) **News.**

When a man wants his handkerchief he reaches around and takes it out of hip-pocket. When a girl wants hers she arises, shakes herself, and picks it up. —**Exchange.**

the mechanics of nature working, then the great mechanic back of the machine must know joy, too; must feel the thrill of beauty, the passion of high hopes. For the parts cannot be greater than the whole.

And God's in His Heaven.[2]

You move toward town with swinging steps. It's great to be alive. There's old Mrs. Jones, 88 and mighty pert. Stop a moment. How does the world look to a women who has lived so much? Pick a quote. Readers will love you for having shown this respect for Grandma Jones.

On to work . . . to open the mail . . . to talk . . . to question . . . to listen . . . and to write in your little notebook.

You will be offered jokes. In general, reject them. Few are original. Unless original, they should be credited if printed. But they can be paraphrased, made into tall tales, or put into dialogue form. Traveling salemen are good folks to know. Their jokes may be risque but they also know anecdotes and have news of markets, styles, price trends, and goings-on in other towns.

People will offer you much advice. They will urge you to "burn down" the city manager because there is a hole in a certain street. You can criticise the city manager, of course; he is a public servant. You may do so. But he may be your neighbor, your fellow Rotarian, your friend. You may desire to take the complainant to the city hall to face the city manager. The chances will be good for clearing up the matter and making friends of possible enemies.

Public officials may come to blows. We read two accounts of a fight between a mayor and a city commissioner. One unimaginative reporter wrote a straight account which could only have made it difficult for the wives of the officials to face each other

[2] *Forty Years on Main Street*, p. 382. Used by permission of Rinehart & Company, Inc. Copyright 1937.

across a bridge table. The other reporter wrote a hilarious account in the jargon of a sports writer. "His Honor led with a sharp left — and missed by three feet, then the commissioner pivoted neatly, countered with a right uppercut . . . and fell on his face," he recorded.

As a columnist, you will hear many demands that things be kept out of the paper. Your column is a good place to explain why news should not be suppressed. Be specific. Offer examples. This one will illustrate the point:

In the early days of electrical refrigeration, a house was damaged when a motor caught fire. Then there was another similar blaze, and still another. The dealer demanded that the third and subsequent stories be omitted. His business was endangered. He was warned about the danger of rumors when facts are suppressed. He insisted that he was a victim of circumstances and should be protected by newspaper silence. Then a columnist asked that he be permitted to put the dealer's dilemma frankly before the public. The dealer was skeptical, but agreed to the experiment. The columnist let out all the stops, telling how the unlucky dealer in refrigerators was losing his health, his hair, his business, etc., etc. Readers were asked to save this man, his business, and his home by expressions of sympathy. The result, in personal and telephone calls, flowers, and other attention overwhelmed the amazed business man, who had the best business in months. And luckily he had no more fires.

As a new columnist, and needing a vacation, you may be tempted to surrender your space to guest writers for a couple of weeks. It is a safe procedure to have the columns in hand before you leave. Mrs. John Bigwig's daughter, just home from finishing school, wrote a snazzy column for her school paper

Is a teacher hired, employed, or engaged? It is our opinion that she is at first hired; after she's been in town six months, she's engaged; and three months later, after the wedding bells, she's employed.—Roy M. Garner, Mobridge (S. D.) Tribune.

The old-fashioned woman who tacked carpet rags now has a granddaughter who thinks rag tacking is tacky.— Dallas (Tex.) **News.**

A family walks to town on Sunday. The sun is bright. The daughter is radiant in finery. The younger son impatiently skips along. The mother is a picture of serenity. The father looks as if his shirt collar were chafing his neck. This is the greatest of American scenes.— **Bill Surber, Shelbyville (Tenn.) Gazette.**

Anybody can cook steak and French fries over a campfire, but in the modern kitchen it takes not only scientific know-how, but lots of know-where. — **Barrie Young, Oakland (Iowa) Acorn.**

and would like to take over your space temporarily, or permanently. But her speculation on local romances may bring a storm of protest and her compliments on Mrs. Brown's hat, seen at the Country Club social, won't be taken at face value. The hat, you see, was a last year's model and Mrs. Brown thinks the writer knew it and is needling her.

And your seemingly innocent observations may result in surprising explosions. One columnist reported seeing a very solid citizen coming out of a downtown watering place of fair to good reputation. But the man had told his wife that he was going out of town that afternoon. He demanded that the publisher keep his name out of the paper forever after.

Printing people's brags isn't always a good idea, either. White lies look black in printer's ink. Public speakers and curbstone orators have some kind of inherent right to exaggerate facts for an effect, such as keeping the hearers awake or getting their attention. It is cruel to print their words exactly, quite apart from the occasion and the mood.

You may note that a few papers are running high school-ish gossip columns. These boy-girl items on who is or is no longer dating whom make severe demands on the heart strings. You have only to remember your teen-age years to know that while the young heart mends rapidly, it must not be assumed that it cannot be "broken." Reader interest in gossip is morbidly high, but you will be a happier columnist if you leave affairs of the heart to the persons concerned. And you may even live longer.

There are three events in a person's life which offer little danger of offending, except with inaccuracies. These are his birth, his marriage, and his death. Treat each of these events with dignity. In fact, it is wise always to remember the dignity of the individual personality. You can make it a basic policy of your column to repeat often the idea that every individual has, under democracy, a precious right in the inviolability of his person and his reputation, and his privilege of choosing his location, his vocation, and his leisurely pursuits.

"Face" is important in a small town where there are few strangers. Tempers have lost some of their mettle in recent years, but we recall how an ordinarily even-tempered man acted when he took his family to a community Christmas tree. Expecting no favors from Santa Claus, he felt vastly insulted when Santa, in high glee, presented him a large, beribboned gourd. This man broke the gourd over a chair and stalked out in wrath. The gourd, we recall, is not held in high regard when it is not a dipper at the well.

Indirect reprimands may take the form of this item from the Goodland (Kans.) *News*:

When you hear some folks you know blow and brag, you are reminded of the time the flea said to the elephant, "Boy, didn't we shake the bridge back there when we crossed it!"

But you will find that it pays to keep a column clean, kindly, and sympathetic. Other columns will have enough of sorrow. Publishers realize today that

. . . a carelessly conducted column may arouse sharp
and damaging reactions . . .

columns are flexible devices for building good will and stabilizing circulation. Conversely, a carelessly conducted column may arouse sharp and damaging reactions.

If you are a kidder, you will be tempted to tease people through the column. Take care. The line between acceptable kidding and being suspected of making an uncomplimentary remark is very narrow. And if people never know when to take you seriously your influence will decline.

We have mentioned the use of news in columns. You will represent your readers as you gather stories on your rounds. You will report things in the spirit of the people concerned. On your beat, you will match wits with your news sources, quip for quip and mood for mood. Calling at an office is a sort of ritual — a proffered cigarette, a what-do-you-know, and an exchange of pleasantries before the serious news is collected. People will probe you for laughs, and they will read your column in the same spirit.

Simple reporting is hard to beat. Note what your friends read, and wear, and say. Watch for new gadgets, black eyes, sprained ankles, chigger bites. Learn why a person is missing from his desk. Replies to questions will elicit news items, of course, but column material also.

We have demonstrated, we hope, that you will never lack for column material; rather, the main lack is time. Keep that little notebook handy to record ideas which otherwise you won't remember. Keep it with you as you read books, magazines, newspapers, and legal documents. Columning becomes a state of mind; an inspiration for a column may come at any time. You're talking to the justice of the peace and it suddenly occurs to you that the history of his office must be interesting. It is, and you can do a column on every public office.

Daylight saving idea came from an old Indian chief who cut off one end of his blanket and had it sewed on the other end to make the blanket longer.— Clarke A. Sandford, Margaretville (N. Y.) **Catskill Mountain News.**

Now, let's wind up this chapter with two musts:

1. Try to say exactly what you mean — and mean it. Words are tricky. Watch for double meanings.

2. When you criticize, be specific. Your targets are entitled to a clean-cut bill of indictment. If you can't bring yourself to name and make your position clear, you are certainly not ready to risk the dangers of partial identification and innuendo, which may lead to libel suits.

Be stubbornly fair, and fear no reader.

Be honest with your conscience, and suffer no remorse.

Remember that people live very close to their emotions, meaning that their first concerns are for themselves. As a columnist you will be examined not only for what you say, but for what you feel. Loyalty to the community is assumed, but its reality may unhappily be cast into the shadow of doubt by some critical remark meant to be constructive. Bob Callan, columnist of the Kaufman (Tex.) *Herald,* puts it this way:

"Readers will follow a journalist through many editions to find out what is in his heart, when they wouldn't give a Chinese dollar to find out what is in his mind."

A St. John vacationist has sent home post cards which read, "Having a wonderful time. Wish I could afford it."—Clelland Cole, St. John (Kans.) News.

## 7.

# Style—and the Light Touch

A GOOD COLUMN STYLE comes from much writing, plus an ability to learn from the effort. It is closely related, of course, to the kind of personality the writer possesses, and to his conversational powers. Lacking an incandescent spark of genius, a writer improves his choice and arrangement of words by imitation, by unconscious acquisitions through selected reading, and by choosing subjects which he knows well. One paragraph catches fire from another when enthusiasm is natural and honest.

Style is much like the personality, although it does not follow that the life-of-a-party can be equally entertaining in print. Spoken humor, which is enhanced by winks, shrugs, leers, and laughter, must in written form convey these overtones by clever choice of phrasing.

Column style is not a matter of following formulas. It consists of choosing words and sentence arrangements suitable to a given subject. Because newspaper columns touch on many subjects, a competent columnist is a man of many literary moods. And, since every man is more eloquent in some moods than others, columning involves selection of materials which elicit from his writing hours the materials which please readers.

Some columnists are by nature argumentative. Their style is direct, challenging, and persuasive. Others, by nature retiring, prefer a quietly expository style in which they teach, rather than preach or demand. To the extent that columnists write what is demonstrably true and generally believed, they can omit the finer points of logic and concentrate on factors which chiefly amuse. But while readers may be pleased to know the columnist agrees with them, they are only bored on discovering nothing to inflate their ego further. Most columnists, therefore, do not drive their typewriters with mathematical directness between two points.

Column style demands frequent changes of pace. Appeals to readers are the familiar ones: use of names, which substitute personalities for abstract qualities; concrete data, filled with mention of earthy, environmental objects known to all; mention of human frailties, which are among the basic realities; and mention of the unique, the heroic, the tragic, the utterly foolish, and the fantastic.

One's style is quickly affected by the viewpoint from which he writes, and by the personality he imagines himself to be. This explains, in part at least, the fad for assuming personalities bordering on the rustic. A waggish columnist not only has greater freedom in selection of colloquial prose, but he escapes another thought which galls him — that of appearing to be writing down to readers. And, afraid of making one mistake, he may deliberately make many.

Furthermore, a small-town editor who most of each day carries his responsibilities with dignity and speaks in dignified language cannot, at the stroke of 4 o'clock, or 8, become a lively columnist without some

**VERBS**

Verbs not only express action; they carry connotations beyond their literal meanings. They give readers a sense of reality. Passive verbs, especially the "to be" derivatives, slow reading tempo. We associate strong verbs with conflict, such as war and sports, but they also are useful in telling of every-day affairs. A worker moving cautiously along a lofty beam may literally inch his way, like a measuring worm. Something of his caution is conveyed to the readers. . . . Verbs are aided by other parts of speech, if not overloaded with them. Clauses expand or limit their meaning, but slow their pace. Clever phrasing enlivens even the garden variety of verbs— those which describe our routine movements. . . . Verbs stand out more strongly in short sentences. Simple verbs are generally preferred. Most people merely die, rather than pass away; they are buried, not interred.

kind of mental transition. But in time a column becomes so fixed in style that it is a writer's habitual manner of speaking. Such mellowness comes with experience.

Consciously or not, most persons adapt their style of speaking or writing to those addressed. A moment's listening to a telephone conversation often gives a clue to whether the person at the other end of the line is young or old, male or female, liked or disliked. Columnists sometimes think of certain persons while writing, so that their product has something of the sparkle of repartee.

The fear of every columnist should be dullness. And nothing is duller than monotony of sentence structure, abstract phrasing, and always saying the expected thing in the expected way. People who would not use worn out expressions still manage to be dull. Well educated people may be boresome because of their weighting of sentences with complex words and their omission of personal mentions. The United Press told how the London Transport Company campaigned against archaic syntax. Plain English, the Company said, is good English. Examples:

Old rule:  Small dogs may, at the discretion of the conductor and at owner's risk, be carried without charge.
New rule:  You may take your dog with you. It travels free at your risk.
Old rule:  The London Passenger Transport Board can not be held responsible for failure to adhere to the scheduled time of the buses, nor can they guarantee the running of the services to be as stated although every effort will be made to maintain them. In inclement weather, on Sundays, certain buses are liable to be canceled without notice.
New rule:  You can not hold London Transport responsible if your bus is late or does not run. London Transport does not guarantee that its services will keep to the timetable or will run at all, although it does its best to see that they do.

**WHICH LANGUAGE?**

Most persons, educated or not, have several types of oral and written expression. They talk freely, spontaneously with daily companions; more formally with new acquaintances, even in the presence of old friends; rather stiffly, perhaps self-consciously, to strangers they hope to impress, or people older or more successful than themselves. Like a public prayer, formal conversation is likely to be phrased carefully before utterance. Similarly, many persons change style of expression when they sit down to write. Such stiffness is fatal to good columning. The trick of writing with seeming spontaneity is worth learning. In learning, beware of trying too hard. Your best, brightest conversational style is probably what you need in the column.

London Transport had discovered, it said, that "simple and homely language is not only more easily understood; it is frequently shorter." Its new signs were filled with "you's" and "your's" and other person-to-person approaches.

Small-town columnists also adapt their style to the people's wishes. Vocabularies of columns are those of the persons met on the streets and in the shops. Hometown language is picked up, polished a bit perhaps, and handed back in paragraphs, anecdotes, jokes, verse, and other standard forms. Hobbies are written about in the hobbyists' vocabulary. Talk about golf is golfers' talk. It is a form of intellectual bungling to talk about another person's chief interest with less than his enthusiasm. It is amateurish, or worse, to retell a story poorly. The columnist is not a ditch-digger; he is a worker with words. He should study how to use his tools. Experimentation is fundamental in all study. In the words of an old advertisement, "How do you know you can't write?"

If you must have a few guideposts along the road to acquiring a better column style, consider these:

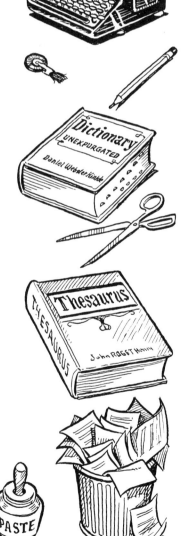

1. Really know your readers.
2. Write animatedly to them.
3. Be yourself, but try to make that self interesting by much reading and careful listening.
4. Seek individualism in your style by observing the mannerisms of others and adapting some for your own use. This is not dishonesty. Originality is almost nonexistent.
5. Don't be afraid to confess human weaknesses or to apologize for the whole human race. Localize and humanize. But stoutly stand for good taste, tolerance, and good neighborliness.
6. Be consistent in your inconsistencies, so that when you put thunder and lightning in your words the readers will not be more shocked than impressed.
7. Learn what stuffed-shirtism is and avoid it as you would a plague.
8. Develop a light touch.

**He should study how to use his tools.**

## NOUNS

Nouns are names; nothing is more fundamental in language. They identify and define. They have dignity and poise. Sometimes they are misused. We hear of name-calling in politics. Such names condemn; they are adjective in effect. But the writer who is clever in choosing nouns can be sparing in use of adjectives. Columnists vary their language by thinking up similes, metaphors, and other figures. There are many synonymns for **man**. At appropriate times, these alternative nouns are more effective than festooning the word with adjectives. The man may be a lion—or a mouse.

### A LIGHT TOUCH PERMEATES COLUMN STYLE

In the years of Fourth of July oratory, editors often blustered and thundered in a pretense of unchallengeable wisdom. They had little to lose but the pretense, for newspaper plants were not worth much and libel actions were rare.

Better times have brought humanness to the small-city press. Reasonableness is both practiced by editors and conceded to be a quality of readers. It is a more honest journalism. It depicts readers as they are — friendly, kind, and generous. But not perfect. Rather than expecting perfection in his people, a small newspaper's editor is not ashamed to report their activities in perspective — the good, the bad, the heroic, the trivial, and the absurd. He finds some of their antics nothing short of hilarious. He mines nuggets of interest in the commonplace. With a deft hand and a light touch he makes life seem an interesting adventure.

In their glass-house simplicity, small-town people must be prepared to face life's triumphs and tragedies without emotional excesses. Maudlin accounts of deaths and funerals have largely disappeared from small papers. People are now conditioned for personal tragedies — children killed by traffic accidents, for example. Perhaps the shock is not much softened, but the reaction to it is less pagan. People take their cues from editor's reporting and philosophizing about events.

The editor's light touch is nowhere better developed than in his personal column, although it also may be found in some editorials and headlines and in feature stories. His lightness of style should not be confused with shallowness. The basic ingredient of the light touch is good will. It exudes good humor. It is the spirit of camaraderie. It is the small-city touch where there are few strangers. For it is in the small town that one finds the neighborly spirit, the harmless prank, kidding without rancor, repartee without bitterness, and laughter that is spontaneous and unposed. People talk roughly, but "smile when they say that."

The light touch may involve both wit and humor, but usually it is not a straight presentation of either. It is a literary stance. It is based, in practice, on the idea that while people in the mass are pretty swell folks, as individuals they run the gamut of human characteristics. In most individuals are capacities for both heroics and plain darned foolishness. Yet the average man, non-existent though he is, is recognized as a long-suffering, home-loving, kindly soul who laughs through his tears. He squeezes some kind of laugh from every situation because he feels an obligation to keep other people from sharing his woes. He loves his comics, laughs with radio and movie wags, and repeats the quips which he finds in newspapers and magazines. He regards long sermons and long articles as stuffy and in general ignores them. He rewards those who make him laugh and may be suspicious of those who make him think. But appeals to his sense of humor and his sympathy bring quick responses. He picks his prejudices and attitudes on the run and therefore has to be speared with barbed bits which he absorbs without realizing it.

Small-town column humor is without sophistication and largely without real or implied vulgarity. Localized, it is lively with mention of people. When a small-town man tells a barber joke his hearers think of a real barber, not a stereotype. Stimulation of the intellect is possible, but incidental. Pegged to current events, column yarns are short-lived. Printable small-town humor is hard to find. But its effectiveness at the moment of publication should not be underestimated. The simple, earthy quality of the small-paper column makes it easy to read by any definition of readability. Often it is the first read

## WORDS

While the language of columns is conversational, in general, rather than literary, many writers like to play with words. Punning continues popular among the paragraphers. Twisting words and using unusual expressions delights the newspaper essayists. Words are columnists' tools; right well do they add new ones and polish their skill in using old ones. Effective words release the shades of meaning which give readers an appreciation of a writer's thoughts. Such words need not be long; they should be familiar to readers or the meaning should be apparent. The history of a word may be worth a day's column. New words can be recognized as they are heard in cafe conversation. Or country club.

## SENTENCES

With verb beginnings or subject beginnings, sentences tend to arrange themselves in monotonously regular structures. If this results from too-careful attention to notes or diction, this fault is probably habitual, and serious. Writing w i t h abandon, largely without reference to notes, promotes good column style. Careful editing and rewriting can be done to shift sentence elements. That is not to say, however, that an ungifted writer can put style and charm in dull prose. But few are the writers who cannot improve their sentences by study and application of a pencil. Improvement of speech, especially through story-telling, may carry over into columning. Gradually, long neglected figures of speech and sentence forms can come into natural use.

department of a paper. It is regarded as personal — a person speaking — in contrast to the detachment of news stories.

Many editors have failed to understand the power of the light essay or witty barb as compared to the serious editorial. Yet they are quick to concede that Will Rogers could deflate a duke, an issue, or an argument with a phrase. Many decry the hiring of newspaper humorists by movies and radio. To a man they recognize the power of the conversational tone in an after-dinner speech, a sermon, or an advertisement. They now concede that the big-name columnists won their place in the press because that place was a void. Readers demanded not only facts, but interpretation. And editors have recognized that readers want material that is a pleasure to read, that has, in short, the light touch that is so descriptive of a small-town man's attitude toward life and his fellows.

Today's small-town columnists use all the familiar devices to achieve the light touch. Some prefer the barbed paragraph, others the anecdote. The news-and-comment method is popular. Comic verse is less common. The light, one-subject essay is well done by many.

Although the quiet tempo of small-town life does not inspire all columnists to distill their ideas into proverbs and sparkling figures of speech, the summations of their philosophy often are quotable. And in increasing numbers they are improving their skill as paragraphers. They are learning the effects of understatement, exaggeration, faint praise, irony, and incongruous comments. Whereas brief wisecracks have the taint of innuendo, light essays permit a writer to choose a subject and turn all its interesting facets to public gaze. Common defects, such as wordiness and leaving too little to the readers' imagination, disappear with experience.

The lighter columns keep readers coming back for more entertainment — and renewing subscriptions. Scolding, prosy columns reverse this readership trend. William Allen White wrote many gay editorials which he called the "foam on the daily newspaper editorial tide."

Variety columns, which well fit the editor's week of contacts, may include news items and comment, doggerel verse, jokes, descriptions of nature, odes to everything from windmills to bobby pins, witty paragraphs, flights of the imagination, nostalgia, and references to concrete things such as the smell of saddle leather, of freshly upturned earth, and of hay meadows and country lanes smelling of sweet locust. Column formulas include a strong dash of whimsey, plenty of warmed-over jokes, jibes at neighboring towns, and sometimes ludicrous references to husband-wife spats and the giddy younger generation.

Cultivation of the light touch pays off in other ways, too. It brightens conversation and correspondence — sells goods — smooths taut committee meetings — brings invitations to speak to civic clubs and chamber of commerce banquets. Another result should be an absence of ulcers, although ulcers are said to be an occupational hazard of the professional gag man.

Relaxed good humor is seldom close to being literature, but it is readable. In this laughingest of nations, the small-town column often merely reports yarns picked up on the street, at conventions, and in normal business contacts. The popularity of donkey ball games is proof of the boyishness of the average American businessman.

. . . lighter columns keep readers renewing subscriptions.

"The Editor's Report" column of the Henrietta (Tex.) *Leader* carried this item:

The Boots and Saddle Club boys really enjoy themselves. For example, Sunday afternoon Harry was roping. He looped a calf. Started to dismount. His horse stopped suddenly. Harry didn't. He rolled about fifteen loops on the ground before skidding to a stop. The audience roared.

Much of the humor of this item is lost unless you know Harry as the Henrietta people do.

Many columns have picked up this advertisement credited to the Danville (New York) *Breeze*:

WANTED—Farmer, age 38, wishes to meet woman around 30 who owns a tractor. Please enclose picture of tractor.

The unexpected ending is one of the most effective of column devices. One columnist solemnly reported that a young lady in his town was flirting with all the men she met. He mentioned the names of several local men who had been favored in her glances. He chided the parents. But local readers were not scandalized when he mentioned the name of the young lady — age 30 months.

From Three Forks to Broadway, the gently chiding column is filling newspaper space. Henry McLemore rode the light touch to his present eminence through items like this one from the St. Louis *Post-Dispatch*:

There is one job on earth I wouldn't have under any circumstances. It's the world's worst. Before I'd take it I would try to make a living by diving off a 100-foot tower into a thimble (with a matinee on Wednesdays), or even by accepting a position that required me to tattoo "Semper Fidelis" on cobras' chests.

The job I refer to is that of saleslady or salesman in a women's hat shop. Why the jails aren't crowded with people who sell hats to women is beyond me. How they resist banging their customers over the head with the handiest and bluntest weapon available shows either great respect for the law or greater control over their tempers. . . .

A small-town version on the same theme comes from the "Russeling Around" column of the Belton (Tex.) *Journal*:

A certain department store in Dallas — and why should we mention its name and provide a thousand dollars worth of free publicity — has hit upon a most humanitarian idea. Presumably to protect the defenseless males from the ravages of competing woman shoppers, it has set aside a special night for men shoppers only. The arguments in favor of this plan are endless. For one thing, men, have you ever been in a store purchasing certain items of clothing for a woman and felt about six hundred eyes, mainly feminine, focused on you in silent ridicule? And have you ever competed with women shoppers in a crowded, impolite city? If you are a gentleman, or weigh under 200 pounds, you haven't a chance. Next year maybe they'll not only segregate the women and men shoppers, but set special hours according to weights.

Random selections from a columnist's reading are presented in a form like this item from the Ronceverte (W. Va.) *News*:

An American insurance statistician traveling in Iran on vacation, but ever conscious of his trade, received a down-to-earth answer when he asked a native chief what the mortality rate in his village was. "Since it is the will of Allah that all men die," the chief replied gravely, "our rate is 100 per cent."

Such stories also appear in dialogue form. This one was found in several columns, credited to *Exchange*.

Jones—How do you spend your income?
Smith—About 30 per cent for shelter, 30 per cent for clothing, 40 per cent for food, and 20 per cent for amusement.
Jones—But that adds up to 120 per cent.
Smith—That's right.

The queer lightness of O. O. McIntyre's first person confessions was typically apparent in this excerpt

**ADVERBS**

What the adjective is to the noun, the adverb is in less degree to the verb. It qualifies, describes, and gives color to the action. Strong verbs may need no such help. The most over-used adverb is probably *very*. People have been described as *very* dead. But unless an adverb has a job to do, why use it? Change the accent to the verb—a verb with full meaning and overtones to most readers. One might say a halfback made 47 yards, running brilliantly. But did he pivot, dodge, spurt, stiff-arm his way, or reverse the field? Another man might be said to move slowly; actually, was it mincingly, crazily, deliberately, or hesitatingly? Say which.

## CHANGE OF PACE

Good writers, like good speakers, change their pace — in tone, length of idea development, and in flights of description, narration, exposition, etc. Paragraph length is varied partly to keep the reader alert. Columnists who always throw out a topic sentence then develop it in obvious fashion give readers no thrills. Why struggle through prosy stuff when it might have been characterized by variety, example, punch lines, and flashes of verbal audacity?

## PARAGRAPHS

In a 12-pica column, paragraphs longer than two inches usually are avoided. However, a single offender may be justified by its content and structure. It is the monotony of successive long paragraphs, one hundred words or more in each, that repels readers. In another direction, the staccato effect of short paragraphs may be distasteful unless the subjects and comments conform to such brevity.

from a column in the Seattle (Wash.) *Post-Intelligencer:*

All my life I've had a terror of policemen. Today, scanning a fresh edition along the street, I bumped into one. I expected to be clubbed silly and thrown into a patrol wagon. Instead, he smiled, stood pleasantly chatting a while, and finally began to tell me a joke he had just heard. At which I rocked and fairly screamed with mirth. I never realized until a block away that I was hysterical.

The late beloved Joe Taylor, a small-town editor whose witty writings carried him to the editorship of the Dallas *News,* wrote for many years a "State Press" column of excerpts from other papers, with his inimitable comments. He also liked to answer letters from readers, often twisting the meaning with mischievous abandon. Example:

A young lady who seems to be hard worked at some university, but who has an inquiring mind and kind disposition, sends to this column a request for an analysis of laughter. The best we can make out of it is that she wishes to know why one laughs when he is amused instead of crying or sneezing. Or why one weeps when heart-stricken instead of sneezing or laughing. The answer must be that the emotions are divided into ganglia or nerve nodules and respond according to which mental filament is twanged. The brain, dear young lady, is like a stringed harp. The tone depends upon which chord is touched. When we weep it signifies that the filament or chord of pity has been struck by the unseen hand. When we laugh it means that chord of comedy has been thumbed. Of course, we sneeze without any consideration of mental pressure. Sneezing is a nasal titilation and is indulged in without regard to mental urge. Laughter is an emotional expression and is accompanied by facial distortion which, fortunately, vanishes after the moment of amusement. It is a response of the same general nature as that which occurs when the nose is tickled by a feather or a straw, except that the nose has to be physically tickled, while the laugh needs only to be mentally touched. Here we find psychology and physiology working in combination. The psychic impression flits from the brain to the face and the latter responds with laughter, which is like a pool being stirred into waves by the wind.

Laughter is, in a sense, a ripple across the physiognomy like a wavelet across a pond. Sometimes laughter becomes audible, but its audibility is only an extraneous factor and has no connection with the source or initial impulse of the laugh. A silent smile is a laugh reduced to its least laborious term, while a giggle is a compromise between the smile and the loud guffaw that bespeaks the vacant mind. This is the best we can do for you, young lady, even if it does sound too simple for belief.

As may be surmised from the example, Joe Taylor had a dead-pan humor which was the delight of small-town publishers at their conventions. With his witticisms, however, Mr. Taylor combined well chosen bits of advice and homey philosophy. He was a favorite of women delegates, with whom he danced with gallantry and grace, and of the men also, who respected his ready wit and appreciated his championing of small-town life. He was a master of the grandiloquent phrase but in general preferred direct speech. Back in the careful 1920's some of his stories were considered daring, but nevertheless in passable taste. Example:

Young woman: Doctor, can you vaccinate me where it won't show?
Doctor: My dear young lady, I think you'd better see your dentist for this service.

William Allen White is remembered for his famous editorial, "What Is the Matter With Kansas?" and for his books and influence, but many who read the Emporia *Gazette* and saw the dumpy little man daily liked to comment on his humanness. His was the light touch, and life roughed him but lightly except in the tragic death of his daughter. He wrote these thoughts at 65:

I have been shaving this funny old face every Sunday, Tuesday, Thursday, and Saturday for years and years.

**IDIOMS**

Although small-town writing is more colloquial than some readers prefer, the historians probably will wish it had been even more idiomatic. As history, small-town articles would then reflect how people talked, not how the editor wrote. Idiomatic sayings are like some old wine; approved more by reason of age than merit. Columnists can be more alert to spot current sayings. Newspaper writers in general have belonged to the "purist" group. Yet language is a living, growing thing. People like to see their characteristic expressions in print. **How** they say things should interest columnists, whose affection is not limited to words as words, but as expressions loaded with pungent but not always literal meaning.

## JOKES

Columnists who are not joke-smiths can see their dentists several times a year—or their doctor, or lawyer, or butcher. Men of professions and trades usually know printable jokes on themselves, or others. They may know local anecdotes. Ministers excel as story tellers. Columnists who regularly pick up these jokes develop dependable sources. Dull columns are written only by dull people —and poor reporters. Everyone **hears** jokes, but many columnists do not print them.

I have come to look on it as a mask behind which the reality that is I has to hide. It is getting a bit battered and shopworn. Perhaps it would not be a bad idea to cast it off and let dust return to dust and if there is any salvage "with God the rest."

In the meantime life has been good, a tremendously interesting adventure. I have never had a bored hour in my life. I get up in the morning now wondering what new, strange, gorgeous thing is going to happen, and it always happens at fairly reasonable intervals. And generally, and this is a part of the unbending curve of my life, adventure comes from afar, from the outside, from things over which I have no control. Lady Luck has been good to me. I fancy she has been good to everyone, only some people are dour and when she gives them the come hither with her eyes they look down or turn away and lift an eyebrow. But me, I give her the wink and away we go.[1]

We'd like to repeat that statement from William Allen White, the small-city newspaper man: "I have never had a bored hour in my life."

It reminds one of another remark by Will Rogers of Oklahoma, another master of the light touch. Will said, "I never knew a man I didn't like."

---

[1] *Forty Years on Main Street,* p. 30. Used by permission of Rinehart & Company, Inc. Copyright, 1937.

# 8.

# The Paragraph

THE NEWSPAPER "PARAGRAPH," referred to in dictionaries as the editorial paragraph, is distinguishable by its brevity and epigrammatic structure. It resembles the paragraph of standard composition mainly in that it is indented and a unit of thought. But instead of developing a thought completely, the editorial paragraph often leaves the reader something to supply; that is an important part of his enjoyment. The technique permits a brevity which is a delight to read, but to write is beyond the skill of all but those who have or can develop this rarest of column-writing talents.

. . . it is easily picked up for use in other publications.

After the young son saw that we meant business concerning his giving away at least five of his dogs, he proceeded to give them to children in the immediate neighborhood. Now it's a case where the cake was eaten and also kept. The dogs came home.—Robert D. Burgess, Opp (Ala.) **News.**

Back a quarter century, nearly all newspaper comment was in editorial columns, and the little quotable stingers appeared as follow-items to the regular editorials. Now, they mostly appear in columns.

We are speaking of small newspapers, which cannot afford the luxury of full-time editorial writers who might also develop a flair for writing paragraphs. The town columnist may deliberately assign himself the duty of writing a few pithy paragraphs each week, or he may produce them in the heat of inspiration while writing news-and-comment matter, anecdotes, and light essays. Sometimes he strikes off a quotable paragraph in summing up his observations.

The paragraph, in the sense used here, is distinguished by its brevity, its independence, and its sparkle. Two to six lines usually suffice. One of the most useable of column items, it is easily picked up for use in other publications as a filler, as the basis of witty comment on its content, and to permit other readers to enjoy its wit and humor. How to make column material quotable is discussed in Chapter 11. As will be noted in that chapter, paragraphs written mainly for local consumption are not as quotable as those based on eternal truths and philosophy.

You don't get ulcers from what you eat. You get them from what's eating you. — Sidney (Nebr.) **Telegraph.**

Rubbing elbows with a man will reveal things about him you never suspected. The same is true of rubbing fenders. — Grimes (Iowa) **News.**

A column containing only independent paragraphs is rare in small papers. Variety columns may contain many, or few, or none. The types found most commonly in newspapers may be roughly classified as follows:

1. The *epigram,* which Webster says is "a bright or witty thought tersely and ingeniously expressed."

2. The *pun,* "a play on words of the same sound but different meaning."

3. The *fact-and-comment* item, in which a bit of information or opinion from any source is presented in a novel way through a witty remark or display of incisive "horse sense."

4. The *news-and-comment* item, in which current news is commented upon in a novel way, preferably with an unexpected twist which points up a truth even when the comparison may be somewhat ludicrous.

Not worthy of classification here, we think, is the smart alec remark, that adolescent outburst which has no basic good sense. The wisecrack was called "the illegitimate child of the epigram and the hoot" by Arthur Peterson of the *Toledo Blade*.

Smartly written epigrams are cartoon-like in their simplicity and lucidity. Their key words hold overtones and content quite out of proportion to their brevity; the reader supplies enough background to permit him to accept the paragraph's economy of construction. In fact, he is pleased because he is able to supply that background. Of course this feat is not difficult because most paragraphers ride the current news hard and also stay close to common problems of living.

The editorial paragraph is worth a lot of time in the writing. It is almost as concentrated as poetry, and sometimes as filled with imagery. It is a distilled sermon. It is the product of a fleeting moment of human insight. It is a flash of mental inspiration. It is a blunt statement of a philosophy which may have been years in the forming. It is pleasant in sound and arrangement, often clever in alliteration, contrasts, or association. It bespeaks the active, well-filled mind.

A charm of many paragraphs is subtlety. Readers discover absurd prejudices in a face-saving way. They can about-face on issues without being bludgeoned in editorials which imply they are stupid fools.

Most great writers have left humanity a legacy in statements of faith. Countless numbers of these are in paragraph form. The Bible is filled with them. Shakespeare was a master of the short bit, and even used

The reason so many women object to their daughters getting married is they are afraid the daughters will make mistakes as bad as the mothers did.—George B. Bowra, Aztec (N. M.) **Independent-Review.**

So live that it doesn't matter if they can recognize your car.—Harlowtown (Mont.) **Times.**

It used to be the family album which scared suitors away. Now it's home movies.—Augusta (Kans.) **Gazette.**

puns more than critics think was good for him. One of the authors received, as a graduation present, a copy of *The Meditations of Marcus Aurelius*. It is sobering to ponder the sayings of that humble old Roman, pagan emperor though he was.

Pick your paragraphers and sharpen your wits—from the literature of any country. Books are made for men, not libraries. In fifteen minutes a day you can share the thoughts of Epictetus, a pagan slave who lived a life of lofty exaltation. Or perhaps you would prefer the translations of Horace, or Aeschuylus, Plautus, or Pliny the Elder. Or Ben Jonson, Samuel Butler, or John Milton. Or perhaps you prefer Alexander Pope, Samuel Johnson, William Cowper, or Charles Lamb. And possibly Thomas Jefferson, William Wordsworth, and James Russell Lowell. All have contributed to the art of paragraphing.

We do not mean to imply that the newspaper paragraph is literature. Or that it isn't. Paragraphs usually are written for the moment. They may live a day, a year, or forever. Those which are clever only in part may survive in part in the form of idioms. Old-time sayings are a part of the folklore of every region. Most of them become dated and belong to a period. Surviving phrases may be broken into words which merge with the general language. Overuse of these items at any time brands them as bromides. They die, but are exhumed by researchers seeking the origins of old expressions.

The paragraph is a natural form of expression. People constantly pass judgment on things. They weigh everything that is new. Crackling criticisms come from grandpa and grandson alike. And a newspaper without a similar critical voice is unnatural and inadequate. A newspaper without pungent observations—paragraphs—is to that extent failing to use an important literary tool. It is failing to use a device appreciated by good conversationalists, after-dinner speakers, judges in their decisions, preachers

When her eyes say "go" and her lips cry "stop," what's a fellow to do, a conscientious contemporary wants to know. Brother, it was our experience that in towns our size, after midnight all kinds of traffic lights are meaningless. — Brigham City (Utah) **News-Journal.**

in their sermons, teachers in their lectures. Even the wisecracks of the immature probably represent youth's grasping at life's great truths and attempts to formulate judgments in pleasant forms.

The relative scarcity of good short bits, compared to the supply of anecdotes and light essays, is inherent in the nature of the paragraph. The paragraph requires reflection, relating of facts, some skill in arranging the conclusion, and extreme brevity. Many columns are the work of persons who are too busy to sit in quiet thought before their typewriters. They have never attempted to perfect independent paragraphs. This is more an observation than a criticism. Skill in any kind of condensation takes time and practice.

Nevertheless, the growing interest in the newspaper column has increased the output of paragraphs and called attention to many excellent paragraphers in the small-city field. Other factors are the larger newspaper staffs, which have been made possible by growth of towns, and the steady movement of journalism school graduates into small papers. And reprinting of column excerpts by newspapers and magazines always inspires writers to try to "make" these publications. Recognition is always a stimulant to activity.

Said the late Marlen Pew in *Editor and Publisher*: "One of the best arts in editorial practice is paragraphing. A real paragrapher is a bird of rare plumage, as you well know if you have ever tried the snappy two- and four-line items which must be 'on top of the news' and give each situation a witty twist. It is doubtful if there are two dozen expert paragraphers in the business." [1]

Skill in any kind of condensation takes time and practice.

[1] Quoted by A. Gayle Waldrop in *Editor and Editorial Writer*, p. 234.

## MOOD AND METHOD

Witty paragraphing is partly a state of mind — a mood or pose which may be habitual or as false as a clown's face. Resourceful columnists permit themselves to react to good and bad news, the weather, and their contacts with people. They gripe and growl, apologize, exhort, and demand. Selecting a mood, they sometimes dash off a string of related witty paragraphs. It is this unpredictable moodiness which brings readers to the column each week—often before other parts of the paper are read.

Those three little words. Well, the most popular are: "I Love you," "Dinner is served," "All is forgiven," "Sleep until noon," "Keep the change," and "Here's that five." — D. E. Carrell, Keokuk (Iowa) **Gate City.**

Mr. Pew was talking of paragraphers of large and consistent output. Few small-town columnists would make claim to this classification. But they are better writers because of their attempts to master this fairly difficult art. Their columns need short, independent items to break up gray masses of straight matter.

Recalling the long-sustained output of paragraphs by the Detroit *News,* the authors wrote to Harry V. Wade, chief editorial writer, for a briefing on paragraphing today. His reply follows, in part:

"The Detroit *News* since the turn of the century has never been without at least one editorial paragrapher, and thirty years ago had three contributing together thirty paragraphs a day. There were many papers at the time that printed as large or almost as large a daily effusion. Funny columns like Luke McLuke's in the Cincinnati *Enquirer,* which were largely paragraphs, ran to great length.

"The art or knack of writing paragraphs has probably not died but in later times has been diverted into other media which invite one of that bent—gag writing for the radio and the panel cartoons, etc. and the writing of light copy in advertising. I recognize my paragraphs regularly in the cutlines under some of the most popular panel comics, illustrating the kinship of the two styles.

"Papers that use paragraphs in any quantity are dwindling in number, and those that persist are papers, like the Boston *Globe,* with a long tradition for good paragraphing that they evidently think worth conserving as an asset. By and large, however, the professional paragrapher today is in about the position of the last horseshoer in town.

"I doubt that one who is not an all-round newspaperman of considerable experience with news and life can produce effective paragraphs in any number day after day. Green hands try it but the vein exhausts itself quickly. The best, most urbane, and penetrating editorial paragrapher in this country in forty years was the late Bob Ryder of the *Ohio State Journal*. He also was the *Journal's* editor-in-chief.

"The paragraph as a form survives sectionally in New England and the Deep South and in the Northwest; but it has largely disappeared in one of its old strongholds, Ohio, and quite generally in the Middle West. I syndicate my daily *News* output through the North American Alliance under the name 'Senator Soaper Says.' It goes to between seventy and eighty papers, a majority of which use the material as *The News* does, following the editorials, with or without the Soaper caption. Most of these papers in the past used paragraphs created in their own offices. Some dress up a daily assortment of five or six paragraphs with a drawn cut, and others frequently pick out a paragraph, title it, and make a short editorial of it. About a third of these customers use the paragraphs as a feature apart or on the page opposite the editorial page.

. . . paragraphing demands as much concentration as anything that goes into the paper.

"I write my paragraphs around midnight in an hour or two. I was brought up on a morning paper and find creative writing, at least, somewhat easier at night. Anyway, it is without interruption, and paragraphing demands as much concentration as anything that goes into the paper.

"At one time or another I have written for sports sections, dramatic sections, have covered all city beats, have been a city editor and overseas correspondent. I think this is the minimum for sound professional paragraphing. Some of the freshest, most exhilarating paragraphs now being written are turned out by Bill Vaughn for his 'Starbeams' column in the Kansas City *Star,* and his background precisely matches my own."

Such is the situation with respect to columning in the daily newspaper field, in which Mr. Wade has an

TIMELY OR TIMELESS?

An entirely local column may die as quickly as the newspaper issue in which it appears. It may have no interest for the next county, or decade, or century. In short, it is geared to events and ideas which soon will be forgotten. Yet life is filled with common denominators. Wit and philosophy may be timeless because man does not change much. The small-town columnist who studies life's greatest subject — man — and reflects on this fearful and wonderful creature is sure to refine some of his thoughts to gems of expression. The pungent paragraph suggests itself when a columnist has reflected not only on man's movements, but also on his prejudices, weaknesses, sacrifices, sins, and h e r o i c s. Such observations should not be confused with the wise-crack of the smart alec.

eminent position. Writing in the Saturday Evening *Post*, Robert Y. Yoder said that "some of the shrewdest comment made on these wacky times comes from Harry V. Wade—alias Senator Soaper—who is a master of the merry art of paragraphing." It was Wade, Yoder added, who wrote about a retiring circus midget, who had reached the sunset of life, and hoped to get on somewhere as a book-end. It was Wade who wrote that the strip-teaser, Gypsy Rose Lee, had arrived in Hollywood "with twelve empty trunks." It was Wade who said of Russia that the misunderstood nation wanted only peace, unity, and its own way. It was he who remarked that while Sherman lived on into the peace, he never said what he thought of it. Wade likes to paraphrase political speeches, such as having the late President Franklin D. Roosevelt telling young voters that youth "must be strong, unafraid, and a better taxpayer than its father."

Mr. Wade, wrote Yoder, thinks the signed editorial paragraph is a break with tradition. He is against newspaper by-lines, believing they "breed a race of ham actors among writers." This is a shrewd observation. Many columns now are signed. While by-lines no doubt arouse a sense of responsibility, they also give writers a feeling of inflated ego which readers can sense. It is a sobering thought that by its flexibility a regular column gives readers a yardstick for measuring an editor's writing skill and probing his innermost philosophical concepts.

Bill Vaughn, conductor of the "Starbeams" column in the Kansas City *Star,* agrees that on big newspapers and some others the paragrapher's trade has been declining in recent years. He wrote in a letter to the authors:

"The causes, I think, are several. One is that the good paragraph presupposes a certain literacy on the part of the reader—a familiarity with current events, coupled with enough background of history (and not textbook history, exclusively, but the history of baseball, beer, and burlesque, as well) and a willingness to be amused by words. In this sense our people are becoming less literate. They seem largely unable to decide by themselves if a thing is funny; they need the roar of a studio audience to reassure them.

"Another factor has been the rise of other types of newspaper columns. We have the syndicated thinkers on global matters, the keyhole school and the chroniclers of anecdotes involving our friends, sprinkled with pleas for crutches for old ladies and homes for derelict kittens. All these columns deliver more zing, apparently, than the paragraph. This not only tends to crowd out the paragrapher, but sends young men who might have been good at the business into other forms of column writing.

"In addition, the paragraph has been the victim of that familiar foe of all locally-produced newspaper features— syndication. By this I don't mean that there are many good syndicated paragraphers—in fact, Harry Wade (the best in the paragraphing business) is the only one that comes to mind. Publishers, however, find that in the package of comic strips and canasta lessons, which they have purchased from syndicate salesmen, is also a paragraph service. These paragraphs are likely to be pretty horrible, but they are paragraphs. They are short and they can be stuck in here and there on the editorial page. The publisher doesn't read them and doesn't really expect anyone else to. But he has paragraphs, and why should he hire somebody to write him some more? . . .

"My own 'Starbeams' appeared in the first issue of *The Star* in 1880, and I think it may be the oldest continuously conducted column in an American paper. One of its best known conductors was the late Charlie Blakeslee. For thirty years prior to my taking it over it was run by Clad H. Thompson— a really fine paragrapher with a highly individual style.

He may have a greasy hat and his trousers may be shiny, but if his children have their noses flattened against the window pane a half hour before he is due home for supper, you can trust him with anything you have.—Katheryn Launtz, Washta (Iowa) **Journal**.

On the way back through Texas we caught up with that story about the boys from the sand country who were caught selling, in lots of fifteen, sand burrs to the boys from Wisconsin as settings of porcupine eggs.—W. H. Conrad, Medford (Wis.) **Star-News**.

Growth of the small-city and town newspapers as business enterprises took increasing proportions of the editors' time, with resultant damage to the quality of editorial writing and paragraphing. But recently there has been a stirring at the grass roots, a rebirth of writing for writing's sake at a time when paragraphing is languishing in the big cities. In his attempts to compose quotable column material, the weekly newspaper editor finds nothing more suitable than the witty paragraph.

The claim is heard that columnists are born, not made. Evidence seems to indicate that good conversationalists are born, but that columnists are made. The relationship between inherited and acquired skills is very close, of course.

O. Henry, a bank clerk struggling in Austin, Texas, to keep alive a little paper called *The Rolling Stone,* wrote in a column many of the paragraphs and anecdotes which were later expanded into short stories. O. Henry was a genius, but much of his column material showed little evidence of it. The main distinction appears to be that some columnists are capable of devising techniques and developing latent abilities, and some are content to remain hack writers. A study of techniques and collecting of good examples of the art are basic essentials for any serious study of paragraphing.

Of course methods cannot be dissociated from the personality and thought patterns of the paragrapher. Real or feigned pessimism adduces a brand of acrid comment which, combined with human insight, mixes the bitter with the sweet in a way that many readers find diverting. Other columnists are warm-hearted and mellowly philosophical. The storyteller can afford to attribute brilliance to others, but the columnist who writes paragraphs stands on his own figures of speech. He is clever or he isn't.

In paragraphing, punctuation must be exact.

**EMBRYO**

freckles
on face
on teeth
a brace

pigtails
down back
her knees
both lack

a space
between
she's skinny
as bean

she's only
eight
but just
you wait

next thing
you know
she'll start
to grow

Points must not be lost in useless words. Arguments should be largely impersonal, disarmingly persuasive, and logically sound. A subtle paragraph may shift a reader's point of view, but he must think his change of heart is achieved wholly by himself. It is near literature when a reader can see, in the words of a writer, golden truths which need exert no force for acceptance.

Since paragraphs make much use of contrast, it follows that figures of speech abound in them. Such figures, being comparisons between things of different classes, must be comparable in some striking detail. Paragraphers are endowed with neural paths along which flash recognition of these unique likenesses. The resulting truism, if apt, is pleasing to readers. But writers who can think only of trite comparisons must paraphrase or delete the figures which occur to them. And nothing is duller than a crude figure, nor more absurd than implausible comparisons about ordinary household articles.

Figures of speech should be fresh, logical, and essentially true. They require some time for contemplation and enjoyment, and should be used sparingly. Use of several figures in the same paragraph is too severe a strain on a reader's imagination. Consider the wealth of paragraph forms in anticlimax, antithesis, euphemism, irony, metaphor, simile, personification, and other figures.

These figures involve use of many forms of contrast, including under-statement, exaggeration, resemblance, and attributing of personal forms to abstract things. Of these, the simile and the metaphor are perhaps in widest use. Mention part of a common simile and most anyone can supply the rest of it: "It was as black as . . . coal, night, etc." Similarly, a mean man is a brute, a heel, a rat, a snake, etc.

Strained comparisons should be avoided: "His oratory writhed and struck like an angry snake."

and just
that quick
this little
chick

will have
complexion
that's
perfection

her teeth
will gleam
like spot-
light beam

her hair
will curl
with latest
swirl

her legs
will pose
for fashion
hose

and she'll
be stacked
and
fully packed

she's only
eight
but just
you wait.

—Bob Bowen,
La Jolla (Calif.)
*Light.*

Far more acceptable: "As helpless as a young mother trying to manipulate the volume control of her wailing infant."—"As We See It," in Chilton (Wis.) *Times-Journal.*

The epigram appeals mainly to the sense. With his somewhat cynical insight, Ed Howe wrote: "Be careful, and you will save many from the sin of robbing you." Said Byron, "Wrinkles, the damned democrats, won't flatter."

Personification in paragraphs is fairly prevalent. Sometimes a column character is created by accident. A mouse shows a quivering nose as he surveys an editorial office from behind a cut cabinet. A society editor squeals. The mouse gets a column mention. He reappears and is named Percy. Readers write in to know more about his antics. Soon he is being quoted. He visits mice at the city hall, and is quoted. Soon he knows more than most folks, and tells some news which might not be printed in other forms. An irate reader would hesitate to name an office mouse in a libel petition——but don't depend on it.

Paragraphs within columns do not require titles, but may have them. Grouped paragraphs have been titled "Twinkles," "Briefs," "Brevities," "Iowa-grams," "Barbs," 'Snapshots,' etc. Columnists' names may be used. "Annegrams" is used by Ann England of the Morton (Tex.) *Tribune.*

Paragraphs require no particular typography. Occasionally one notes indentions and alternate boldface and regular type.

Types and techniques of paragraphing are further discussed in Chapter 11, and examples are printed in the margins.

**If telephone operators could talk back, they probably would say, "Get that cigar, pipe, cigaret, or pencil out of your mouth and put your teeth back in so I can understand you."— Frank Hall, Hill City (Kans.) Times.**

**. . . visits the city hall, and is quoted.**

# 9.

# *Anecdotes and Essays*

Oꜰ ᴛʜᴇ ᴠᴀʀɪᴏᴜs ᴛʏᴘᴇs of column materials, the short narrative article is one of the most effective. In the form of anecdotes, it has a flexibility ranging from the humorous to the fantastic.

While ranking below the expository essay in frequency of use, the brief narrative is an indispensable element of the newspaper personal column. Several of the little stories may fill a day's quota of space. One or two local stories in each issue cause it to be one of the paper's first-read departments. Or a brief story may become the subject of an essay which follows it.

Other reasons for the popularity of the narrative article include:

1. It resembles ordinary conversation; from birth to grave, people tell stories.

2. It involves literary patterns—news, features, etc.—which are most familiar to newspaper writers.

3. Anecdotal material is fairly abundant, especially if readers know that the columnist needs and will print contributed material.

4. Narratives such as are often told columnists can be commented upon with a minimum of preparation

**ANECDOTES**

Few columns are composed almost or entirely of anecdotes. Such writing would be a full-time job, and a hard one. But short narrative stories, actual or imaginary, have an important place in newspaper columns. Sharp writers are good story-tellers. They know how to search out anecdotal material and how to elicit it through interviews. Few skills are more important to small-city columnists.

because the writer can draw upon his philosophy, his conversational skills, his imagination, and his basic policies.

5. Reporting local incidents as anecdotes permits a writer more freedom of style and structure than do other forms, such as rhyming verse and humorous paragraphs.

6. Both anecdotes and light essays may be used to further campaigns, point morals, and through subtle or direct exposition build a public understanding of the paper's policies — and without scolding.

But not everything printed under a standing heading in twelve-pica measure is a "column." Some departments taking this form are filled with news items, announcements, or straight editorials. Dully composed matter presented in this form may be typographically attractive, but it would be inaccurate to call it a column of the kind usually described as "personal."

The column under discussion here is characterized by the previously described light touch. It uses literary forms which follow distinctive patterns. The anecdote is one of these. The effectiveness of the brief narrative story, or yarn, is well understood by traveling salemen, evangelists, lecturers, and teachers.

An ancedote is a brief, polished narrative. It has a point — creating a laugh, a tear, or some other human reaction. Having a good story to tell is fundamental, but the skill in the telling largely determines the reader's response. Every word adds to or detracts from its effectiveness. Each well-turned phrase gives the reader a sense of exhilaration, the writer a thrill of accomplishment. One moment of inspiration begets another. The writer's mind, like his reader's, races ahead probing for phrases, discarding bromides, thinking but consciously discarding the obvious.

*. . . the skill in the telling largely determines the response.*

As the writer proceeds, he separates significant facts from the trivial and the unusual from the commonplace. He edits sharply, knowing that logical transitions can be supplied by readers, who will derive satisfaction from doing so. He refrains from pointing out obvious conclusions and from making unnecessary explanations, for the same reason.

The parts of a simple anecdote usually are three: (1) The introduction; (2) the details, or build-up; and (3) the climax or conclusion.

This conversation was heard:

"Say, did you hear what happened to Joe Blow?"

"No, what?"

"Well, it seems that Joe was driving out to the corn field the other morning, and . . ."

The yarn continues as the narrative moves chronologically to the climax of the story — Joe's breaking his leg in a freakish manner. The structure of the story is clear:

A—Introduction of the subject and whetting of the hearer's interest.

B—Presentation of details, each of which contributes something to the suspensive effect.

C—The conclusion, which leaves the reader satisfied because he has had his thrill and he now has a story which he can repeat, with such variations as he may contrive in his own version.

The hearer might repeat the story as follows:

"Say, did you know that Joe Blow broke his leg yesterday?"

"No; how?"

"Well, he cracked a whip at a wasp nest, the wasps organized a quick attack, and Joe broke his leg jumping off a wagon. . . ."

This second version, even more than the first, uses the element of surprise, or startling statement. Suspense is sacrificed in the swift statement of the main point of the story. Yet small town folk wish to know

**RELATE and LOCALIZE**

Small-town columnists have no obligation to save the world. But when hometown boys are fighting or serving on distant fronts, many items from the outside have local meanings. Readers crave information which relates outside information to their problems of taxes, wages, style, food, and employment. Columnists at the national and international levels must mention prominent names; local columnists can mention the butcher down the street, the baker, the banker, the farmer. Readers are pleased by local reactions, not by platitudes and generalizations. Therefore, **relate** and **localize**. Reflect the result of national decisions through local incidents. Keep the light touch in writing.

everything about a minor tragedy affecting an acquaintance. The narrator continues:

"It seems that Joe was driving over to a corn field at the time and. . . ."

The story is concluded without artifice, ending when the last pertinent fact is given.

Less exciting anecdotes may take a more leisurely, chronological form, using the familiar "Once upon a time. . . ." or "That reminds me of the story of the man who. . . ." In any case, an anecdote must be told so quickly and so interestingly that the reader's interest is held all the way. No tame vocabulary will do. Too many facts will obscure the main narrative thread. Trite phrases will destroy freshness. Concrete words full of imagery must whet the reader's imagination. Good writing demands an easy, flowing style, rhythm, simplicity, and precise placement of emphasis.

The over-all effect may be intimate or reserved, exciting or restrained, slow-paced or abrupt, didactic or quietly narrative. The totality of the effect is to create in the reader the impression which the writer set out to give. For having read the item, the reader will be conscious of having been entertained, warned, praised, or instructed.

In subject matter, anecdotes may be either real or imagined. They are most effective when they concern subjects, people, and incidents which are familiar to readers. They are highly quotable. They are the vehicles of rumor and gossip. Exaggerated, they are known as "whoppers." They often are only "relatively true"; they might or should have been true, or they are true except that the person or locality involved is disguised.

In reporting anecdotes heard in the streets, a columnist must remember that story-tellers habitually "improve" their yarns. But what may be told on Main Street, with grimaces and obvious jest, may

## ANALYSIS

What is a "fairly good" friend? This euphemism has m o r e meaning than meets the eye. Earl Tucker of Thomasville, Ala., heard a colored maid use the term, then developed a full column on it. He included some humor, his personal philosophy, several anecdotes, and a clever ending. The fairly good friend was a first cousin to the better known fair-weather friend. . . . A columnist analyses incidents and picks up the language of the participants. If he has strong feelings on national affairs, he may draw some farfetched conclusions. Readers appreciate the confining of such P.S. material to brief suggestions. To explain the obvious is to imply that readers are dumb.

look coldly factual in type. Men who shrug away being the butt of a Rotary Club joke may take offense if the yarn is printed.

Anecdotes which do not concern local people are often composites of persons, times, and happenings. They include parables, fables, and other forms designed to achieve a planned effect. Speakers use them to appeal to the emotions. Propagandists use false anecdotes because of the believability of the narrative story. When readers can identify a fictitious character — of known qualities — with a local person or issue, the power of the anecdote approaches, or may surpass, that of the serious editorial.

The imaginative yarn is perhaps too little used by the columnists. Perhaps we should see more tastefully presented fables after the manner of George Ade or Robert Quillan:

"Once upon a time there lived in a little town three well-known women — Mrs. Bigwig, Mrs. Middle-sized-wig, and Mrs. Smallwig. And it happened that one day . . ."

But profundity is certainly not a requirement of the small-town yarn. Minor comings and goings of citizens evoke chuckles because the readers can supply characterizations and backgrounds. Moreover, columnists gain reputations for having quaint attitudes; their stories are read with a consciousness of the writers. While many items have twists and surprises at the end, others are mere pleasantries in which the endings are "sweet." In any case, local anecdotes are more effective than jokes because they are more plausible and because they represent local people, or types, in action.

No one seems to know for sure what people want these days, except that they won't accept a cent less. — Homer King, Hemet (Calif.) **News.**

We have said that column stories need not be long. Here is an example of brevity from the Corona (Calif.) *Independent*:

Marcia couldn't think of the word for jackknife when she was telling how her grandfather fixed his shoelace.

"He did it," she recounted, "with that little knife which hides itself away."

And, even briefer, is this one from Fred D. Keister's "Round About" column in the Ionia (Mich.) *News*:

Wife to husband, after several rounds of drinks at a local cocktail party:
"Henry, don't take another cocktail. Your face is already getting blurred."

W. J. McHale of the Chilton (Wis.) *Times-Journal* asked his daughter, 5, what she most enjoyed on a summer day. He said she replied, "Chewing bubble gum, riding my bike, and running and screaming and hollering." McHale commented in his column that while this program probably wasn't conducive to developing her brain or making a perfect lady of her, "we can't think of anything we'd rather have her do."

Simple little stories have a high readership when the characters are locally known. This one is from the Fallon (Nev.) *Standard*:

Shorty Burton and Jimmy Allison were down watching our new lithographic press in operation and were quite fascinated by its smooth operation at 6,000 sheets an hour.
Jimmy leaned over and closely watched the automatic paper feeder air-sucker pick up the sheets and start them on their way to be printed. Finally he straightened up and asked, "What picks those sheets up so fast and accurately?"
Before I could answer his question, Shorty Burton quick-like exclaimed: "Why, Jimmy, dontcha know that? It is the same little man picking 'em up that turns off the light when you close the door of a refrigerator."

Telling stories at the expense of other states or regions is a favored diversion in many columns. A New England spinster was credited with this one in the *Back Bay Ledger* and *Beacon Hill Times* of Boston:

She was struggling with a hot cup of coffee in a small Texas railroad station, trying to gulp it down before

Things can be so pure they have no taste or savor. Distilled water is so pure there is little satisfaction in drinking it. Most of us would rather drink out of the creek. Pure gold can not be used. Baser metals must be added. Pure copper has no market. Pure English could not be understood. All of which encourages a person, doesn't it? — Nelson Brown, Mason (Mich.) **News**.

the train pulled out. A cowboy, seated a couple of stools away, noted her plight, and seeing the conductor waving at the woman, came to the fore—

"Here, ma'am, you can take my cup of coffee. It's already saucered and blowed."

Anecdotes and morals have long had a peculiar affinity in the small-town press. The following example is from the Belle Glade (Fla.) *News*:

They tell a story of a chap who found himself alone in a New York hotel on New Year's eve. The lobby teemed with people. Merry-makers thronged the streets. There was gaiety and laughter and a carefree atmosphere on every hand. Lonely and blue, the stranger sat feeling sorry for himself. Finally he could stand it no longer. He decided to do a bit of celebrating even if he had no one but himself for company. Going from tavern to tavern he accumulated a very mellow glow. Life took on a rosy hue. Finally, a few minutes after midnight, he staggered into a swanky hotel lounge. Seeing that he was inebriated, a bouncer took him in charge and escorted him to the street.

Not far away he saw a brilliantly lighted building. Men and women were entering, richly dressed. The place seemed to breathe with a quiet dignity. That was where he belonged. Those were his kind of folks. Making his way to the door, he entered. Looking for the bar, he shuffled down an aisle paying no attention to his surroundings.

Unwittingly he had entered a great cathedral when midnight mass was in progress. Pushing his way to the altar rail he loudly demanded a Scotch and Soda. "Hurry," he shouted, "I want one more drink before the whistles blow; make it snappy, bartender." The priest, seeing his condition, and realizing that the unfortunate man did not know where he was, signalled the choir to march by, singing an anthem.

Unsteadily clinging to the rail, the inebriate stared in amazement for a moment and then, turning to the priest, he cried, "To heck with the floor show; I want a Scotch and Soda."

I do not present this story because of the humor attached to it, but rather because of its pathos and the fact that it seems to typify the spirit of reckless abandon and inability to understand what exists everywhere today. The whole world, it appears, has lost its sense of values and is looking for the answer to its problems in another Scotch and Soda.

Ten years ago I often forgot to lock the office door when I left in the afternoon. Now I'll worry for an hour or two after I get home, wondering if it was locked. Finally I'll get up and go back just to see. Sure enough, I hadn't forgot to lock it. That's one reason why I think my memory is getting better. Not one time have I found it unlocked. — Earl L. Tucker, Thomasville (Ala.) Times.

*Swimming Together* was the title given to an occasion for philosophical observation by Madeline A. Chaffee in the Cranston (R.I.) *Herald*:

The bronzed young man in the swimming trunks knelt on one knee, his eyes on the progress of a small toddler in a bright blue bathing suit coming toward him over the sand.

"Swimming with daddy?" he inquired, as the blond, curly headed little girl made her precarious way from an attractive young woman, apparently her mother, seated on a beach blanket.

Clearly the idea found favor with the miniature bather. Laughing with the delight of a 2-year-old, she reached his outstretched hand.

The man looked over her head at his wife.

"I'll take care of her," he said.

"Of course," she smiled at him. "I'm going to be lazy and sun a while longer. I'll be down."

What an attractive family, we thought, watching from our background vantage point. The thought passed through our mind that happiness is contagious. We smiled just looking at them; they were so obviously glad to be together. He's probably back from the wars, we thought.

The bronzed young man stood up.

With perfect balance he stood there — and we thought for a moment our eyes were playing tricks on us. It couldn't be. It just couldn't.

But it was.

He had but one foot.

The other had been amputated just below the knee, so that, kneeling as he had been, the loss was not apparent. Now, standing, he held the stump close to his good leg so that the effect was somewhat that of the traditional one-legged stance of a crane.

Our immediate reaction was that of sympathy, followed with a tremendous feeling of admiration.

That takes courage, we thought, as he wheeled and started down the beach at a one-legged hop, with no support of any kind, his small daughter toddling at his side.

"He didn't learn that balance overnight," our companion remarked. "That fellow has got what it takes."

"So has his wife," we said, glancing at her as she followed them with her eyes, trusting his independence, as they reached the waves and waded in.

"I'll bet there's a story behind that amputated foot,"

Some of Cupid's shots must have been the result of a wild ricochet. — Douglas Meador, Matador (Tex.) **Tribune.**

our companion mused as we watched the man lose his balance as a wave hit him, and come up laughing.

We watched as he left the little girl on the beach, watched her scamper back to her mother, turned and hopped back into the water. When it was deep enough he dove and swam, with powerful strokes, into the blueness. Presently his wife joined him and they swam together.

They swam together.

We sat on the sand and watched a Coast Guard cutter offshore, a sail on the horizon, a plane circling overhead, and mused on this business of togetherness.

It's a very satisfactory sort of word: together. With tremendous ramifications. Not only the togetherness of families, but of friends, of races, of nations. It's when we lose our sense of togetherness and go our separate ways that tragedies occur; when we lose sight of fundamentals.

The waves danced up the beach, frill upon frothy frill. The sun shone warmly. Out in the frothy blueness, two heads turned toward shore, where a small girl sat playing in the sand.

It doesn't matter so much, we mused, what happens to us, just as long as we keep swimming.

Together.

An example of building up suspense until the last line is this story from the Laurens (Iowa) *Sun*:

Once upon a time there was a newspaper publisher who was inordinately fond of fishing. In fact, he'd hightail it out of the office and up the nearby river the moment his paper was out on Thursday.

Came a week end when the moon, water, and bait were just right, and the fish bit so fast and furiously that he couldn't tear himself away from the spot on Sunday, Monday, or Tuesday or Wednesday. But on Thursday he awoke with a start to the enormity of his sin. Here it was press day and not the first lick hit on the paper. Frantically, he threw his tackle into the boat, speedily rowed down the river to town, his mind meanwhile outracing the current.

At the shop his worst fears were confirmed. Judging from the empty bottles lying around, his one printer and general aide had been on his annual spree. And the bookkeeper-reporter, of course, had fled the moment the printer hit the bottle. The publisher glanced at untouched forms from the previous Thursday, then broke down and wept bitterly. Then out of bleak des-

The gossip of small towns is just about the same as that in large cities, but it is more unanimous. — J. E. Sterling, Hugo (Colo.) **Eastern Colorado Plainsman.**

Things are so confused at present that even four-way cold tablets don't know which way to go.—Gaffney (S. C.) **Ledger.**

peration flashed a brilliant idea. It took but a moment to set a line of type in 24-point boldface, which he inserted above the head of the front page before trundling the forms to the press: "REPRINTED BY REQUEST."

Probably because the pastime is a favorite of editors, fishing provides many anecdotes for columnists. Here is another one, as recounted by Richard Stanton in his column, "From What I Hear," in the Sussex (N.J.) *Independent*:

A man who discovered the joys of fishing rather late in life became even more insistent than ordinary anglers are upon telling his triumphs to skeptical acquaintances. Enraged by their thinly veiled hints that he was a liar, he bought a special pair of scales, installed them in his library, and made his friends watch while he weighed the fish he caught.

One evening a nervous neighbor (about to be a father) burst in and excitedly sought permission to borrow the scales. He was back in ten minutes, his face flushed with dazed delight.

"Congratulate me," he cried. "I'm the father of a 48-pound baby boy!"

War talk starts, so we put longer-lived old folks to making ammunition to shorten younger lives.—El Reno (Okla.) American.

True stories have an especial appeal because they usually have happened to many readers. This one is told by J. C. Peck in the Cazenovia (N.Y.) *Republican*:

Early Sunday morning, the horn on George Tessier's truck, parked in front of his house, short-circuited and started to blow. George, solicitous of the neighbors' sleep, leaped out of bed, scrambled into a few clothes, and tore downstairs. Just as he reached the porch, the blowing stopped. Much relieved, George went back to bed but had hardly pulled the covers up against his chin when the horn let go again. Another race downstairs and this time he made the sidewalk before the horn cut out.

Back to bed again but this time as a precautionary measure he laid out his clothes like a fireman so that if necessity arose he could almost slide into them as he left the bad. It was a good thing he did because, just as he was getting drowsy, the horn started on another rampage. This time it really meant business and George had an audience of interested and much amused neighbors as he frantically cut the wires to the horn.

Disgusted, he decided he was too wide awake to go

back to sleep, so he stayed up and polished the children's shoes.

Equally believable is this story from Mrs. Rosamond B. Hanson's column, "Chat and Comment," in the Manassas (Va.) *Messenger*:

One very warm Friday evening, Sheriff Kerlin peeled off his coat, hung it on the rack in the hotel lobby, and joined his fellow Kiwanians at dinner. Came time to go home, and the sheriff's coat was gone from the rack, badge and all. The sheriff was cagey. He said little, but his eagle eye was on the lookout for the miserable thief who would walk off with the sheriff's own coat. In the meantime, an unsuspecting but innocent sheep went to midweek church services — a sheep in wolf's clothing, so to speak. It was not until just the other day that the Rev. Len Weston discovered that he had two coats, identically the same, hanging in his closet, reminiscent of the days when a fellow could get a two-pant suit. From the pockets of one he extracted a legal summons, a stock sale certificate, and a bottle of nitro-glycerin (tablets, not explosive). It was not long before the sheriff arrived at the parsonage with a fanfare of siren blasts to recover his property from the "thief."

A woman can see an old rival's virtues a lot better after both of them have to wear glasses.— Raymond Duncan, Ellaville (Ga.) **Sun.**

A bit of whimsey now and then is relished by many small-city writers. The following tale is from the "Sand Dunes" column of the Sierra Blanca (Tex.) *News*:

A tourist had been mountain climbing near Sierra Blanca and on his return to the sand dunes and cacti-covered mesas he told me of going above the clouds.

"Yes," said the climber, "I stepped right off the side of the mountain onto a big fleecy cloud and walked for some distance before I really knew my feet no longer were on terra firma."

"Weren't you awfully scared?" I asked.

"Oh, no, not until the clouds began to scatter and left a wide space between the mountain and my cloud," he replied.

"Good heavens!" I gasped. "Did you ride that cloud 2,000 feet to earth without it deteriorating?"

He laughed and said, "No, the cloud drifted over to another peak and I just stepped off."

I was about to nominate him for president of the local Liars Club to succeed me when I looked down and saw pieces of the cloud clinging to his shoes.

The only time that liquor makes a man go straight is when the road curves. — Everett M. Remsburg, Vista (Calif.) **Press.**

An examination of these and other typical examples of short narrative articles will show the importance of the final statement. In fact, in the composition of an anecdote the final twist frequently is conceived first, then the facts are placed before it. Ability to think up good punch lines is important in many forms of writing. A good line is readily adaptable to verse, essays, cartoon captions, and advertising display. A dramatic situation is lame without a clever summation or characterization. Sharpening of one's ability in narration pays dividends in better writing, better conversation, and in development of a more vivid personality.

### THE ESSAY DEMANDS LITERARY POWERS

Most newspaper writing takes the form of some kind of essay — descriptive, expository, argumentative, editorial, biographical, personal, etc. In its very wealth of types, as well as in literary devices, the essay calls forth all the creative ability of a writer. Given an idea and some details, a columnist must still decide what kind of essay he shall attempt, as well as its aim, its mood, and its method.

*. . . readers never know what to expect.*

Everyone writes and talks essays. They are the stuff of diaries, speeches, papers, sermons, and reports to stockholders. They represent facts and ideas passed through a human mind and delivered in some order, in a form and format suited to the need, and in a style dictated by the intended use.

Columnists can succeed if they are good reporters only, or good paragraphers, or are skilled in versifying, but a reputation for being a "good writer" usually implies something more. Versatility in a columnist means that readers never know what to expect. They look forward eagerly to the writer's seemingly spontaneous forays into an endless variety of fields.

A first-rate column essayist will venture, not far but gaily and frequently, into discussions of everything from woman-hating to raising of guppies, from observations of nature to the composition of music, from wood-carving to the way of a man with a golf club.

The essay can be as heavy or as light as the columnist desires. For column essays, unlike anecdotes, short stories, and other forms of composition, depend relatively little on organization. Their charm is inherent in the subject matter and in the writer's way of presenting it. Arrangement may be entirely logical or it may be almost formless. Many essays represent merely a columnist's "I think" approach to current local problems. What he thinks is less important than that he entertain and inspire readers with keenness of observation and a flair for interesting combining of words. A simple exposition demands accuracy and understandability. A fanciful essay depends upon flights of the imagination and an ability to associate ideas in unique ways.

The kind of beauty that wears best is the kind that grows on one. — Freehold (N. J.) Transcript.

Having struck a pose and advertised a point of view, column essayists are found frivoling or philosophizing or sermonizing according to their bent. To set them expounding, merely mention such words as safety pins, debts, peanuts, war, peace, blondes, farming, and traffic. Columnists have well defined ideas on these things. They like to pick up one of these subjects and rattle a typewriter with it. The result is not necessarily good, of course, but much readable material is being produced.

Many of the best column essayists combine the arts of paragraphing and exposition; that is, their essays are studded with epigrams. Their summations are sharp and quotable. Their style is crisp, their methods variously quaint, whimsical, apologetic, exclamatory, gossipy, etc. Everything they see and hear has column possibilities. A visit from grandma will inspire a series of charming light essays, as also will the presence of daughter's roommate from college. A vacation trip by the columnist calls for a report to readers — not a routine one, but the recording of impressions and delights of a person sensitive to the changing scenes.

There's not much difference between shutting one's eyes to temptation and a couple of winks. — Jonesville (Louisiana) Booster.

Letter excerpts from readers to the columnist show a similar technique. The education and life station of the writer is less important than his outlook, which should be distinctive, and his style, which should be interesting. But hometown readers don't object to colloquialisms and occasional banalities if the report "sounds like" the writer. It is also true that many columns are on the borderline of being boresome, saved only by the fact that they deal with local materials. The popularity of a column cannot be estimated, however, in terms only of its technical excellence or presumed importance of subject matter.

But, on the other hand, the influence of a column may not be in direct proportion to its popularity. Beneath his often clownish pose, a columnist craves the respect of his readers. Although his subject matter may seem light, the purposes of the columnist may be quite serious. And periodically he will vary his topics to include critical local issues. He knows that the greatest piece of column material is truth — concrete, unadorned, specific truth. Truth illumines not only affairs at the city hall, the courthouse, and other public places, but the ways of life of citizens generally.

An "inside story" essay grabs top rating for readership. When argumentative, it may be as exciting as a dog fight. The column spotlights a person instead of a corporation or a firm name. This projection of personality will be discussed in a later chapter.

In the column, the writer's mood and spirit may be exploited through subjective reactions to commonplace things. Women as columnists seem to excel at this sort of thing. Here is an example written by Mrs. Erma Freesman, "The Girl of the Gumbo," in the Manhattan (Kan.) *Tribune-News*:

Immaculate housekeepers never have any thrills. I just know they don't. A car comes down the road; I hold my breath and sure enough it's driving into the lane and my house looks like the devil had been having an auction in it. What do I do? I grab a bath towel and wrap it around my head and wrap a dish towel around the broom and am busy cleaning house right up until they stomp in on the porch. Then I explain I am cleaning house and they'll have to excuse the mess. It works, or anyway I hope it does.

If he shrinks from such first-person writing, the columnist may attribute his feelings to an unnamed person of like profession and problems. Thomas D. Clark includes this description of a southern small-town editor in his book, *The Rural Press and the New South*:

In 1874 an ink-stained Georgia country editor dreamed that he had died and was standing just outside the Pearly Gates when he was greeted from within by a loud, hysterical outcry. This noise came from a group of former subscribers who asked most embarrassing questions in this moment of his entrance upon the celestial life. One wanted to know what the editor had done with the curious egg which he had left in the newspaper office. Another cried, "Where's the piece you promised to write about my new soda fountain?" A familiar voice asked why Old Peddle's new picket fence attracted so much attention while his went unnoticed. Above all this medley of angelic protestation rose the painful demand as to why one outraged soul's name had been misspelled. A female seraph wanted an explanation as to why the account of her wedding had been recorded among the death notices. A David Harum in a southern accent demanded an explanation as to why the editor had written such a sensational story about a runaway scrape in which the reputation of his horse was completely ruined for trading purposes. The village poetess was there, and in a petulant whisper she accused the poor old editor of having botched her verse. A tedious literary companion was most embarrassing of all because he demanded the return of his manuscript. Thus, standing on the very threshold of a glorious eternity, the old Georgian was

If all the cars in America were placed end to end on one long hill, some fool would try to pass them. — Raymond Duncan, Ellaville (Ga.) **Sun.**

reminded of many of the reasons for publishing a country paper, and of most of the local editorial sins.[1]

Vivid description is a quality of many of the best columnists. Familiar scenes are described so concretely that readers share the writer's impressions. The following example by Kay Metz is from her column, "Between You and Me," in the Lamoni (Iowa) *Chronicle*:

I like hens. I like the soft crooning off-key song that accompanies their leisurely search for whatever it is they find when scratching in the petunia bed. I like their business, the way they dust themselves in the middle of the road, and, above all, their sensible contentment in motherhood.

I even enjoy their audible pride on having laid an egg, the hen-house gossip as they gather on the roost for the night, and I do not object to the squawking of pretended panic that lady chickens indulge in when startled by a sudden "shoo!"

It's nice to watch them dip a wing in the dust, feathers separated like an old-fashioned fan, and then stretch a leg far to the back, just like a danseuse taking warm-up exercises back stage.

But even such an admirer as I will have to admit that the term "dumb cluck" is not an idle phrase when applied to most hens. But dumb or not, our old Dominique biddie once taught this former farm girl an important lesson.

It was a drowsy, quiet day. Just the kind of a day that the click of ice cubes in a tall glass sounds as pleasant and inviting as temple bells. Suddenly the still air was split by a loud, shrill sound from the chicken yard and we be-stirred ourselves enough to rush out and see what was causing the commotion.

There was that disgruntled old Dominique trying to get out of the wire enclosure. The gate was wide open but biddie was so busy scurrying to and fro trying to find a way through the fence that she didn't see the gate or realize that freedom was just at hand.

And so today, when I find myself scurrying around to get things done, working at a frenzy to finish up a lot of little tasks, I remember that foolish old hen and pause long enough to look for an "open gate."

In case of gas attack we are supposed to rush to the attic, and if it's bombs, to the basement. If the enemy begins alternating attacks, war is going to be tough on some of us old short-winded guys. — Selbyville (Del.) **Delmarva News.**

---

[1] Pages 1–2.

Richard B. Swenson of the Monmouth (Ore.) *Herald* reported a different parable in this manner:

Spading in the garden the other morning, we found a half dozen choice worms and dropped them one by one in a can as a treat for the chickens. The worms were fat and long. One might suspect the hens would divide them out among themselves, taking half a worm apiece.

But when the worms were dropped there was a rush and scramble of wings and heads. One hen got two worms. She swallowed Number One with remarkable rapidity, then grabbed the second and made off with it. The other hens paid no attention to the many worms before them, but pursued the hen which had two worms —just like human beings.

Gaining a little, the hen would halt and swallow an inch of worm but when the pursuers would catch up she was off again. And so on until worm Number Two was fully taken care of, but with the flock in hot pursuit all the time.

Meanwhile, the other fat and long worms stayed in the can, unnoticed.

An awareness of life at its many phases leads columnists into appraisals like this one by Hazel Murphy Sullivan in the Sun Prairie (Wis.) *Star-Countryman*:

There's magic in being 5. At 5 one is old enough to cross streets without holding a grownup's hand, but young enough to snuggle into a parental lap for a bedtime story. At 5 one can be very big and brave and businesslike in carrying out an errand at the grocery store, but very little and loving and sleepy when it's a bit past bedtime. A 5-year-old can live in a gingerbread house and pick tid-bits off the sugar-plum trees, all the time hob-nobbing with the fairies and elves and make-believe folk, and still boast gleefully over a recently acquired mastery of roller skates and zippers and knots that really stay tied.

At 5 one can marry the little boy next door one day and subsequently vow marital allegiance only to her daddy. At 5 one can spank and scold dolls and say grace at the table with equal dexterity. A 5-year-old is still blissfully unaware of the common identity of Santa Claus and Daddy. In a 5-year-old's world there's scarcely an ill that an ice cream cone won't cure.

Five years is the age of decision. Dresses are discarded for blouses and skirts; one cuts her own meat and butters her own bread; one has stridently verbal and voluble

Children speak of God with such intimacy that it sounds almost indecent. — Justin Hammond, Corona (Calif.) **Independent.**

preferences in breakfast foods and hair bows and cousins. The passion for cleanliness involves long sessions in the bathroom, though it rarely includes ears or above the elbows.

At 5 one can still bestow sticky kisses with strict impartiality and sit through a church service without squirming; at 5 one can go to kindergarten and play at lessons. At 5 one is queen of hearts and mistress of all she surveys. It's great to be 5!

Gene V. Davis of the Boonville (Mo.) *Daily News* offers a later version:

So short a time ago I stood upon the curbing, holding tightly to her baby hand, and said firmly, "Don't jerk away, darling. The cars whiz by so fast."

But today, standing on the selfsame curb, she put out a restraining hand to me, and said, "Wait, mother. The light is red." And then with her hand tucked casually within my arm we crossed the street as the signals changed, and I was warmly conscious she was taking care of me.

Long hours she spends brushing her flowing hair into lustrous waves. Daily or twice daily she must have her perfumed bath, her change into spotless clothes. But when I protest shockedly, "Those shoes! Surely you are not going downtown in those shoes!" she looks down at her saddle shoes, grimy, shoddy, and says in mild amazement, "What's the matter with my shoes?"

When we enter stores to choose her fall school clothes, she is still my little girl, barelegged, short and childishly chubby. But when she emerges from the fitting room to parade a new fall costume, she is suddenly no longer my little chrysalis, but a shining butterfly. Her skirts swing smoothly from trim hips, her sweater molds her young girl figure. She moves with grace, with sweet awareness, with a new-found poise — and something clutches my heart.

In quilted robe, curled up in the big arm chair, she thrills away the afternoons with love stories and romances. But with the cool of the evening she is transformed into a hoyden in gaudy shirt and rolled up jeans, kicking the can with the gang, tusseling over balls, sprawling in the grass, climbing trees. And before she goes to bed she must read the latest "traded" comics.

Craving change, she must have a different frock each day, yet the frocks themselves must be just like those of all the other girls lest she feel conspicuous.

The best security for old age is to be respectful to your children. — Jim Cornwall, Stanton (Neb.) Register.

Criticism breaks her heart. Love and patience and endless tact are her requisites. She is a shoulder to lean upon in trouble. She is but a weeping child in one's arms. She is April showers and April sunshine. She is fourteen.

A simple little story, with a lead which invites reading without destroying suspense with too much detail, was written about a dog by Darwin Lambert in his "Among Virginia Citizens" column in the Luray (Va.) *Commonwealth Review*:

> The man was not even Mickie's master; he simply was a friend. (Mickie is a dog.) It was a hot Saturday night, and partly as a result of some things which happen occasionally on Saturday nights, the man had gone to sleep at the entrance to our lane.
>
> A wooden gate is there and just beyond it the lane slopes abruptly to the State road. En route to town that night, I stopped the car while my father, who was visiting us, opened the gate. My father got back into the car, and I started to drive through the gate.
>
> Mickie suddenly appeared in front of the car, barking. I blew the horn, but the dog refused to get out of the way. I stopped and got out and called Mickie to the side of the lane. The lights of the car shot over the downslope of the lane but lighted the road beyond. It didn't occur to me the first time to look into the shadow.
>
> I got back into the car and started forward again, but Mickie leaped in front of the car, barking furiously and jumping up and down, unwilling to yield an inch. I stopped the car again. My father and I both considered his behavior very queer, and we sat a moment talking about it.
>
> Then I got out and looked carefully in front of the car, and there in the shadow, already too close to the car to be seen from the driver's seat, was the man, sprawled across the lane, asleep. As soon as I went to the man, the dog was content and calm.
>
> Dogs have personality and character, much as do people. They are part of the great pattern of life and by knowing them we inevitably learn more of life.

But not quite as happy was the dog story told by Edward T. Mundy in the Dodgeville (Wis.) *Chronicle*:

The smart man stays a step ahead of those who oppose him and a step behind those who urge him. — Hamlin (W. Va.) **Democrat.**

Many churches have a driveway all around the building these days. That's so Dad doesn't have to back out after delivering the family. — Vic Green, Pekin (Ind.) **Banner.**

Red Evans of this city had been proud of his German police dog. He placed great confidence in the canine and when occasion came to use the animal to guard property he did not hesitate to put him to the test.

Dodgeville has no city sewerage system and the matter of disposal is one for individual solution. Consequently, there are many small buildings of a certain architecture, of course. Hallowe'en pranksters have the rude custom of overturning these edifices, and to guard against such a catastrophe, Red chained his trustworthy animal to the building.

Not a yip or growl did he hear all night, and with the first rays of the rising sun the owner went out to reward the faithful animal. He found the dog, still chained to the building, which, however, was not in its upright position.

If anyone wishes to purchase a police dog at greatly reduced rates, see Red Evans.

A suspenseful chronology about his dog was carried in his "Chatterbox" column by Glen R. Fockele in the Maryville (Mo.) *Tribune*:

My dog Prince was partly responsible for a near catastrophe when he accompanied the Boy Scout troop on a hike. It was in early autumn, and we had taken enough food for the day, planning to return to town late in the afternoon.

But, under the guidance of the Scoutmaster, we had constructed several lean-to's from saplings and leaves, and it seemed a shame not to use them. So we tramped across a cornfield to a farm house, where we found a telephone, and obtained permission of our parents to camp out all night.

It turned right chilly that night, and each lean-to kept a roaring fire going at what was considered a safe distance in front of it. I was wearing an almost new corduroy suit. Prince, of course, was my bed partner, and as the night grew chilly he snuggled closer and closer for warmth.

Suddenly I was dreaming that I had become uncomfortably hot. I awoke to discover the tail of my corduroy suit blazing merrily. Prince had snuggled me right out into the fire.

Small-town people have a strong sense of appreciation for the pioneering of people who preceded them in the community. Many columns are written in praise of old settlers. The following example is from Douglas Meador's "Trail Dust" column in his Matador (Tex.) *Tribune*:

Worn blankets of gray clouds hung for a long time in the west and rain-sweetened wind twisted them like sails of drifting ships. Riding with an ease born of the saddle, the old man topped a low range of hills and his horse became motionless. He braced himself with a wrinkled blue-veined hand on the saddle horn and studied the landscape. With the battered hat pushed back on his head, he looked at the winding river bed to his left and the music of phantom spurs were ringing in his ears. A few grass-covered trails remained but the mold of memories would not fit the image of reality.

For an instant he wished he had not sought this last visit to a remembered camp ground. He had read the letter from the hospital several times and thought of the white, barren room that awaited him.

He rode on slowly and the strong wind pressed his hat brim upward. The saddle creaked with a comforting sound; laughter of old cowboys seemed to come from the swaying mesquites. At last he found a trace of the wagon road and followed it south to the big flat where roundups were once held, but a taut wire fence blocked his advance. A plowed field covered the memory like a brown tarpaulin. He turned his horse and rode back. The wind was blowing sweet and clean; gray sage nodded to his passing like old friends who remembered him.

Another tribute was written by Mrs. Lucille Ellingwood Morrow of the Collinsville (Okla.) *News* in her column, "Just Thoughts of a Plain Country Woman."

The oldtime cowboy was as hard as nails, loyal to his outfit, quick to flare up, afraid of nothing but walking and a decent woman. There are very few, like old Bud Morris and Bill Ericksten, left. Bud was foreman of what we called our Avant Ranch and was true blue. When the cattle stampeded, Bud rode four days, hatless, rounding up the herd; his head and face were burned to a crisp, but the cattle were all located. Bill Ericksten was a cattle foreman of the home ranch and what Father called a "Prince."

We often wondered how Bud knew when nothing was missing since he could neither read, write, nor count.

A report says that three-fourths of the children of the U. S. are undernourished. Most of them are never home long enough to get a good meal even if their mother were there. — George B. Bowra, Aztec (N. M.) **Independent-Review.**

Residents of little towns are much like tadpoles in a small pool. As they grow, neighbors can see them change. Some become chirpers; some turn out to be pretty; some are fast swimmers; some make a big noise; lots of them just set on the log and blink their eyes. Now and then there will emerge a big fat bullfrog — far too elegant for the little pool of his tadpole days. So he moves on up the creek, and waxes fat on the lazy bugs of other places. Though he has the loudest basso on the bank, he is unhappy. He longs for the days before he shed his tail. So in the middle of the night he crawls out on a log and blows his top for the frogs back home. He hopes they're admiring him; but they're not. For they remember when he wasn't any bigger than they were; and when his croaking is over, they go back to sleep in the little pool. That's life in a small town. — Hugh Park, Van Buren (Ark.) **Press-Argus.**

Came to find out that he carried a lot of fence staples, and at the round-up he dropped one for each animal, into a separate pocket, then took them home for his wife, Doll, to count. So they kept the record true and straight, and never was there a hoof short.

Bud was about six feet one, weighed about two hundred. Doll could walk under his outstretched arm, and weighed about a hundred. He swore eloquently, but used no tobacco or liquor; the worst fault Doll found in him was . . . whittling! It was old Bud who said to his horse, which had somehow caught his hind foot in the stirrup, "Well, if you're goin' to git on, I'm goin' to git off."

I was never a bronc-riding cowgirl and my roping was confined to fence posts, but I knew better than to mount my horse, lean forward, and whisper, "Let's commence," in his ear. If there was any hard riding to do in the round-up, I let the men do it. Once I let two steers get away, and after a hard ride, Bud brought them back and shouted to me, "Sit up close to 'em like the other boys do."

A man's estimate of the fabulous oldtimers was given by Giles L. French of the Moro (Ore.) *Journal*:

When the spirit of any of us ventures beyond this mortal coil something goes out of the life of those who remain. Occasionally such a passing seems definitely to terminate an era, to mark the end of a way of life. To those who knew him, the passing of Dave McKelvey will be one of that kind.

In the days when life was rough and men were tough and each depended on his own fists or his own wits for his place in society, Dave McKelvey was a man among men. He was said to have been as quick and as lithe as a panther and to have a punch in either hand that required no second. Not quarrelsome, but never one to evade an argument or a battle, he went his independent way, letting no one dictate to him about his actions.

There were others of his stripe in those days, men who walked any street confident that they could take care of themselves without benefit of police, the law, the customs, or the manners. No emergency dismayed them, no event nor man could make them fearful. If a rattlesnake bit them they cut out the bite, sucked the wound, tied it up in their shirttail, and went on their journey. If a wagon wheel broke they chopped a few saplings and braced it up with a lasso rope and whatever wire was at hand. If a man wanted to curse and brawl they accommodated him briefly, effectively — and often successfully. They just didn't need any help.

They often lived on the coarsest of food — beans, potatoes, bacon, sometimes seasoned with the fruit of the corn, and despite the prattlings of the nutritionists these old men of another time lived on and on, hale and hearty at seventy, still living and liking it at eighty, and turning to the ministrations of women and man-made comforts only as grey hair and ninety approached.

Their stories were filled with direct action; of man against man, of man against nature. There were always tales of men who had to place reliance on nothing outside themselves. They had but one life and they lived it, and the rest of the world could be damned.

In these effete times beds have sheets on them instead of being wooley, unwashed blankets covered with canvas; men work an eight-hour day instead of until the finish of a job; a man can hardly take a drink of whiskey without some woman putting water in it; there's a bathtub in nearly every house and the rough old days are history.

Life is softer, but not fairer; quieter, but not kinder; easier, but less stimulating.

Fern Lee of the Towner (N. D.) *Press* completed the picture in this short item:

Speaking of cattle ranches, how times have changed. In olden days people expected a rancher to be a sort of tough appearing, grizzled, bewhiskered man with a six-shooter on each hip. Consider the difference in that picture and that of the man from Kansas, who with his $17,000 plane arrived in a few hours to attend the Schultz sale. He cooly laid out $7,600 for one animal and $3,700 for another and then returned to Kansas for supper.

. . . balance between town and country is now quite complicated . . .

Small-town editors have to balance news coverage and policies between town and country, a task now quite complicated because farmers are maintaining houses in town and towns-people are buying farms.

The economy of the smaller towns rests on agriculture, and the editor won't forget the fact. If he has had a rural background himself, he isn't likely to let the readers forget it. If he is a town man, and if he has a columnist who speaks the language of R.F.D., he will happily print material which rings true to out-in-country readers.

The authors, having boyhood acquaintance with the subject matter, liked this discourse on threshing time, written by Hazel Murphy Sullivan of the Sun Prairie (Wis.) *Star Countryman*:

Threshing time, like the old gray mare, "ain't what she used to be," but it is still enough like it to make an interesting study in contrasts and similarities.

My mental image of the oldtime threshing day is a hodge-podge of bearded men in overalls with red bandanas tied around their bronzed throats; air charged with excitement and thick with chaff and smoke; strident noises which sent the mother cat scuttling out of the granary in three rapidly repeated trips, each time with a baby kitten held tightly by the nape of the neck; red hot coals in the firebed of the snorting, chugging engine, while the blue-eyed fireman, black as the smoke which bellied out of the smokestack, sweated out his day; neighbors' wagons parked at noon all over my mother's carefully kept front lawn; wash basins and towels placed on orange crates outside in the rear of the house; much good-natured bantering, jocular and often a bit on the ribald side; stampedes to be first to the table, and the seemingly endless supplies of roasted meat, heaping bowls of mashed potatoes and the accompanying gravy, the cole slaw, pickles, pies, and doughnuts. . . .

The members of the young fry at our house were stationed outside the screen door wielding broomsticks to which strips of old shades had been tacked. It was our business to see that the men got in and the flies stayed out. Often it was a draw.

Newspaper readers appreciate columns which deal with farm scenes in whimsical style, for these little essays echo popular attitudes. An old saying, "You can lead a horse to water, etc." suggested to the late O. E. Bramson of the Dunlap (Iowa) *Reporter* a

**The best check-writing machine was made from a rib.** — Welch (Okla.) **Watchman.**

better version of the old wheeze. He addressed the following to "My Dear City Cousin":

Until you have tried explaining to a week-old calf the secret of swallowing up hill from the bottom of a pail, your education has been neglected. There is nothing to which this business of smartening up a baby bovine can be compared, and there are no books on the subject. The whole thing is strictly between you and the calf — and may the better man win.

Now it happens that calves, like people, rats, and kangaroos, are born with instincts. From the moment they utter their first baby bawl, they know through instinct that breakfast, lunch, and dinner are up in the air in a hammock that mama has — a hammock that looks like a cross between a Scotch bag pipe and a four-legged stool. The calf never has been told about this free soda fountain — this lacteal tap. He knows about it, that's all. He raises his head and roots around, pretty soon connects, and goes after it in earnest. This is instinct in the raw.

In the first few days of their lives calves develop a will of their own. At times I have thought a calf was fifty per cent instinct and fifty per cent temper. If I didn't shudder at such puns, I might go so far as to say a calf is just plain bull-headed.

When a mamma cow's milk is ready for back porch delivery, and the baby must be weaned, you put about five fingers of warm milk in a bucket and walk into a stall where the calf is already demanding in loud bawls that his source of foodstuff come back.

First off the bat, the calf wants nothing to do with you. He wants mamma; and no matter how you look, you still don't look like his mamma. You get one arm around the calf's neck, and you hold the milk bucket in the other hand.

"Nice calfie; put your head down."

But he doesn't put his head down, so you gently but firmly press his head down to sort of assist him like. This is when the nice calfie gives a mighty lunge and sends the bucket skyward with his nose.

You retrieve the empty bucket and get more milk and return to the scene of action. You wet your fingers with milk and stick them in the calf's mouth. This makes him happy. Again, with the same results. But just as his nose is about to touch the milk he remembers his instincts and rears his head.

Same thing over.

You repeat the whole process a dozen times. He fol-

Tomorrow is wonderful, for it releases today. So today I can forget all the unpleasant things in the past, forgive others and myself for errors, clear from my thoughts all belief in defeat, and wait quietly and serenely for the leads that will direct me into worthwhile achievement. I can do this because there is always tomorrow when I can return to worrying, to regrets, bickering, and fears — if I choose. — Clarke Sanford, Margaretville (N. Y.) **News.**

lows the finger down, down and finally you get his dear little nose in the milk. Hooray, he drinks! You take your finger away; the calf rears his head. Same routine all over again, and again.

Well, to make a long story short, after three or four thousand times, civilization overcomes instinct and the calf knows how to drink uphill. Then he not only wants to hurl his whole body into the milk bucket, but insists on chewing the handle off, too.

Lead a horse to drink? That's a laugh. Give me a horse any day — you take the calf.

The experts say we should not upset the child when we correct him, but it's difficult otherwise to reach that part of him we work on. — Willow City (N. D.) Times.

What a country editor thinks of his farmer friends was neatly told by Matt Vernon in the New Iberia (La.) *Iberian*:

There never has been anything wrong with farming that a few profitable crops wouldn't cure. It has always been the most satisfactory existence of all the trades and professions. The dividends in good living, independence, outdoor work, and the enjoyment of association with Nature and growing things put it high up on the list of desirable occupations. The good farmer is seldom lazy, yet can find time for recreation. . . . And he has the means for full enjoyment of his leisure time. His shotgun is always handy, his fishing pole and bait convenient, and the field and stream lie just over the way.

The good farmer is also a good businessman; he has to be. Once upon a time we wrote something about farmers, and we want to reproduce it here today. Keep in mind that this was written by a country boy who knows both sides of farm life — one who has lived in both country and city, yet prefers the rural life. We called it "The Farmer's Creed," and wrote it for a farm celebration held in June, 1943, in Mississippi.

I am the farmer.

I live by hard work and the sweat of my brow.

I work in the sun and the rain and my hours are long and my duties unending.

I seek not fame nor fortune but my life is one of little things, humdrum to the city man, full of drudgery, but rich in contentment and peace.

I am the first stop on the production line of mankind for I start the raw materials of food, fiber, and timber down the channels of trade to feed, clothe, and shelter the people of the world.

I am an idealist who will not sacrifice my freedom and independence for a weekly pay check, but value my way of life above all, no matter what the cost in toil or sweat or sacrifice.

I plow my own row, keep my own time, vote my own ticket, choose my own company, burn my own fuel, raise my own feed and food; I am Freedom's child and her most ardent champion.

I am a home builder and a family man and my children give life and leadership to the nation, for they know the meaning of work as the real purpose in life, a reason for being as certain as the processes of nature itself.

I am a God fearing man and a believer in the church, for under God's supervision I have charge of the beasts of the field, the soil I tend, and the plants I bring to fruition, and through His teachings I learn my responsibilities and duty and in His inspiration I find my solace and strength.

I am a specialist in an intricate profession with skill and knowledge acquired only through years of planting, cultivating, and harvesting, through producing and marketing, through butchering and building, through blacksmithing and animal husbandry and many other trades.

I am the foundation of civilization and its hope for the future, for neglect of my way of life is the most certain sign of decadence in any race or nation.

I am the farmer.

Town people live close to nature, and their columnists are moved by the changing seasons — inspired to flights of description and appreciation:

October is a month that puts a new drive in my heart. Its nippy mornings, air filled with a bracing effect, lift me up and make me look forward to nice cool days laden with hours of warm, comfortable sunshine. Not the hot, sweaty days of summer that make me gasp for a decent breath of air — but balmy days that cause me to say, "God, I'm glad I'm livin'."

Yes, indeed — October, the great invisible hinge on which the door of summer closes and the door of autumn opens. The October that creeps into our midst on the hazy edge of summer's lazy air that is drifting away like a gentle lamb running across hilly pastures. . . . away . . . far away. The October when patches of crystal white frost deck the lawns and fields . . . when gay flirty banners of smoke break the early morning blue or the evening's golden sunset as they merrily chase themselves up from the chimneys of houses . . . houses that then seem to be so clustered that you like to think they are embracing each other to ward off the sting of a snappy morning.

—Tol Solinski, "Impressions One Gets," Salem (Ind.) *Republican-Leader.*

Alimony is next to worthless on a cold night. — J. O. Jewett, Fairfield (Calif.) **Republican.**

October always baffles us. It's death in the midst of life; it's a door closing, and corridors opening; it's dead fields, with living harvests to produce death and then life again; it's a ball game reeking verse and din, tumult and laughter, and life at its highest, while all around the dead leaves, the trees, the birds — all animal and vegetable life — are at farewells; it's a school bell, a funeral knell; it's the end, it's the beginning.

—Jean Olson, "But Incidentally," Story City (Iowa) *Herald*.

Tongue-in-cheek essays, half in jest and partly serious, and sometimes ornamented with extravagant phrasing, have long been standard column items. Whether they stem from popular attitudes or help to create these may be debatable. But many waggish writers delight in veiling their ideas in verbal spinach, implausible tales, and clownish comment.

The following tidbit from the Belton (Tex.) *Journal* probably was inspired by advertising claims for cold remedies:

In the good old days when you wanted a horse to stand still, you tied him to a hitching post. Today you place a bet on him. — Bells (Tenn.) **Sentinel.**

People in Belton are now divided into two classes: who have just recovered from a cold, and those who now have one. The Research Department of the *Journal,* staffed by eminent medical authorities and a smallish man with a protruding Adam's apple that twitches when he is thinking, has concluded that colds can be prevented by proper diet. One quart of llama milk upon arising, followed by a dozen mockingbird eggs is recommended. Later in the day, one should eat plenty of gnats' livers, together with second-joints (only the left ones, mind you) of young female pheasants, fried in butter. In case this diet cannot be followed — for butter is hard to find — a cold can be cured by drinking a mixture of lysol, mercuric acid, buttermilk, and Temple (Tex.) water. We tried this on a friend and he didn't sniffle again — he just lay there, looking so natural.

Advice to a town fretting over the lack of direct rail and highway connections was written in somewhat the same spirit by T. A. Lally in his column, "A Voice in the Wilderness," in the Bridgeport (Neb.) *News-Blade*:

A recent press dispatch records that Hartington (pop. 1700), county seat of Cedar County, Nebraska, decries the lack of a direct highway or rail connection with Omaha. And not only that, but the lack of direct transportation with any place. It sits on a spur railroad and a secondary highway.

Now, it seems, the people of Hartington are after something. They aren't quite sure up there what it is, but it sounds like they want a few trans-continental trains zipping through town, at least a couple of paved highways with buses and everything, and maybe two Mainliner air flights a day.

Well, listen, Hartington. Don't do it.

You may feel that the world is now passing you by. But the shape the world is in today, you're not missing a thing. Your town, in the press dispatch, is quoted as "making progress" in spite of its isolation.

We'll bet it's making progress (whatever that is) without help from the outside world. Keep up a good school system, support your churches, subscribe to your local newspaper, surface your streets, teach your kids to blow their noses and to say "thank you" and "please" and "sir" as the occasion warrants, give them jobs to do instead of letting them parade the streets at midnight, jail your speeders before they reduce the population to 1699 or 1698, throw your drunks in the clink instead of letting them run loose insulting women and scaring children, stir up a batch of taffy for that Saturday night shindig after the movies, hold a weekly bubble gum contest, and take the car keys away from the kids.

You may feel out of it now, but believe us, brother, your day is coming.

Philosophizing in a homespun manner has made H. B. Fox of Taylor, Tex., a dirt farmer and sometime editor, one of the most widely quoted columnists in his region. The following example of his work is from the Carrizo Springs (Tex.) *Javelin*:

Dear editar: Last week I was writin you about a outfit that's worryin over how the farmer is gonna spend his "surplus" money, which is like worryin over a hole in your raincoat during the worst drought on record, and now I've discovered another group of thinkers which is worried over the problem of plenty.

Accordin to these thinkers, science with the help of atomic energy and a few other things is liable to stumble on a method of makin food out of thin air, without the

I feel very unworthy when my cocker spaniel sits on the floor and gazes at me like I am God. It takes a lot to live up to what a dog thinks of his master. According to him I can do nothing wrong, I am noble, kind, a defender of the weak, a good provider and he trusts my judgment. Sometimes people think dogs are a nuisance, and that in this day when food is expensive they are an unnecessary expense. But mine is worth his salt if he only reminds me occasionally, when I need it, that there still is left in the world such real true attributes as friendliness, constancy, trustworthiness, love and loyalty. — Laura M. Klinefelter, Adams (Wis.) **Times.**

The trouble with depressions is they come at such inconvenient times — when everybody is out of work. — Orin Taylor, Archbold (Ohio) **Buckeye.**

trouble of plantin and cultivatin and raising cattle, and they're afraid if everybody got enough food for nothin it would demoralize things.

Bein somethin of a pioneer, I been experimenten with just such a problem for some time; that is, I've tried livin without doin much plantin or cultivatin, and I ain't found it demoralizin, although some folks would differ with me on what demorilizin is. Also, I have noticed that farmers with smokehouses full of meat and cellars full of canned goods and potatoes, enough to run em a year more, ain't demoralized by havin all they want to eat. And also, the millionaires I read about, with enough money to feed themselves the rest of their lives without hittin a lick, still don't seem to be disturbed, and I ain't heard of a one frettin about his situation and wantin to go broke so he could be happy again.

If you ask me, some folks is hard-pressed to find something to worry about. I say let em come out here and worry about somethin practical — how to keep a cow in a pasture that ain't been rained on in eight months, with a two-wire fence; or how to keep a woodbox full when there's newspapers to read; how to draw water from a dry well; how to make four bales of Johnson grass hay last all winter; how to patch a roof that's got holes in the patches you put on last year; etc.

However, if the people who spend their time worryin about what'll happen to folks if they don't have to worry about anything, could find out how little time I worry about anything, they'd have something to worry about. And if you're worried about the money for my subscription to your paper, you got a right to be.

Examples of essays which have been expanded to full column length will be found in the Appendix.

# 10.

# Column Verse

THE COLUMN, least dignified of newspaper departments, would seem a good place to run light, humorous, and clever verse. And it is. But the small-town press makes relatively little use of verse. Most hard-worked editors have neither the time nor the energy for expression in rhythm and rhyme. Contributed verse, moreover, is likely to be rather awful.

In the formative years of the column, content was more literary and humor was expected. Hallam Walker Davis wrote in 1926:[1]

Sure-fire humor in America got its start in the sixties. It was evolved largely in the West and in a way marked the beginning of newspaper column writing. George Horatio Derby, writer of the "John Phoenix" papers, is generally credited with being the father of the new school of humor. Charles Farrar Browne (Artemus Ward) and Henry Wheeler Shaw (Josh Billings) are much better known. The work of David Ross Locke (Petroleum V. Nasby) was also well known to our fathers and grandfathers. Edgar Wilson Nye (Bill Nye) was another of the school.

---

[1] *The Column*, p. 82. Used by permission of Alfred A. Knopf, Inc. Copyright, 1926.

We have noted that Eugene Field gave a literary turn to the column. Contributors' columns, such as the Chicago *Tribune's* "A Line o' Type or Two," encouraged writing of humorous verse.

In any acceptable form, good humor is good sense. It helps keep the world sane. Many persons have grieved because Will Rogers' untimely death lost to the world the sanity of his comical but basically solid perspective. As community builders, editors sometimes forget to live in the present. An all-serious newspaper can hardly escape being dull.

Small-town people have readily accepted verse in their magazines, but in general they have not preferred this literary type as a means of local expression. Similarly, their editors have liked alternative forms, such as the anecdote, the tall tale, the humorous paragraph, and the light essay. The college magazine has continued to exploit possibilities of verse, doggerel and otherwise, and not infrequently naughty. Serious rhyming has been considered "longhair" in regions which prefer Edgar A. Guest and Ogden Nash to the poets laureate.

By verse is meant writing in poetical forms which are considered in contradistinction to prose. Poetry is hard to define, and we need not concern ourselves long with it here. Poetry is usually musical, or at least rhythmical. It may rhyme, or not. Poetry uses distilled diction — imaginative, emotional, idealistic, tender or impassioned — and in subject ranges from the lightly fanciful to the deeply philosophical. Of course, given similar motivation, prose partakes of many of these same attributes. For prose, too, can move on wings of high purpose, beauty of expression, and flights of imagination. Some great sermons and orations have the form of prose and the concepts of poetry; they may be called prose-poems. Prose is usually differentiated from verse by its full lines and by paragraphs indented only at the beginning. Poetry

**GET AN IDEA**

A cute idea, usually expressed in the final sentence, may quickly result in acceptable newspaper verse. The idea differs little from the humorous or witty paragraph. With a little practice, anyone capable of expressing an idea neatly should turn out clever verse. Expanding the idea and giving it a title and an opening are relatively simple. It is not surprising, then, that much brief verse is written from bottom to top. The whip must crack at the end.

usually is set in shorter lines, which have a regular appearance because of the repetition of metrical units. Free verse, however, has irregular lines which are fitted to the thought only, and a line may contain one word, or many, and rhyme is not essential. The goal of free verse is perfect expression of a thought.

Not everything which has short, indented lines is poetry, however. A short, simple verse, with or without rhyme, intended only to entertain or perhaps to carry a radio commercial, is not poetic in conception. It is a jingle, or perhaps a doggerel verse. This is said not to condemn but to define it. But it may be bad verse, just as prose may be bad prose.

From couplet to limerick, simple verse is well within the abilities of many columnists. It also appeals to many contributors who are not interested in prose. In fact, its appeal may be so wide as to embarrass a columnist who must decline to print some of it. Old people, especially, turn to maudlin verse and are quite hurt when jingles which their friends call good are not printed. And some readers are shameless in taking even copyrighted verse out of scrapbooks and sending it in as their own.

Nevertheless, it is likely that future columns will use more verse, not less. Some pump-priming will be necessary to encourage readers to contribute. Hodge-podge columns, which have the greatest need of verse, sometimes carry offers of prizes for last lines of limericks or other forms.

Much of the good light verse written today is flowing into magazines and children's books. Newspapers could get more of it by being more hospitable to amateurs' efforts. Strangely, publishing houses are accepting manuscripts from housewives, school teachers, and other beginners whose efforts are given no outlets in local papers.

Contributors need patterns; they learn best

### RHYTHM

The thought that simple rhyme is unworthy of a columnist seems to suppress this kind of writing. Some consider it too difficult. Sports columnists have been among the notable exceptions. . . . Telling a simple incident or idea in rhythmic verse is mainly a matter of learning, or imitating, a simple pattern. Soon it becomes as easy to versify as to write headlines. The idea, not the rhyme, comes hardest.

through imitation. Nothing is a greater stimulant to endeavor than a bit of success. Few contributors will develop the light and delightful style of a Franklin P. Adams, but addition of verse to a column, by the columnist or anyone else, broadens the base of popular acceptance.

Writers of column verse compose for the day, not for eternity. A jingle may be as timely as a paragraph based on the latest news headline. Its mischievous variety is its greatest charm. In the small-town press, column verse is clean. It is simple. It is brief. Mechanically, it may miss a meter now and then. In subject matter it ranges from the nonsensical to the evangelical. It is less subtle than the comic paragraph in that its meaning is not half-concealed and its charm usually is in its wide-grin good humor and tuneful swing.

Versifying takes a little more time, but the change in form is pleasing to readers if the verse is passably clever and has an unexpected verbal twist. This example is from "Annegrams" in the Morton (Tex.) *Tribune*:

> That life begins at forty
>   I've read in book and verse,
> But does in then begin to get
>   Much better, or much worse?

Another single, simple idea:

> I hate to see a puppy's tail
>   With nothing much to measure,
> For what is there for him to use
>   To indicate his pleasure?
>     —Lebanon (Ohio) *Star*.

And this one, in an election year:

> I've always been rather lucky,
>   As I went my weary gait.
> So now I feel fine and ducky,
>   Because I'm not a candidate.
>     —Hays (Kans.) *News*.

The Editor practically never writes good English, as much as he appreciates the art of those who do. In the first place, he is too lazy. And in the second place he finds it so difficult to be himself. There are so many other people he would rather be. — Paul F. Watkins, Ashland (Va.) **Herald-Progress**.

And this rhyming birth announcement:

> Smiling Sam, the colored cop,
>   Is a mighty happy poppie;
> His wife has given him a son—
>   A little carbon cop-y.
>           —Lyons (Kans.) *News.*

Of deeper discernment is this bit of verse by Kay Noel (Mildred Wamberg) in the Glenwood (Iowa) *Opinion-Tribune*:

> God,
> Give me
> Insight to stay my hand,
> Enjoying a moment now those little
>   fingerprints
> I wipe away.

Rhyme which has the added cleverness of a surprise is especially to be desired in columns:

> Our canary won't sing, though
>   we've had him a year;
> To inspire him we've tried
>   every day.
> But since he won't warble
>   in spite of our care,
> We've decided to give HER away.
> —C. C. Caswell in Clarinda (Iowa)
>   *Herald-Journal.*

The same author, in a more thoughtful moment:

> I've lost half an hour somewhere,
>   I don't know where it went;
> All I know is that it's gone,
>   Vanished, squandered, spent;
> But there's no cause to worry if
>   It's merely gone unused—
> The consequence would be more dire
>   If it had been abused.

Column verse is without pretense, and if colloquial speech intrudes nobody minds. Homey ideas look better in verse form because even the typography suggests lightness or at least a departure from prosaic observations:

I would like to live in 1951 wages, 1932 prices, 1926 dividends, 1910 taxes. — Clarke A. Sanford, Margaretville (N. Y.) **News.**

Whether a lady should wear a hat
Depends on when and where she's at.

\* \* \*

Once people frowned on gentlemen
Who in public wore no coat,
But nowadays the opposite
Is what one seems to note.
For the coatless man is now the thing,
And those who cannot bear 'em
Frown upon the fellows who
Continue now to wear 'em.
—Kingsport (Tenn.) *Times-News.*

Timeliness is enough to support a rhyme when otherwise it might not be acceptable:

Hoardhogs are members
Of that self-centered clan,
Whose cellars hold more
Than their bellies can.
—June Paschal in Des Moines *Register.*

The gift of merging idea and rhyme is not inherited full blown, but it must be cultivated. Many reporters would do well to doodle with words instead of figure-eights. A scrapbook of verse one has had printed may be the source of much pleasure. The following column verses, written by Morris Midkiff of Austin, Tex., are taken from his scrapbook:

### Left of Center

Too many motorists lose sight of
The way I'm sure I have the right of.

\* \* \*

### My Sweet Is Occupied

Who blocked the punt? Who made the score?
Does My Fair One see that? No, verily;
But she does know just what each woman wore,
And comments on them all so merrily.

Who caught the pass, made touchdown run?
To My Dear One all that's a mystery;
But she derives much big-game fun,
From gossip swaps with sistery.

Pity us if the time ever comes when the teen-agers do not think they know more than their elders. — Grants (N. M.) Beacon.

### The Hyphen

Hyphen, pesky little pest,
Horizontally at rest;
  You, I know, are quite syntactical,
  But why can't you be more practical?

You're no good, 'tis plainly seen
Except to serve as go-between
  For certain words that need compounding,
  But that's what makes you so confounding.

Stand up, hyphen! Out with chest!
Look your military best . . .
  No, you've got no lung inflation;
  You won't do for exclamation.

Lie back down, you may as well;
For, standing up, you look like "l."

More fanciful is this bit of verse by "Sandra Ames" (Mary Jo Niendorf) in the Earlham (Iowa) *Echo:*

A flash of red against the blue,
  His crest . . . a brilliant crown
Arched high, above each gleaming eye
  As he sat . . . looking down
Singing to me . . . "Oh, do not weep,
  The world is bright, and fair" . . .
And slowly plucked a feather bright,
  And dropped it . . . on my hair.

Verse sometimes grows like a chain letter. This exchange probably ran through more stanzas then these:

### Gates Ajar

Oh, shed a tear
  For Luther Stover;
He tried to toot
  Two State cops over.
          —New York *Sun.*

Please wail one wail
  For Adolph Barr;
He just would drive
  A one-eyed car.
          —Macon *Telegraph.*

Bill Muffet said
  His car couldn't skid;
This monument shows
  That it could, and did.
          —Newark (Ohio) *Advocate.*

Now the scientists are trying to dehydrate water. It's something like taking the him and her out of love. — Gardnerville (Nev.) **Record-Courier.**

Toying with words has not been disdained by many columnists and some magazine wits. This bit appeared years ago in the London *Tit-Bits*:

O, MLE, what XTC
I always feel when UIC,
I used to rave of LN's eyes,
4 LC I gave countless sighs,
4 KT, 2, and LNR,
I was a keen competitor.
But each now's a non-NTT,
4 UXL them all, UC.

### Easy Does It

Heppelwhite or Sheraton,
Empire, Mission, Chippendale;
　I do not care
　What style of chair
Just so it fits my hippentale.
　　　　　—Morris Midkiff.

Free verse looks easy, but demands close attention to order of elements, choice of words, and conclusion. Extreme brevity may be used to produce a well-indented appearance in a twelve-pica column. An extreme example by Bob Bowen of the La Jolla (Calif.) *Light* follows:

### Competitor

somehow
a salad
is pretty
as ballad

the way
it's arrayed
when it's
displayed

on 24
sheets
around
our streets

beyond
belief
each
lettuce leaf

in full
and green
tomato's
sheen

is glowing
red
on
leafy bed

the
mayonnaise
is color
of maize

but home
at table
i'm
never able

to make
a salad
pretty
as ballad

**Free verse looks easy, but . . .**

lettuce
is limp
tomatoes
like shrimp

are small
and pale
and i
always fail

to make
a dressing
without
messing

my clothes
and floor
it makes
me sore

i can't
compete
with
24 sheet

The same newspaper also printed this appealing verse by Louisa Boyd Giles:

### Applicant

Description: Lost, alone.
Parentage, unknown.
Skills? The useful ones locked up
In a homeless pup.
Occupation? Just a stray
Unemployed today.
But hold a quiet hand and wait—
Loneliness will take the bait
When cautious exploration ends
And nose and eyes say "friends."
Food and drink are only part
Answer to a canine heart;
Human love is daily bread
To loyalty unlimited.
Now the long-sought god has come . . .
Petition granted. Found — a home.

Observation of nature has through the ages inspired poets to song. And the following verse was written, from a similar urge, by C. R. Spencer in his "Free Speech" column in the Ouray (Colo.) *Herald*:

### Call of the Hills

Along high south exposures, where the warm,
   bright sunshine falls,
There's a greening in the nitches of the
   mighty, ageless walls,
Starting sap is bringing color to the
   hibernating pine,
And, released, the streams dash singing from
   the heights at timberline.
There's a stir and urge and promise 'neath
   the snows in gorges dim,
And the ice is creeping backward from the
   yawning canyon's rim.
Rocky trails that toil far upward
   to the tundras on the heights,
Where the towering peaks blaze crimson in
   the last bright evening lights,
Are calling me up yonder where the present
   meets the past,
Where time runs on uncounted, each new
   aeon like the last,

As a matter of fact the ant is a horrible example of the life we are trying to avoid. The ant works as hard as he can every waking hour every day in the week, every week in the year of his short life, fetching, carrying, storing, building, feeding, propagating, without an hour off for play and recreation, with never a day to bask his soul in rest and reflection and all to what purpose? Does he leave the world better than when he entered it? Does he entertain the world by the beauty of his song or the gaiety of his plummage? Does he consider the plight of others besides himself or provide food and shelter for anything but ants? Does he serve any useful purpose to anyone? No indeed. He works his legs off and his heart out his whole life just to keep himself and his colony alive. And the only fruitful consequence of the ant hill is more ants.— Paul F. Watkins, Ashland (Va.) **Herald-Progress.**

Where the sharp, clean air untainted by
   smoke-belching mills of men
Starts my stagnant blood to racing and stirs
   my youth again.
Lead me far from all this turmoil, this self-
   seeking human strife,
Far from those long-winded speeches on the more
   abundant life;
Let me grab a pick and shovel, throw once
   more the di'mond hitch;
With a jackass and a grubstake, turn me
   loose: my old feet itch.

Verse compresses thought so much that readers may not sense the overtone felt by the writer. Ray Murray, writing his numbered items for the "Murray-Go-Round" of the Buffalo Center (Iowa) *Tribune*, occasionally uses a prelude, like this:

Each of us has, filed away deep within the hidden recesses of his mind, small but sweet somethings which we seldom parade before others but never neglect in our own thinking. . . . Mother's cradling arms, Dad's so-seldom tears, a woman's kiss, your baby's first cry. Not so important, but also hidden there, are memories of fishing in the creek, the feel of rain in your hair, of mud between your toes. Mayhap the luxury of just loafing in the sun or walking through autumn's leaves. I have no doubt but that many of our fighting force in Korea may harbor some of those same thoughts as they live with death.

*Even as the Leaves*

Life holds a host of little pleasantries
Like shuffling deep through brown October leaves.
Today, that pleasure brought me little joy,
I sensed the marching feet of every boy
That once trod Autumn leaves, so crisply dry,
But now walk ways where men, too, fall and die.

This philosophical idea of living one day at a time is all right, if today's the aay you're using. — R. B. Lockhart, Pittsburg (Tex.) **Gazette.**

*The American Press* commented that Grant Utley, publisher of the Cass Lake (Minn.) *Times* had received considerable fame for the verses he runs under the heading, "Timely Tunes — Current Comments in Cubic Centimeter." His verses have the appearance of prose. Example:

"It's in McGuire's Coffee House that village trades-men meet — where problems of the day are solved — from atom bombs to wheat. Each morning, at the stroke of nine, the tradesmen gather there; and fill that little java joint with superheated air. We won't attempt to call the roll — we've tried it, and lost track — for if a man attends just once — you know that he'll be back. More fish are caught in Calvin's booths — by measure and by weight — than in ten thousand spring-fed lakes, around the North Star State. More deer are slain, more ducks are shot, more bullhead nets are set, than's done in any other place that's been discovered yet. Whenever you can't find a man around his store or shop — call 'six' and if he isn't there, he's bound to make the stop. There may be places in the world, where one can get more pay, for what he sells or what he gets for working by the day. But money isn't everything — in Flint and Pontiac are men who'd give a sack of dough, if they could wander back, and gather with the gang at Cal's, where o'er a cup of 'joe' all tongues are loosened in a spell of Wis-dom's fluent flow."

There's nothing much wrong with love, except it shoves you around. — Jonesville (La.) **Booster.**

A similar style was noted in the Three Rivers (Tex.) *News.* However, paragraphs were equal in number of lines. Example:

### I Like to Go to Meetin'

"I like to go to meetin' where the folks extend the hand; and a word of friendly greetin' seems to be at their command. Where the stranger finds a welcome, no matter how he's dressed, and in that sort of atmosphere he's comforted and blessed.

"I like to go to meetin' where all may have a part; in all the ways of worship that may touch and warm the heart. I like to sing the good old hymns of worship and of praise. I like responsive readin' and we need it in these days."

We're told it takes self-made millionaires about six years to get over being startled by v a l e t s. — North Canaan (Conn.) **News.**

A smiling picture of Chris Reese is printed at the top of his "Rippling Rhythm" column in the Algona (Iowa) *Upper Des Moines.* A mischievously comical example:

I often wonder at the plan
(It beats me; I can't understand.)
By which we live and love and die,
The reason therefore, or the why.
Mankind is given everything
By way of brawn and reasoning,
Is fitted out with talents, brain,
That he may over kingdoms reign;
And though he lives in sundry sins,
Consumes of toddies, beers, and gins,
St. Peter never overlooks
But makes entries in his books.
So man goes on in careless way,
Considers not the judgment day;
He aims to reach a ripe old age
Nor worries he about a page
Where entries by St. Peter's pen
Sets out the senseless sins of men.
The smelly goats at twenty die
Yet never tasted Rock and Rye;
And sheep but eight short years attain
Tho they have never sipped champagne;
Few horses live to thirty years
And they know naught of wines or beers;
Some mules at times reach twenty-eight
Nor care for whiskey mixed or straight;
Man's friend, the dog, at ten's all in
Yet never once has lapped of gin;
The cow all alcohol taboos,
At twenty years her hide is shoes;
The cat drinks milk, of ale has none,
At twelve its micing days are done;
The bone-dry hen for nogs to mix
Will furnish eggs, then dies at six.
In fact all animals are dry
And sinless, too, yet soon they die.
But gleeful, sinful, rumful men
Live on for three score and ten.

. . . Encourage verse writing —
even at the cost of having to
reject much of it.

Popular targets draw column verse, as in this item from the Bryan (Tex.) *Eagle*:

> The weatherman dreamed that he
>     was dead;
> That he stood by his monument tall,
>     and read
> The message thereon
>     and hung his head;
> For, "probably warmer"
>     was all it said.

It's always a good plan to carry your bride over the threshold. Thus, you always can feel that you supported her until she put her foot down. — Cottage Grove (Ore.) Sentinel.

Descriptive verse frequently is written in tribute to a town or to the native soil. This example is from the Sierra Blanca (Tex.) Hudspeth County *News*:

### Rain in the Desert

The hot sun parched the drying land;
No vapor rose from earth's parched face.
For months the skies the ranchmen scanned
For signs of rain, through endless space.
Then flashed the lightning, thunder roared;
Wind-driven rain flooded ranch and street;
Tanks, long dry, now depths of water stored,
And sound of frogs, extinct before, was sweet.

Composing light verse is for those who enjoy doing it . . .

Racial foibles are used, as in this "new Indian love song" from the Greenville (S.C.) *Observer*:

> Comb 'um hair,
> File 'um nails,
> Paint 'um mug,
> Watch 'um males.

Writing light verse is for those who enjoy doing it, but the number who enjoy reading it is much larger. If newspapers are written to be read, and if reading can and should be fun, doesn't it follow that small-town columnists should encourage verse writing more than they do, even at the cost of having to reject much of it?

If you drive fast enough, your car will probably last your lifetime. — L. S. McCandless, Craig (Colo.) **Empire-Courier.**

## 11.

# How To Write Quotable Columns

*[ This chapter is presented to help readers to write columns that will be quoted. Probably that can be done more easily if the reader draws his chair up closer, and we get chummy. ]*

THERE IS ALWAYS a possibility that quotable newspaper columns will be given more credit than is due them, as compared to less quotable ones.

This lies in the fact that when a person sees a quote from a column here and there in the newspapers of the country, and sees it often, he concludes that the column from which the item was taken must be excellent, or he wouldn't see the quote so much. Maybe it is excellent, but it probably is no better than the column in the newspaper in the next county seat, which doesn't get a quote in a decade.

The difference in the two could be that the quoted one has the advantage of universality of interest and timelessness which made it easily quotable, whereas the other did not. For instance, the first may have been something

about marriage, which is of interest almost anywhere at any time, while the second urged the city council to pave Third Street before winter sets in. The latter would hardly be quotable in any other town.

But so far as real benefit to the public was concerned the former may have been just another wisecrack about men and women wedding each other — which comes at a used dime a dozen in columns — while the latter resulted in a needed improvement.

Or length may have made the difference. Both may have been about that subject of universal and timeless interest, marriage. The quotable one of but a few lines may have made the complete comment, while the other ran to a full column, with the length necessary to make the comment complete. Few publications have space enough to quote a whole column. And possibly, in addition, the individual paragraphs of the latter column were tied into preceding and succeeding paragraphs in such a way that lifting one out for quotation would be difficult.

So, a reader should not assume that because a column earns many quotes it is superior to its less quotable fellow. As a matter of fact, it may be inferior in accomplishing the prime purpose of columns, which is to entertain and inform the reader.

Of course, a paragraph is lifted out of a column and reprinted in another publication because the editor doing the lifting thinks it will interest his readers, and is of interest at the time he publishes it, which is later than the appearance of the original item. It follows, then, that to earn quotation, a paragraph must be of widespread interest and somewhat timeless. And the greater the interest and timelessness, the more likely the extensive quotation.

Reverting again to marriage: A paragraph like "the greatest circus of all time is the two-ring, with Cupid as its manager," could be used at any place that

**ETERNAL TRUTHS**

Probably the ancients observed that often by the time a man is able to do something he is too old to enjoy it. Back in 1926, the old **Literary Digest** attributed to a St. Louis newspaper this p a r a g r a p h: "About the time one learns how to make the most of life, most of it is gone." . . . In 1950 and 1951, many columnists used phrases saying that a man ". . . rich enough to take two hours for lunch is probably on a milk and crackers diet," and ". . . who can afford a rich sweetie, is too old to attract her."

has readers acquainted with circuses, and could be published at any time. But suppose the column cracked, "Mayor Bill Smith likes to live dangerously. He says he will wear his new red tie at the bull exhibit next Saturday." It would hardly be quoted widely, and certainly not later than the date of the exhibit.

So, the initial requirements of a quotable column are:

1. Universality of interest.
2. Timelessness.
3. Brevity.

As to the actual writing, suppose we have universal interest in our topic, with a quick comment that we can get into two or three lines, one which could be as pertinent next year as now, how shall we word our little hopeful?

We've spent much of an enjoyable lifetime analyzing column quotations, and we think they can be summed up: *Unexpected comment on a familiar topic, made by implication.*

Of course, that's an over-simplification, so let's go along together and do some writing, aimed at getting our column quoted.

Generally speaking, it is the unexpected comment that piques interest. For instance, if you say, "There was a beautiful dawn this morning," and your companion replies, politely, "There was?" his comment doesn't arouse much interest. But suppose your companion quipped, "Who told you?" then you're alerted. That reply implies you didn't get up in time to see the dawn, and you are challenged to parry his sally. Maybe you don't do anything better than reply lamely, "Well, it certainly wasn't you!" But you are more interested.

We want comment that is unexpected, to insure interest. We want unexpected comment that gets a chuckle. The sure-fire way to get a chuckle is use of the incongruous, the comment that is ten thousand miles from being logical, although it is pertinent. For instance: "An Illinois man was found by police to be living in the same house with two wives. Imagine! Not a place to hang his clothing."

Or this one: "Scientists say a baby thinks three

. . . Unexpected comment on a familiar topic, made by implication.

months before it is born. . . . From such thinking by the baby three months before its birth probably came that old alibi, 'Unaccustomed as I am to public appearance.' "

The incongruous is divided into exaggeration and understatement. As an example of the former we have, "Sizes often are deceiving. Sometimes a woman's thumb has a man under it."

Or, "Then there was the egotistical nurse, who always deducted two degrees from her men patients' temperatures to allow for the effect of her personality."

And then there is understatement in which the chuckle comes from a comment way down lower than expected. And it is here we find 99 per cent of the current column or paragraph humor. When we checked through files for examples of exaggeration and understatement to cite here, we had some difficulty finding exaggeration; none in finding understatement.

The explanation is easy. Exaggeration is the broader, plainer, less subtle humor. It is the kind used by children. They get a laugh by telling of the mouse that was as big as two and a half elephants; the fire engine that was "as tall as our house, and the Smiths' too."

The use of understatement comes along in later years. Here are a few examples of readily evident understatement:

"The college boy's contention is that today's best value is a nickel for a phone call — to the right girl."

"Some nudist colonies have suggested a new plan for world peace. . . . If none of the armies wore clothes, it would be impossible to recognize the enemy, and peace would be automatic."

Or, "You'd think there would be less murdering, the red tape a man has to go through."

Too, young man, if you run real fast after one woman, you may distance the other women who are after you. — Bells (Tenn.) **Sentinel.**

Here's one that is a little longer, but perhaps more plainly emphasizes understatement:

"He may be in red at the bank. His crops may be blighted, his business headed for the rocks. He may be contemplating having his teeth extracted, or expecting his wife's relatives on the next train. But, wealth or power or fame have little to offer the man with a watermelon under his arm."

We have now developed the thought that the paragraph to be quotable should be pleasing or laughable, and to get this we should make unexpected comment on some fact, and that the comment should be incongruous; and being incongruous it should be exaggerated or understated — preferably the latter.

Now we consider the touch that makes the difference between an almost-quotable and a quotable paragraph, between the kind that has unexpected, understated comment and *doesn't* experience that wonderful feeling of the scissors snipping around its edges, and one that does.

The difference is exactly the difference between a joke in which the point is explained and one in which you are required to get the point by an instant's thought:

"High heels for girls probably are dangerous, but probably we'll always have them. At least so long as girls prefer to be kissed elsewhere than on the forehead."

We had to think just a split second to realize that the girls wanted the heels to lift their lips high enough for the business at hand.

But what a flat paragraph we'd have had it been written:

"High heels for girls probably are dangerous, but probably we will have them for a long time because they lift the girls up so their lips are higher for kissing."

A thesis on which we are doing some investigation is based on a belief that Will Rogers' statement that he'd never met a man he didn't like, should include women. — John Peterson, Walton (N. Y.) **Reporter.**

Note the difference? The latter paragraph was funny, perhaps, but certainly not very subtle.

Here is another:

"Have you heard about the mind reader who went to Washington? He couldn't find a thing to do."

Suppose you had written: :

"Have you heard about the mind reader who went to Washington? No one there was doing any thinking, so he came back home."

So, we can agree that the unexpected comment, to be really subtle and sophisticated, and to pique the maximum of interest, should not entirely reveal its point. That point should be given by implication. So the reader has to reflect just a split second to get the meaning; but, having got it, is very pleased with himself, and with the paragraph, and with the writer.

Here are four or five that, for want of a better term, we may call "complete" paragraphs. That is, very plainly, there is a statement of fact, then unexpected comment is made with the point not quite revealed.

"Life, in a community like our own, is a series of adventures in contentment. If company arrives unexpectedly you can borrow a bottle from the neighbor — and chances are you've seen the cow that filled it."

"If you can't find it in the dictionary, don't give up. Ask for it at the drug store."

"Sports authorities say a triple somersault is not recognized in the books. So what you did carrying an armload of canned fruit down the basement steps was unofficial and doesn't count."

"Six feet of moist earth is said to be effective protection against atomic bombs. So all you have to do to be safe after death is to keep the earth moist."

"One of the reasons we have divorce courts is because many husbands who promised they would die for their wives haven't made good."

Pollsters say 8 percent of the people have no opinion. So you see you have about a 1 to 12 chance of meeting a genuinely charming person. — Grove Hill (Ala.) **Democrat.**

"Doctors say that thin people usually live longer, being harder to hit by automobile drivers."

As you read these you may recall this or that paragraph quoted in a newspaper that doesn't fit this formula. Perhaps there was no preliminary statement of fact, or maybe the comment was not implied.

Perhaps half of the paragraphs quoted today are like that. A little different. Not exactly the complete paragraph of unexpected comment with an implied point. But, if you will analyze them closely, you'll note that they are complete in effect. Maybe it was not necessary to state the fact because it already was so well known. For instance, if we were going to comment on a chap named Lincoln, we could make a quip about the presidency without having to say Lincoln was president.

Actually, there are many variations or adaptations of the complete paragraph. The complete paragraph is like the 1, 2, 3, 4 of the waltz. As long as we stick to that 1, 2, 3, 4 we shall be waltzing. But there are many variations of the 1, 2, 3, 4 that also are enjoyable. Here are some of the classifications of paragraphs, all of which are based on the unexpected comment, with implied point, formula:

1. The *pun,* or play on a word, or words:

"Of course, the really big Orange Bowl contest is in China, where the Yellow Peril and the Red Menace are mixing it."

And the one we have cited as causing mild embarrassment:

"The meanest man in the world is the restaurant proprietor who goes around pinching the waitresses' tips."

2. The *metaphor,* which satisfies the reader's desire for pictures:

"A good many men who talk bass downtown are tenors at home."

The world weighs only 36,000,000 sextillion tons, but seems heavier than that to newspaper columnists carrying it around. — Roosevelt (Utah) **Standard.**

I wonder if the people in other professions and trades are as stage-struck with the supposed glamor of their jobs as we who toil over a lukewarm typewriter all day. Does an engineer climb down out of the cab of a passenger local and then run over to get the autograph of the railroadman that just brought in the Ponce de Leon? Does the construction foreman who's just knocked together a two-story frame house wonder if the man who built the Empire State Building will ever condescend to nod to him on the street? — Joe Parham, Macon (Ga.) **Telegraph.**

"Many couples say that children brighten up a home. That's right — they never turn out a light."

3. The *aphorism,* or precept:

"Some people are like blotters; they soak it all up, but get it backwards."

4. The modified quotation:

"To the victors belong the broils."

5. The *homily,* or moral truth:

"With chilly weather here, it is time for some motorist to warm up his car in a garage with the doors shut — and fly off on a pair of wings."

6. The *distorted proverb*:

"Of course a cat still may look at a king, but it will have to hurry."

7. *Ironical explanation*:

"Speechless banquets are becoming quite the thing these days. Maybe it's the price of food that makes them speechless."

8. *Paradox,* or Irish bull:

"If there's anything that hurts more than paying income tax, it is not having to pay income tax."

"All Gaul is quartered into three halves."

"The trouble with the Irish is that too many Irish want what too many Irish don't want."

9. *Innuendo,* producing an effect by a hint:

"A wife can stand almost anything about a husband, until he begins to weigh less than she does."

10. *Human nature*: — a broad term, but by it we mean comment on human foibles:

"If human nature would only work as hard for pay as for more pay."

"The owner of the back lot that is filled with old cans, rubbish, and broken crockery can usually be found somewhere discussing the orderly adjustment of international affairs."

11. *Satire,* especially on institutions:

"The next president is rapidly increasing in numbers."

Now, let's consider a few examples of the right and wrong ways of writing paragraphs.

Right: "The truly contented husband isn't afraid to come home unexpectedly."

Wrong: "The truly contented husband isn't afraid to come home unexpectedly, because he knows he won't find another man there; that's why he's contented."

The last part of the sentence is unnecessary. It spoils the paragraph because the reader resents the explanation.

Here are more examples. Parentheses indicate the parts to be supplied by the reader, not the paragrapher.

"The curfew law is being revived in some towns where the parents want someone in the house during the second show." (The curfew bell will bring in the kids so they can stay in the house while the old folks go to the second show.)

"The Michigan woman sentenced to prison for life at hard work isn't worrying. She's reared ten children." (And, therefore, is used to hard work, and doesn't fear the sentence.)

"Insurance statistics show most accidents happen over the week end. Bathtub bottoms are as slippery as ever." (It is laughingly said that we bathe only on Saturday nights, and while we are bathing we slip and get hurt. But I'm clever enough to see that automobile accidents and such are meant.)

If the dog is the best friend of man, why doesn't he come home sometime with a bone with some meat on it? — Charles A. Knouse, Perry (Kan.) **Mirror.**

"The reproduction of Sir Joshua Reynolds' 'Age of Innocence' is being done from a pose." (The artist can find no girl today who is innocent, so he has to get one to pose as innocent.)

"Municipal officials say the practice of dumping hooch into sewers has almost eliminated sewer clogging. But, they say, they have to repair the pipes more often." (The hooch not only eats away the clogged places, but eats the pipes, too.)

Now, let us consider some "ideas" and their expression in paragraphs:

Idea — Joan of Arc failed because she couldn't get help for her king. King. Modern women play cards, and use kings; try to get help or support for them.

Paragraph — "Modern card-playing women aren't so new. The Maid of Orleans was forced out because she couldn't draw support for her king."

\* \* \*

Idea — It often is said that "Life is just one damned thing after another." People in love follow each other around. How about modifying *life* to *love?*

Paragraph — "Life is just one damned thing after another. Love is just two damned things after each other."

\* \* \*

Idea — In most homes guest towels are for looks, not use. So much so, it often is said a wife should kill her husband if he uses one of them.

Paragraph — "In an eastern husband murder, they couldn't find a motive, until someone discovered a used guest towel."

\* \* \*

Idea — About everywhere you see girls nowadays, they are smoking.

Paragraph — "Nowadays, where there's smoke, there're girls."

\* \* \*

Idea — Even the smaller towns are having their murders.

Paragraph — "It's a pretty small town nowadays that hasn't one street pointed out as that on which the body was found."

\* \* \*

Idea — Half the prisoners in a certain penitentiary are studying law. Since so many of them are doing it, let's pretend that is the natural thing for them to do.

Be patient with the girl who walks to the front seat late to church, in order to show a new hat. In a few years she will drop into a back seat, to get out quickly if the baby cries. — Atchison (Kan.) **Globe.**

Paragraph — "Half the prisoners in an eastern penitentiary are studying law. You just can't get the criminal tendencies out of some prisoners."

\* \* \*

Idea — This thing of divorces isn't so new. Often, a present day divorcee is the son or daughter of divorced parents.

Paragraph — "Often the bride of today can't run home to mother, because mother has already run home to grandmother."

\* \* \*

Are paragraphs hard to write? We think they are not. Let's see if they are. We'll give you a rather interesting statement of fact that almost invites some paragraph comment:

"At a recent huddle of college professors, it was agreed that 16 new letters should be added to the alphabet."

There are all sorts of possibilities to that one. Bowls should have to be bigger for alphabet soup, wives could say more, the unsaid things would be all the more unsaid, the letter "I" would get needed help. Write your own.

So, we conclude agreeing, we hope, that the quotable column is one that has its brief comment on a topic of timeless and widespread interest, the comment being of an unexpected nature and made by implication, rather than directly. If we want to write a quotable paragraph on quotable paragraphs we can say:

"The world is listening, expectantly, for the man who doesn't quite say what it doesn't expect him to say."

. . . the world is listening.

## 12.

# Editing the Column Copy

**UNIFORMITY**

Column editing includes checking for parallelism in the form of question-answer matter, group interviews, and other copy where uniformity is desirable. The result is easier reading. Brevity also adds force. But watch for unintentional repetition of similar words in opening sentences of paragraphs, or adjoining sentences. Such repetition is to many people as grating as sand in the celery.

IT IS PROBABLY NO EXAGGERATION to say that most personal columns in small papers could be improved considerably by careful editing. For lack of incisive and creative work with an editor's pencil, a column paragraph or essay may lack the unity and clarity which would permit it to speak in clearer tones. Wordy English is muffled composition. To say less may be to say more. To say only approximately what one means will not win any bravos from readers. Yet most of us constantly struggle for words to express imperfectly matured thoughts.

The fundamental purposes of editing include these:

1. Correcting errors of fact.

2. Correcting errors of grammar.

3. Eliminating bad taste.

4. Guarding against making of actionable statements involving laws of publication.

5. Marking for desired typographical effects.

6. Fitting a given space, if this is required.

7. Improving the column in detail and in structure.

[ 148 ]

This list is not as formidable as it appears. An experienced newspaper man will do most of these things almost instinctively and simultaneously, especially in handling news copy. Editing column material is more exacting in that choice of a word or phrase may not only involve accuracy, but effect. The columnist sets his own standard of excellence in most cases because he alone dares make changes in copy as personal as humorous paragraphs, verse, etc.

There are no errors of fact which are peculiar to the column. However, some columnists who would withhold rumors and hearsay items from news stories yield to the temptation to mention them in the more informal climate. And inasmuch as these writers inevitably assume an air of some infallibility, their making an error is especially irritating to readers, and to themselves. There are some tests which a columnist must make for himself, but careful reading by another person is desirable. And editing out errors in proof is unsatisfactory and costly.

Second readers are likely to be more alert than a writer is to errors in grammar and expression. Some mistakes may arise in straining for literary effects, but most of them are traceable to the haste in which most newspaper work is done. Constant use of standard reference works is a must for every journalist. Reproducing the statements of others, especially those telephoned, is a major source of errors.

Bad taste is not as easily detected as might be imagined. It often is a matter of opinion. What is regarded as unpardonable in one set of people may be considered sophisticated and smart in another. Of course there are clear-cut offenses: the risque joke, racial and religious intolerance, ill temper, and flagrant displays of egotism. Yet who knows when he has used "I" and "us" too often, mentioned his family too frequently, or over-publicized his club? It is easy to offend an advertiser, a political candidate, or an

**WORD LENGTH**

The informal language of most columns does not invite use of multi-syllable, unfamiliar words. In fact, columns generally rate high in both readability and readership. Rather than worry about word length, small-town writers probably should concentrate on using better style and more descriptive language, in polishing their story-telling ability, and in developing patterns of column organization. Long words may be acceptable if familiar to readers; short ones may be less acceptable because they are known only to certain professions or to the well-read. A columnist who habitually uses long words probably is not using his conversational vocabulary, but one reserved for talking to strangers or sophisticates. If he keeps his readers in mind as he writes, stuffed-shirt talk will not develop.

**CHARACTERIZATION**

In every situation, at every scene, there are details which may be expressed in a few words—if they are the right words. In addition to the key words, such as nouns and verbs, there are descriptive words and expressions. Some of these may be used to fill out leads and headlines. The column, having few or no headlines, must grab and hold readers by clever phrasing placed near and at the beginning. In the editing process, the characterizing words should be given close attention. Fast writing preserves the spirit of the moment and improves style, but careful editing weeds out weak characterizing words, supplies others, and sharpens punch lines. It also guides the pace by shortening or lengthening sentences and paragraphs.

ardent sports fan. The prayer of a careful columnist is that, when he does these things, they shall be deliberate and in his advance knowledge. Yet, human nature being as it is, he knows he will unknowingly give offense now and then, and will have to make amends as best he can.

The columnist remembers, too, that some readers are sensitive to the slightest criticism and that others "can't take a joke." In this respect he may have a mental black list of not-to-be mentioned individuals. He remembers, too, certain individuals who regard his lighter remarks as trivial; that others think his profound observations are stuffy. Probably he will ignore these when he writes his day's output, but will remember some of them when he passes a black pencil over the copy.

In regard to legal entanglements, columnists have to remember that the costs of winning an action may be only slightly less than those of losing one. And even threats against a paper may cause it to take costly precautions.

The laws and regulations involved include:

1. Libel.
2. Contempt of court.
3. Copyright.
4. Plagiarism and piracy.
5. Postal regulations.
6. Miscellaneous federal and state prohibitions.
7. The common law, under which actions for damages may be brought, or restraining orders obtained.

Libel actions under criminal law, prosecuted by a government, are rare and are of little concern to the columnist. He isn't likely to advocate a breach of the peace or scandalize an instrument of government. But civil libel, instituted by individuals, is an ever-present danger. Because of space limitations, only some of the more pertinent aspects of libel can be presented here.

Columnists recognize these dangers, as defined variously in state laws:

1. Imputing a crime, loathsome disease, unchastity, dishonesty, or other defamatory characteristics, to a person in printed matter.

2. Making any person an object of ridicule, scorn, or hatred.

3. Injuring a person in his profession or business.

4. Damaging a business firm, which can sue for pecuniary redress.

5. Damaging the reputation of the dead, which usually affects the social and business or professional standing of living relatives.

Writing in anger, a columnist might accuse a professional man of malpractice or negligence, refer to a lawyer as a shyster, call a physician a quack, question the moral standards of a coach of athletics, hint at corruption or bribery in a public office, question the trading practices of a firm, or challenge the professional ability of a craftsman. In most states, these allegations by a paper are libelous *per se* and actionable.

Other libels may result from imputations which can be drawn from associations of facts printed and facts already known by readers; from innuendo, if the plaintiff can be identified, even when not named; and from slurring and contemptuous references. The very fact of trying to disguise a libel with allegory or anonymity may indicate malicious intent as seen by the jury. And malice, whether of the garden variety or the result of pure carelessness, forfeits most of the defendant's defenses except truth.

Defenses against libel actions, *which are not absolute,* include: (1), the truth, when it can be proved; (2), legal privilege,

. . . libel actions may result.

subject to limitations set up by the state laws; and (3) , the right of fair comment and criticism, which varies state by state. Additionally, defendant papers may cite in mitigation those facts and circumstances which tend to sustain its claims of public service and good motives, and to question whether the plaintiff was damaged and whether by his actions he invited the publication involved. And evidence of retractions and corrections may be introduced.

The fear of libel may be more damaging to a paper than libel itself, and newspapers constantly take calculated risks. But it is unwise to take risks based on the presumed — but not yet proved — guilt of the accused, on his being an apparent down-and-out vagrant, on the remoteness of the person or firm accused, and on popularly believed guilt of persons deceased.

The columnist must learn to differentiate between a *comment* upon matters of public concern and public entertainment, and an allegation of a personal nature derogatory to the person mentioned. It may be proper to describe an act, accurately and fairly, but not to judge it in terms of *general professional competency* or private morals.

And most writers know that in printing a column, letter, or advertisement a newspaper assumes joint responsibility and may even be exclusively sued by a plaintiff.

## CONTEMPT

While few columnists expect to be charged with interfering with administration of the courts, a militant writer might be held in contempt for refusing to reveal the source of printed charges, for lowering the public's confidence in a court, and for grossly inaccurate reports or comment on a court trial. Newspapers are constantly asserting their right of fair comment and criticism on public matters, including the courts. A point at issue is whether justice is obstruct-

## QUESTIONS

Some columnists are over-fond of rhetorical questions. These can be irritating. Amateurs like them because they take the place of harder-to-write leads. On occasion, nothing else is as good; save them for that time. . . . Questions asked but not answered constitute a form of insult. They carry insinuations and innuendo. Worst of all, perhaps, is that venerable question, "Have you quit beating your wife?"

ed by comment before, during or after hearing of a case, and pending appeal. Newspapers claim the constitutional right of comment while a case is of public concern, and in several states have been upheld in recent tests.

### COPYRIGHT

A fact is public property, but the manner of expressing it in words, photographs, and art work can be protected under provisions of federal law. Titles cannot be copyrighted as such, but a court might restrain use by another person under some circumstances as unfair competition.

Strictly speaking, a columnist cannot use any copyrighted material without permission except on risk of infringement. By custom, however, fifty words or less are used in reviews of books, plays, etc. It is safer to get written permission.

Copyrighted data cannot be protected as facts, but unusual theories, bodies of statistics presented in unique ways, and other information obtained through much expense or effort cannot be appropriated by others with impunity.

A columnist might wish to copyright a poem, a puzzle, or an essay because of presumed merit in the wording or arrangement. The procedure is to obtain the required form from the Register of Copyright, Washington, D. C.; print the notice of copyright ("Copyright, 19–, by _____") thereon, and send in printed copies and fee as required. Such copyright, lasting 28 years, can be renewed for 28 more; at the end of 56 years, or 28 if not renewed, the material becomes public property. Matter printed without copyright goes into the public domain immediately.

Newspaper syndicates have reported rather widespread infringement of copyright on feature material sent with advertising services.

### ERRORS

Reading copy for detection of mistakes is not a job for a person gripped by one of the livelier emotions. Concentrating on one category of possible errors may at times be advisable. Such limited readings may include only accuracy, or whether questions are raised but not answered, or whether there are grammatical and style errors. Again, libel may be the main fear. We think it is no exaggeration to say that few columnists are complete critics and wholly capable correctors of their own copy. Other minds more quickly detect ambiguities and fact errors.

Literary piracy is unauthorized use of another's production, often involving sales. Plagiarism is taking the work of another and passing it off as original. In the world of fiction, property rights customarily are protected by copyright. In the columnists' world the issues are more confused in that copyrighting is infrequent and ethical considerations are more involved.

Although a columnist may wish to claim no property rights in his output, he does expect credit for his work when he sees it reproduced with or without his consent. Plagiarism is clearly unethical. Yet filler material, including humorous paragraphs, jokes, fact items, and brief verse, is widely reprinted without credit to the sources. Sometimes the matter is merely credited to "Exchange." The prevalence of the practice has been inversely proportional to the size of the papers; small papers have needed much filler. Perhaps one distinction has been the fact that readers have not regarded the pickups as original with the small papers.

It is especially irritating to see one's uncredited work in a paper in the nearby territory. One midwestern editor put it this way:

> All newspapers have a newspaper exchange list. This is for three particular reasons. First, there is a chance to get advertising suggestions; second, it is nice to see how other papers do it; third, there is a chance to pick up some news. . . . This newspaper, when it finds items we desire to reprint, always gives credit to the paper from which we clip. That is customary and common courtesy. We note, however, that one newspaper has reached the habit of clipping news and then not giving credit. . . . That's a cheap way to do business.

Adapting of editorial and business ideas of another non-competing paper to one's own needs is approved and even facilitated by press associations. But there are other practices which are in the shadowy border-

## SENTENCE LENGTH

Long sentences are bookish, and for leisurely and concentrated reading. Columns are read at a faster pace. Column sentences average as few as fifteen words and, acceptably, as many as twenty. Subject matter makes a difference. Columnists who think much and write slowly are likely to qualify many statements. Those who like description let sentences lengthen. But writers with strong convictions and those who prefer narrative prose use shorter sentences. . . . Not the average length, but variety of sentences which make up that average is important. Watch averages, but don't overrate them. Use two-word sentences now and then. Or three, or four. Study the total effect.

line of ethics. One of these, so widespread that nothing probably can be done about it, is the rewriting of column material. In most cases there is nothing illegal in the action because exact wording is not duplicated. Certainly the practice is more ethical than running items without credit.

A humorous paragraph soon becomes the substance of a radio gag, a joke, or a comic strip caption. An uncredited brief may be credited to the one who clipped it. The experience of a Missouri columnist is not unusual. One of her paragraphs was picked up, with proper credit, by a daily newspaper, then by a magazine. Later with few words changed, it was reprinted by another national magazine and credited to a big city paper.

Of course the proof of such rewriting is not always implicit in the mere fact of finding an idea credited to another source. When a paragrapher writes a rather obvious gag about a news event he must concede that others might do the same. Headline writers, who also think alike, have been known to write identical headlines on the same news story.

### POSTAL REGULATIONS

The federal government and most states prohibit publication of matter concerning lotteries, except the bare announcement of winners, and of matter deemed obscene. Sending of the prohibited matter through the mails may cause barring of an issue or suspension or loss of a mailing privilege.

Mention of bank nights, turkey shoots, and other lotteries is sometimes seen, but the law forbidding such details is clear. Lotteries involve chance, a consideration, and a reward, but even the need to be present at the time of drawing is by definition a consideration.

Columnists sometimes support through favorable mentions the promotions, clearly lotteries, of church

### TRANSLATIONS

Everyone uses double-talk. It may be false or literally truthful. Usually it conceals facts and conditions. People in trouble turn to it to soften public criticism. "We are doing everything possible to locate the trouble" may really mean that "We know what the trouble is but there is nothing we can do about it at the moment and we hope you will forget the whole matter." Translating public statements, with levity or satire, is a favorite device of many columnists. . . . Finding himself guilty of double-talk, the columnist can eliminate it while polishing his offering.

and fraternal organizations. While some postmasters pay no attention to these "worthwhile" games of chance, others demand that regulations be followed.

### OTHER PROHIBITIONS

In the editing of columns and other material, copy-readers also must remember the taboos on altering of official weather reports, accepting advertising of fraudulent stocks and illegal mail schemes, and re-producing pictures of stamps, certain legal documents and money—except as provided by law. Re-printing of matter used by another publication is no defense. Cold war regulations affecting national security are little less troublesome than the voluntary censorships of wartime. Some columnists have erred in printing letters from men in military service— letters which revealed troop movements, use of certain materiel, etc.

Another purpose of editing a column is to mark it for the printer. It is not necessary to indulge in the typographic orgies sometimes seen. But effective yet sparing use can be made of initial letters, indentions, bold-face type, etc. All marks necessary for these innovations and for insertion of illustrations should be carefully made and checked for error. Linotype operators, never made happy by typographic frills, lose valuable time when instructions are confusing. At the same time, it can be ascertained that the column is long enough, and flexible enough, to fit the space allowed for it.

Of course the larger task is improvement of the column in detail and in over-all structure. The amount of pruning is likely to be proportional to the experience of the writer; the experienced columnist does most of his editing in his head and before com-mitting it to paper. For many persons, however, the better practice is to write at top speed, using the

If ever there was a wet blanket and a spoilsport, it's a con-science! — Justin Hammond, Corona (Calif.) **Independent**.

language of the moment and trying to make full use of one's creative inspiration. Later, this enthusiastic but wordy and somewhat lame account is sharply edited . . . cutting a word here, a phrase there . . . substituting a word . . . inserting a clause . . . supplying connectives . . . smoothing continuity. Then it may be necessary to rewrite to clean up the copy.

A second way is to make a rough outline of the intended essay, then write it paragraph by paragraph on half-sheets of copy paper, rewriting each page as often as necessary to polish each bit as it is written. Finally, the sheets are gone over for consideration of all the factors previously mentioned here, if involved. Paragraphs are of course written and perfected one by one.

Civilization doesn't always time things right. Lipstick would have wiped off the old celluloid collars. — Princeton (W. Va.) **Observer.**

The copyreader, usually the columnist, also takes an arm's-length look at the whole piece. He will read it in its entirety, and quickly, to get the impact it may have on the readers. He realizes that this is the last legitimate chance to edit the column deeply. Is there anything in it in bad taste? Is he "in character" or has he pontificated a bit today? Does he end on a pleasant or effective note?

When a column has been written in anger, or in full voice for any reason, this question is always in order: DOES THIS STATEMENT MAKE THE WRITER, AND THE PAPER, APPEAR RIDICULOUS?

In some cases it may be advisable to put the column on ice for 24 hours. If it doesn't cool off, the writer may. The resultant revisions may save a situation, a libel suit, or some friendships. A real editor is . . . one who really *edits.*

. . . take time to cool off.

## 13.

# One Hundred Column Ideas

**ASK—AND RECEIVE**

Publicity offices spend millions preparing material for newspapers — a fact that should suggest to the latter that they try to turn these sums not only into advertising, but also into usable news and features. Columnists could write more letters and ask more questions. Even postal cards bearing the column imprint are acceptable. One minute and one card may bring highly interesting data from Hollywood or elsewhere.

ONE DELIGHTFUL ASPECT of the small-town newspaper column is its endless variety. Below are listed some of the ideas which appear in such columns.

Keeping in mind various formulas and devices is a stimulus to inspiration. Furthermore, repeated use of a device brings readers back to a column regularly. Circulation is stabilized by such continuing features.

A good idea may have a universality which commends it to writers of columns everywhere. Adaptations to local conditions make other devices usable.

Many columnists have found these worth giving readers:

1. *Departments.* Some writers classify materials by divisions or labels. Examples:

Edge-of-the-seat department.

Room-for-research department. (Did bridge drive men to golf or did golf drive women to bridge?)

Minor disaster of the week.

Man of the week.

This week's orchid for public service.

The week's bonehead award.

Today's wacky definition.

There-ought-to-be-a-law department.

2. *Characters*. Many columnists put words in the mouths of fictitious characters. These include well-known types — an unnamed grouch from a certain part of town, a stenographer, an old bachelor, Teen-age Tessie, etc. Also noted are the Office Cat, the Boss Rat in Jones Alley, and the Broadway Mocking Bird. These characters speak not only from their animal perspective but also from man's viewpoints.

3. *Items Overheard*. Facts are sometimes handled as rumors, and nameless persons are heard to comment on affairs of current interest. Also, actual remarks picked up in a crowd may be interesting although fragmentary. A few writers have planted wire-recorders in gossipy meetings with hilarious results. Speakers usually are not identified.

4. *Contributors*. While few small-town columns show a steady flow of readers' contributions, the opinions of local people on current issues are valued. Sharing column space with friends and readers seems almost an obligation. Quoting well-known local people makes a column seem alive. Acceptability of readers' verse and essays is a more debatable question. Some columnists turn down all verse rather than reject most of it.

5. *Philosophy*. Manners and morals are standard column subjects. Writers try through precepts, proverbs, parables, and paragraphs to voice the philosophy needed by their generation. In time a columnist builds into a recognizable pattern the ideas and convictions by which he lives. The more skilled he is as a writer, the

Many columnists put words in the mouths of fictitious characters.

less like a sermon his column will seem. He will present the main structure of an idea but leave to readers the phrasing of the moral.

In the following example, Lynn Landrum of the Dallas *News* satirizes the tendency of institutions of higher learning to ignore certain fundamentals while worrying about others:

Episcobapterian University, founded in 1950 by the Evangelical Reformed Episcobapterian Church South of God (Unigational Synod), is having trouble. Opposition has come up against the official policy of the university on bubblegum on the campus. School authorities have ruled against the gum. Throughout this fair land of ours the young men · and women of our choicest families are everywhere upset by the temptations and enticements of commercialized indulgence. Besides, some imp of Halifax went out and parked his gum in the internal workings of the check–signing machine and all the salary checks for May are not out yet. Moreover, Episcobapterian faculty people have come out for bubble gum liberalism. They say self-expression must not be circumscribed. They say that the psychological id of the norm must not be regimented by the reflex ratio of the idem sonans. They hint that crackerdemic freedom is involved. It is true that an academician might become the more firmly attached to his seat of learning, but it is hard to see how bubblegum enhances tenure. But it looks like concessions will have to be made if next year's football schedule is to be met successfully.

6. *Part for a Whole.* Emotional values in cold statistics can be made more apparent by pointing out localized effects, even on a single individual. The average man comparison has grown stale, but columnists find it effective to describe an event through the mind and heart of a child, a blind person benefited by a civic club minstrel, or a bond issue as seen by a laborer. It is perhaps remembered that the New York *Times'* "Hundred Neediest Cases" is still a good publicity device.

7. *Teen-Age Talk.* Juvenile delinquency is, more than is generally recognized, a failure to understand and influence the adolescent mind. Yet every parent

knows that teen-agers have sound ideas about parks, playgrounds, traffic, and other local issues. Instead of imposing early curfews and other restrictive measures, some communities put their youngsters on civic committees and challenge them to help build sound public programs. No alert columnist will wish to be without some quotations from his future subscribers.

8. *Wisdom of the Ages.* Put the same question to persons 10, 20, 30, 40, 50, 60, and 70 years of age. The variations in viewpoints will be amusing, and possibly enlightening. What columnists write about depends much upon their ages. Here is a pertinent item from the Fountain Inn (S.C.) *Tribune*:

### THIS IS LIFE

At five the youngster says: "The stork brought us a new baby."

At ten: "My dad can lick any man twice his size."

At fifteen: "Girls are — blah!"

At twenty: "Just give me a chance. I'll show 'em."

At twenty-five: "The system is all wrong; there should be reform."

At thirty: "In a few years people will wake up and demand their rights."

At thirty-five: "I'd be rich if I'd stayed single."

At forty: "Give me another, and a larger bottle of that cure-all tonic."

At forty-five: "I'm sick of reformers."

At fifty: "Thank God I've got a good comfortable bed to sleep in."

At sixty: "I was mighty lucky to pick such a fine woman for a wife."

At sixty-five: "I feel as young as I did at twenty-five."

At seventy: "I don't know what these modern young people are coming to."

9. *The Weather.* People are so subject to variations of the weather that they never cease to talk about it. Columnists who neglect it do so at a sacrifice in reader interest. Weather history is interesting, especially as it concerns extremes. Forecasting the weather is popular. Readers help by reporting the thickness of fur on animals, bark on trees, moss in the pond, etc.

### ADVERTISING

Don't sell advertising space; sell results. Yes, but also sell interest in advertising. What was John Jones' hardware store advertising 25 years ago? Look it up. Write it up — then and now. Mention John. How did he get about in the old days. If he rode a high-wheel bicycle, the thought may be shocking, in contrast to his present dignity and Cadillac. But chances are that he'll brag of his prowess on the old high-wheeler. It's an item.

10. *Old Sayings.*   From the pig in a poke to a cock crowing before a door, people have interpreted life in stories and idioms which make up a region's folklore. The American language is dynamic, colorful, growing. Rather than hamstringing it with rules, columnists are recording it in folk tales, brief quotations, and light essays. Some writers run a few old sayings each week and ask readers to send in others.

11. *Folk Tales.*   Every region has its legends, haunted houses, and Indian tales. There are stories about people and about things, about plants and animals and about lakes and streams. After exploiting the better known stories, columnists can try for others which will be lost unless the old folks recall and record them. Local newspaper men often regard themselves as historians. It is a wholesome attitude.

12. *Apologies.*   Corrections and retractions usually are run in news columns, but minor apologies appear in many columns. A variation ran in the "Etaoin" column of the Somerset (N.J.) *Gazette:*

> A very nice lady just called in and scolded hard about a story we had promised to use. She demanded to know why it wasn't printed. She was hopping mad. We told her to look right smack in the middle of Page 4 and there she'd find the story. She thereupon apologized and said she must have read too fast. She felt very silly. Little incidents like that make us chortle with unholy glee. We don't often get a chance to have fun. We're mostly wrong.

The lady mentioned probably doesn't exist, but the item will make readers look over their papers carefully before calling the editor to complain. On the contrary, a columnist on the Ripon (Wis.) *Commonwealth* had to eat his words:

> The paper (chomp, chomp) isn't so bad, (chomp) but the words . . . ugh!
> These were the Commonwealth sports editor's feelings this week as he proceeded to eat the words in which he proclaimed that "there ain't no sich animal" as a divided

**SEARCH—AND RESEARCH**

Musty old records make good column material. Columnists have promoted cleaning out of attics, and front-porch sale of antiques for welfare causes. Few columnists make good auctioneers, but there have been exceptions. . . . Many public officials and court clerks, aw secretaries, and accountants are constantly turning up interesting material. They don't know that columnists could use it, either in the column or in by-line features. Let them know.

season in the Central State League. The sports editor was misinformed.

13. *Brevitorials.* Although columns have replaced many formal editorials, some publishers retain both forms and find them complementary, not competitive. Nevertheless, terse little editorials are found in columns, and these are sometimes called brevitorials. One paragraph is usually enough for such terse comment.

14. *What To Read.* As an advocate of the printed word, a columnist can afford the time it takes to write short reviews of significant new books and magazine articles. He can establish the idea that it is pleasant to browse in the public library. He can broaden the base of his column by quoting from what he reads. He can quote friends who have read other material. He suggests that reading is fun and he backs his argument with examples. It would do his business no good to give the impression that he spends his evenings listening to Amos and Andy *et al.*

15. *Promotions.* Readers like action and appreciate success. Many columnists try to have some campaign or promotion going all the time, and they share leadership in many local projects.

16. *Half-Minute Interviews.* Under this classification a columnist can introduce newcomers, give brief biographies of new club presidents, mention advertisers just back from market, and quote students home from college. Quotes are good, whether from beggars, tourists, or prize-winning steers, real or make-believe.

17. *Seen.* Under this heading the columnist's eyes make their contribution. Perhaps he drives over the country on Sunday afternoon. It's safer to see *things* than some people in some places.

18. *Heard.* This heading is for items heard and overheard — children playing, frogs croaking, a new

**A disadvantage of living in a small town is that when your cat gets too high in a tree you have to get it down yourself.—Merrill Chilcote, Maryville (Mo.) Tribune.**

father boasting, brakes screeching, firecrackers exploding, dinner pails rattling.

19. *This 'n That.* Things which deserve only a sentence each can be bunched in a single paragraph and separated . . . like this.

20. *Trade at Home.* Transient dollars and regional trade support many small cities. Columnists stress ideas for exploiting local recreational resources, places of historical interest, and scenic spots. Columns offer opportunities to repeat slogans — "What Centerville Makes Makes Centerville," "Advertising Pays," etc.

21. *Family Names.* Check old county records for family names on original documents. Write up the old families and how they came to the county. Similarly, farms and firms bearing old names may be subjects for one-topic columns, which really are feature stories. Shorter material may be used on origins of family names.

22. *Old Subscribers.* "While renewing his subscription for the nineteenth straight time, John Blank told us that. . . ." The suggestion here is that people like and read the paper, but the item may be expanded on its general merits.

23. *Letters.* Communciations from readers which are too hot to handle in letters-to-the-editor departments may be run in personal columns, where analysis and comment are easy and pruning of the contributions may be explained. Usable, too, are letters from former residents and reports from local people on trips. Some columnists share their thoughts and findings as they open a typical day's mail.

24. *Gripes.* Editors, like readers, like to complain. Here is an excerpt from the Laurens (Iowa) *Sun* which has a universal application:

> Where our subscribers are concerned, we like to feel that the Sun is THEIR paper; and we'd like the privilege of being first with such news. It doesn't matter one

If you must tell your troubles to someone, the psychiatrist costs more than the old-time bartender, but not as much as the other woman. — Havertown (Pa.) **Haverford Township News.**

iota to the city papers if we have it first, but it kinda knocks the frosting off our cake when we read it in them first. . . . We'd like to make a desperate plea to all couples intent on committing matrimony, particularly to the brides-to-be and their mothers, to see that the details are written up in advance or immediately afterward, and gotten to us.

25. *Unusual Signs.* One paper, noting that an excavating company advertised that it "would go anywhere to dig up dirt," started printing other unusual signs. It also noted the frequency of misspelled words and the strange lettering of amateur calligraphers. Encyclopedias and advertising texts gave interesting historical data on signs.

26. *Phone Calls.* Errors made through misconstrued telephone calls would fill a joke book. A phoned-in ad offered for sale "two used sheets"; it ould have read "two ewe sheep." Ask readers to of other telephone blunders. Interview a tele- one operator. Do a bit of research on telephone etiquet. Study local telephone voices. Offer a modest prize for the local secretary having the most gracious telephone manners.

27. *Close Calls.* The home is a dangerous place. Calling attention to some of the hazards may prevent accidents. Shooting at shadows, climbing on old ladders, going alone into old wells, filling a house with extension cords — these are settings for tragedy. But there are many other hazards likely overlooked. Call on readers to furnish examples of queer accidents in the home. Look through fire records to find causes of home blazes.

28. *Then and Now.* Nostalgia quickly palls, but there is no harm in noting these changing times. Many farms, for example, have no draft animals; some have no pigs, chickens, or ducks. Many farms have no cows. And it has come to pass that some farmers' sons cannot tell what a well-dressed horse

Editorials are something of a tradition in the newspaper world. They're like the buttons on the sleeve of your coat — they serve no particular purpose but for some reason they are supposed to be there. The presence of an editorial column, convention speakers say, gives the newspaper a certain tone and prestige, which may be true, but it's hard to put one's finger on the values. Such claims must be accepted in blind faith and sublime hope.

The easy — and maybe the best — way to do an editorial column is to buy the stuff already written. We can buy it by the ream, turned out by top-flight writers who by their abilities have crashed the syndicates. You would thus read better editorials and know what the bigger minds are thinking about, but there is one thing those fellows can't provide — that's the local angle, the home-town atmosphere. If the local newspaper is to live and move and have its being at the grassroots, we think it should try to express that viewpoint. — Ralph Shannon, Washington (Iowa) *Journal.*

should wear. Make up a list of parts — reins, bits, suspenders, hobbles, knee boots, head poles, etc. — and test your theory that farms are not what they used to be. Ask a hardware man to compare his stocks of today and 25 years ago.

29. *Scrapbooks.* Some columns are carrying items labeled "For your scrapbook." These include verse, recipes, puzzles, odd news, tributes to this and that, and regional folk tales. Of course, recipes are worth separate attention. Readers will enjoy a run of recipes for sauces, chili, scrapple, chigger ointment, stomach bitters, and snakebite remedy.

30. *Pet Peeves.* Unlike gripes, which are ill-tempered, peeves may be humorous, good humored, comical, etc. Consult garbage collectors, night watchmen, park attendants, delivery men, and steeplejacks. Talk to ministers about their many strange experiences in times of crisis, death, marriage, and divorce.

31. *Finding Lost Articles.* Very real is the gratitude of a person for whom a columnist has found a lost pet or purse. Some columns run free mention of such losses. Sometimes a small reward is offered by the paper. Free mention may be limited to lost pets so as not to detract from the classified ads.

32. *Gratitude.* Readers, too, do things for others. Each community has persons who are quick to give flowers, food, and attention to the sick. They would likely be embarrassed by publicity, but a columnist can praise the spirit which prompts such unselfish service. Sometimes an elderly individual can be singled out for praise, or some honor can be arranged, presented, and reported.

33. *Eccentricities.* People are funny, and should not be ashamed to admit the fact. Some have long unfulfilled desires, such as the eating of ice cream and cake *before* the main course at luncheons. Mention this, and old Mrs. Jones, who supervises Methodist ladies who serve the Rotary Club each week,

Home is where you turn the catsup bottle upside-down and get catsup. — Vic Green, Pekin (Ind.) *Banner.*

will see to it that the queer one gets his dessert first. Once started, confessions of odd desires may become epidemic. Drop the subject while readers are still talking about it.

34. *Habits.* People like to occupy the same pews in church each week. Children are broken up even by a move across town. Old folks are site bound. Not everyone likes a new house, a new pair of shoes, new golf clubs. Not everything that is new and shiny makes for happiness and comfort. Columnists write much about the habits of people — and themselves.

35. *Tours.* Outlining of Sunday afternoon tours, logged by miles and stops and things to do and see, not only please many readers but also develop possibilities for advertising. A columnist on tour is able to mention accommodations both good and bad — within the limits of the libel laws.

36. *Allergies.* Not many years have passed since people with peculiar tastes and reactions were considered offensive. Tolerance of people whose only abnormality is a different physical reaction to their environment is not marked in some communities. And some physicians have harsh words for parents who force children to eat things they don't like and wear clothes they don't want. Columnists note these differences, and also comment on the effect of wallpaper tones, noise, tight places, altitude, and other phenomena.

Grandparents think kids are wonderful because their perspective is better than the parents'. — Helper (Utah) **Journal.**

37. *Public Figures.* The average reader is interested in the personal life and habits of persons known to him through news articles. Columnists describe the mayor's desk, his trophies, his golf score. They note how firemen use their leisure. They tell of school teachers who open hour quizzes with prayer, others who serve tea midway of final exams, and of professors who can never remember where they parked their cars.

38. *Special Days.* Unimaginative columnists say

only the obvious things about Halloween and other special days. Others try to tell readers things they don't know. Keeping a clipping file is one way to do this. A visit to the public library may suffice. Or the columnist may interview a veteran's foreign-born bride about holidays in other lands.

39. *Mistakes.* Pointing out errors in bigger papers may be a mistake, but many columnists indulge in it. Textbooks, which tend to be based on other textbooks, may be astonishingly inaccurate. Check the geographies used in the public schools. What do they say about the region in which the children live? Encyclopedias aren't perfect, either. What is hominy? Ask your grandmother, then see if her definition agrees with a dictionary. It may be a good idea to explain why newspapers are not, and economically can never be typographically perfect.

40. *Classified Ads.* This lively section is unexcelled for reader interest. But many ads leave readers curious. Wholly apart from promoting the section, columnists can find many little features by telephoning advertisers.

41. *Conversation.* To what extent does conversation waste time while stupid questions are answered? Are you offended when you get a complete answer to the question, "How are you?" How does barbershop conversation differ by seasons? To what extent do people agree with others while secretly believing the opposite? What is a "brilliant conversationalist?"

42. *Reactions.* Not all the good actors are in Hollywood. How should people act when they have heard a joke before? When they get bad news? When they get wonderful news? Why do people laugh? Should back-slapping be discouraged? What is the best way to break shockingly bad news? How should one reply to a compliment which isn't deserved, or even to one that is?

. . . a complete answer to the question, "How are you?"

43. *Reviews.*    Movies take a lot of time, but columnists can salvage some of it by commenting on the shows. Exhibitors' press books have data on stars and on problems encountered during production. . . . Columnists can dig out unusual facts in interviews, at dress rehearsals, and by consulting technical staffs. What other writers overlook, columnists can report. This often is the most interesting part of a show or event.

44. *Success.*    How to get that first job is the serious problem of many high school and college graduates. Some guidance, and much news interest, may be found in the stories of how local business men got their start in life. . . . And many young people need advice on how to apply for a job. One business man reported this phone call from a high school graduate: "Hey, you got any jobs open down there now?"

45. *Procrastination.*    Having confessed that he habitually puts things off, a columnist can look around town and see alleys which need cleaning, church lawns uncut, signs needing paint, fences drooping and gates off their hinges. Comment on the alternative of (1) trying to live happily despite these eyesores and (2) taking the time and energy to keep a neat house, a clean store, an attractive town.

46. *Prevention.*    Press services constantly remind us that this world is filled with wells to fall into, ditches to cave in, stairs which may collapse, dogs which may go mad, and bridges which are unsafe. Why not make a survey of such hazards in your area.

47. *Animals.*    Animals are of human interest; i.e., they live with and are loved by people. Column subjects include unusual pets, barking dogs, poisoning of pets, dogs and mail carriers, dog shows, etc. But don't overlook cats, nor the animal hospitals with their lying-in rooms.

48. *Beauty.*    Beauty is for those with eyes to see it. The columnist can point it out. Readers can offer

Mothers always are better cooks than mothers-in-law. — Tallahassee (Ala.) **Tribune.**

their versions. Housewives report finding rainbows in soapsuds, children find them in lawn sprays, and motorists see similar colors on wet pavements. Aviators report that the city dump is beautiful when viewed from 3,000 feet up. In season, trees and flowers form beautiful patterns of interest to amateur photographers. What is beautiful in your town?

49. *Life at Forty.* "When a man passes forty, no photographer can do him justice," wrote Earl Tucker in the Thomasville (Ala.) *Times.* He described the person he imagined himself to be and contrasted it with the picture recorded by an impartial lens. Columnists approaching forty write in mock dread of the date but manage to express some good sense and no little humor.

50. *Spelling.* The argument goes on: Children are, or are not, being taught to spell as well as formerly. How is spelling taught today? Do teachers change their methods in a decade? What is the effect of listening — to radio — rather than reading? In a variation of theme, the Chilton (Wis.) *Times-Journal* rejoiced that the government had eliminated the first "c" in Kinnickinnic, but suggested cutting it to Kinnic, or even Double Kinnic. It added, "If we were running an august federal board we would run Kinnickinnic through the silage cutter, save one nic, and send the rest back to the Indians. Nic Street."

51. *Proposals.* People often say, "There ought to be a law . . . ." Columnists make many such statements. The Adair (Iowa) *News* endorsed having all holidays on Monday in the belief that everybody would be better satisfied and business would be less disturbed. "A holiday hooked onto Sunday is so enjoyable and so sensible in its minor interruption with business that it seems strange that a demand for holidays on Mondays is not general," the paper added.

And the Thomasville (Ala.) *Times* suggested this election year sign: "Jim's Place, 6 miles — 7 votes."

Words can hurt as much as any weapon, and it's so difficult to know whether they are loaded. — Frances Olin Gowen, Bainbridge (Wash.) **Review.**

52. *Work.* People commonly think they work harder than other folks. What is work? What tires a white-collar worker? How tired is a postman at the end of a day? Here is a chance to clear up some misconceptions. And you might try to find out what it is in a shopping round with his wife that makes a man approach a state of collapse.

53. *Birthdays.* The "Shinglediggins" column of the Coloma (Mich.) *Courier* keeps a birthday book on local people. But in addition to reporting birth dates of readers, Joe E. Wells, the columnist, gives facts about famous people born on the same dates, and events of history.

54. *Thinking.* Education, it is said, should teach people to think. What is thought? How can the validity of thinking be tested? Why is there so much faulty thinking? And consider the relationship between thinking and moods. Consider the mood — and thoughts — of a man with an aching molar. Consider, too, that — no matter what emotions tug at them — people such as teachers, ministers, and clerks must face their publics with cheerful moods and thoughts.

55. *Day by Day.* The "Sun Beams" column of the Spring Valley (Wis.) *Sun* has the unusual paragraphing of being written by days of the week. Paragraphs open with the day set in light caps, followed by a dash. The matter following, however, is not limited to that day. A few columns run calendars of promotional events. Others remind readers of deadlines for taxpaying, voting, assessing property, etc.

56. *The Ill.* This is a doubtful classification, but some columnists issue simulated bulletins on conditions of persons — and pets — who are ill. In small towns, black eyes and sprained ankles need explanation. Columns do it best.

57. *Dialogue.* Instead of the usual prose comments, some columns use quotation forms. Example:

We are happy when we hear the patter of little feet because we know then where the little rascals are. — Fred D. Keister, Ionia (Mich.) **News.**

Jones — You can't cheat old Father Time.
Brown — No, but some of the women drive a mighty close bargain with him.

—Rosetown (Sask.) *Eagle*

58. *Change.* News columns report what is new in a community — schools, people, smokestacks. Columnists can go a step further, analyzing what a new factory means in terms of new schools, playgrounds, and utilities. Growth imposes needs and penalties and there is no need to avoid inevitable adjustments. Columnists make them easier because they are better understood.

In the pursuit of happiness, some babies are hundreds of headlines ahead of the others by the time they get born. — Upton (Wyo.) **Gazette.**

59. *Styles.* Some columnists rant at style changes, but most of them are more amused than disgusted. A feature angle may be found in the history of the wedding ring, throwing of rice, and other customs. Male comfort vs. adherence to male styles is worth analysis.

60. *Correspondence.* A columnist complained that while his writings had explained how legislators should handle the economy of his state, only two of them took the paper. Another columnist wrote letters to legislators and printed their replies. For three cents and the time it takes to write a letter, an editor may obtain needed information not only from legislators, but from corporations, colleges, museums, libraries, and many other sources.

61. *Flabbergasted.* "So help me," wrote a columnist in the Southwest, "I will take an oath. I swear that among the tourists I saw over the week end was a little girl, not more than eight years old, upholstered with falsies. Her mother should be jailed."

62. *Displays.* Displaying in show windows materials mentioned in columns is good promotion. Such items may include oddities, photographs, garden produce, articles manufactured locally, letters, war relics, etc.

63. *Longevity.* Long and faithful service merits column mention. Included are longtime employees, old settlers, old machinery, antiques, and other subjects to which age has lent dignity, honor, and possibly enchantment.

64. *Quiet Living.* Columnists frequently champion sanity, safety, moderation, and similar virtues. "Simply sit by the fire and wiggle your toes," urged one as an antidote for the usual week-end traffic fatalities.

65. *Do You Know?* Under such subheads are put facts from many sources, including state almanacs, encyclopedias, and textbooks. An hour's work will produce enough for many columns, since they will be used sparingly.

66. *Subheads.* Small titles may be run in at the opening of paragraphs. The "This 'n That" column of the Howard (S.D.) *Miner County Pioneer* begins paragraphs with a word or phrase, followed by a colon. These include "orchids," to those it approves; "worth a try," "how true," "school days," etc.

67. *Kibitzing.* Where people gather, there's news. The "Looking and Listening" column of the Somerset (Pa.) *American* devotes some of its space to descriptions of kibitzers. Subjects vary from dog fights to the inevitable steam-shovels.

68. *Words.* A columnist, being a writing man, is likely to develop into an amateur philologist; i.e., a lover of words. He learns the common origins of clerk and Clark, Dick's son and Dickson, wagon maker and Wainright. He finds that the word *derrick* originated in a hangman's device; the hangman's name was Derrick. He learns the power of Anglo-Saxon words as contrasted with multi-syllable words which obscure meaning.

69. *Direct Address.* Not very often does a columnist address an essay to "Dear Mayor" or other public or private figures. Used in anger, the device may be

A gentleman minimizes the quantity of a lady's past and maximizes its quality, in that order. — Weiser (Idaho) **American.**

extremely distasteful. Used in good taste and good humor, however, it may be an effective literary device.

70. *Sponsorship.* Real or fictitious clubs are sponsored by many columnists. These include bachelors' protective associations and societies for the advocacy of this and that. Targets include postoffice pens, wearing of neckties and coats on blistering summer days, and allowing low-hanging limbs over sidewalks to annoy tall men and ladies. Timeliness of such sponsorship adds much to its humor.

71. *Puzzles.* Reader responses to puzzles have been surprisingly good in many instances, particularly if the "dumb columnist" is weak in decimal fractions and some of his fans are strong. Preferably, problems are fairly easy but tricky. One columnist asked his readers to write a sentence explaining that the English language contains "to," "too," and "two." Incorrect, he said, is the statement that "There are three two's in the English language." Then readers went to work on it.

72. *Skills.* Columnists can balance personal mention and content by recognizing physical as well as mental skills. A quick survey will point to the baker, the barber, the bootmaker, the welder, and other craftsmen. Others are the skills of the housewife, the boys in their workshops, and the girls in their 4-H clubs. Some columnists sponsor hobby exhibits and the work of Scouts, home demonstration club women, and amateur photographers.

73. *Pictures.* What is a proper picture for a home? Should it be an original or a lithograph? How many local people encourage regional artists? How many pictures express the personality of a person, and a home? These are proper column subjects. Some columnists have convictions which lead them into wild controversies over trends in art. A few comment on art in libraries, schools, and courthouses.

We hope the pastors hereabouts will understand and forgive, when we say that newspapering can be sort of a religion. Some of the most financially successful newspapermen never acquire it but all of the happiest ones have it. "The Paper" is your life, your love and, as we have said, almost your religion. Not just a newspaper; not just your job, but "The Paper." — Ferndale (Mich.) **Gazette.**

74. *Prayers.* These usually are timely, as suggested by the season. They are seen infrequently, and necessarily must be in good taste.

75. *Adventures.* Few columnists figure in crises worth mentioning, but sometimes they have hilarious times in imaginary happenings. Tongue in cheek, they write up adventures met in driving home over streets full of holes, crossing vacant lots at night, pushing their way through Saturday crowds, escaping a snowball fight between school kids, and fighting their way past a bargain counter to deliver a proof to a merchant.

76. *Funerals.* Comment on funerals and burial services usually is limited to important persons. Dignified yet sympathetic, these remarks avoid sentimentality and pagan attitudes toward death.

77. *Thanks.* When a paper is asked to express the Lions Club's appreciation of minstrel props lent by a local lumber yard, the column may seem the proper place for this chore. The columnist may simply say he heard Lions President Joe Jones thanking Bill Smith, the lumber man, for the materials. If he knows both men well, he may clownishly add that the lumber will never be the same again, but that it probably was knotty anyway. He avoids giving the impression that it is a formal note of appreciation. Such notes are paid ads.

78. *Ifs.* . . . Lacking other ideas, a columnist may engage in "iffy" speculation. If he were rich, he would do so and so; if he were mayor, he would do such and such. He may ask readers to join him. Serious notes and hints for public officials may evolve.

79. *Confessions.* Admitting faults common to most persons is a columnist's way of saying he is a regular fellow. He confesses that he is a poor husband (poor memory for anniversaries) ; a poor father (gives children too much money) ; a poor business man (gives more to charity than he can afford) ; a

poor insurance risk (sees his dentist when he has to and his doctor, ditto).

80. *Firsts.* Most people are interested in first things — first cotton baled, first robin, first blooming century plant, etc. And things historical include first trial, first school, first fire station, and other local and regional beginnings.

81. *Questions.* Big questions perplex but little ones annoy. What little ones annoy you? Examples: How do you feel? Where have you been? Where are you going? What do you know? What do you want for dinner?

82. *Male World.* Some women say they detest being always addressed in terms of their femaleness — in styles, manners, thought, etc. And it may be a mistake to talk overmuch of the man's world. But columnists do write of dad's prerogatives in other lands, about male beauty vs. female plainness in other than the human species; about women in male attire, etc.

83. *Bitter and Sweet.* Under this heading go all those it-could-have-been-worse items, alibis, moral victories, and picking up the pieces after minor disasters. But remember that some people detest alibis and others seem to like to suffer. And a community, like an individual, can take itself too seriously.

84. *Treasures.* These are where the heart is. Columnists sometimes attend household auctions and report reactions of children to parting with toys and pets. But communities have treasurers, too. Some cling to outmoded city ordinances, ancient fire engines, and antiquated courthouses. Antiques may include a few librarians, politicians, and school teachers. But be kind; columnists also age. And by their writing columnists name their own treasures.

85. *Reprints.* These are hard to evaluate. Previous column material may be reprinted "by request." Choice bits are chosen, of course.

You're not really old until you like to be home on time. — Charles V. Mathis, Wildwood (N. J.) **Independent-Record.**

86. *Elder Statesman.* In some communities, essay-type columns are written by leading citizens who have large followings because of their long prominence as business or professional men. An instance is that of Dr. J. A. Hill of West Texas State College, now president emeritus of that institution. He writes a "Hilltop Views" column in the Amarillo (Tex.) *Times.* And to that column he doubtless took the interest gained by making countless speeches in his region over a period of thirty years as college president, and friendships with thousands of ex-students and fellow educators.

87. *Pest Control.* Household pests rank with the common cold in affecting people, who spend much time fighting flies, ants, termites, and rodents. Sometimes queer devices are used. The Fountain Inn (S.C.) *Tribune* reported seeing little wads of cotton fastened to screen doors. Flies avoided doors so treated. Other people electrocute flies. People's reactions to common complaints are almost legendary. A famous editor is said to have sent a substitute to read his speech when he took to his bed with the rash of poison ivy. One person wrote him to compliment the speech, but six hundred sent remedies for poison ivy.

Our doctor tells us that breakfast should be eaten in silence. Of course we understand that he means we should not start anything so early in the day.— Edgar T. Harris, West Point (Miss.) **Times Leader.**

88. *Relatives.* Bob Burns is not the only humorist who talks about kinfolks. Columnists describe some mighty queer and some mighty wonderful relatives. For example, the "Read 'Em and Weep" column of the Park River (N.D.) *Walsh County Press* has written copiously of Uncle Dan. Dan was an unforgettable character with a sixth sense which told him when unseen persons were in a house.

89. *Births.* Clowning seems inappropriate when a child is born. But the Ada (Okla.) *Times-Democrat* manages something novel: "We have it on good authority that it was a blue cloud E. T. Carson was walking on Monday — and with good reason. Wife

Betty presented him a son Monday afternoon. But it was a pink cloud for the Rev. Paul Stephens Wednesday. He has a new daughter to go with his two boys."

90. *Variations.* Readers appreciate some departures from normal column organization, providing these are not too frequent. Don Whitehead, from an advanced regiment post in Korea, sent back an item reporting the soldiers' lives as a society editor might write it. Clever columnists have written events through the eyes and ears of various people. Harvest time does not look alike to all persons. State fair is one thing to a first-time goer and quite another to the jaded oldster whose feet are "killing him." Also readers' entry into a subject can be guided by an introductory line. Examples: "Give your sense of justice a workout on this." "Thoughts while waiting for a freight train to pass."

91. *White Lies.* Many half-truths can be defended. Some are condemned. Columnists make the distinction. Turn through a college catalog, a tourist guide, a legal petition. Note the exaggerations, the wishful thinking, and misleading statements. Hometowners on vacation trips can send back reports on prices, availability of tourist accommodations, and whether the fish are biting. But don't forget the libel laws.

92. *Greetings.* Some columnists write ponderous essays at the year's end; others contrive easy ways to fill the space. One column was blank except for "Season's Greeting" centered near the top. Another ran "Our Best Wishes for 195-" in vertically set 48-point type, filling the column.

93. *Biggest Mistakes.* Embarrassing moments and "The biggest mistake I ever made" are standard column subjects. Some readers don't mind confessing that they quit school too soon, chose a wrong profession, failed to keep up music lessons, and experimented too long before starting a lifetime trade or profession. Similarly, local business men can tell

Maybe it is good that men don't understand women. Women understand women, and don't like them. — Duncannon (Pa.) **Record.**

how they got started. Such articles can be timed to coincide with graduation of high school seniors who think on such things.

94. *Salesmen.*   Traveling men know the value of the anecdote. In a way, they are columnists afield. Ask them for their latest printable story. They may be worth a short sketch if they are well known to store people. And they can tell about style trends and prices. Many of them influence merchant attitudes toward selling and advertising. They are part of the local scene.

95. *Snappy Comebacks.*  Plant a leading statement and record the comebacks by the town's wiseacres. An editor or reporter covering a beat can quickly assemble reactions to a question, with or without names. These can be as timely as the latest headline.

96. *Kids.*  Less civilized peoples make much of playing with children. Small-town columnists like to be known and liked by town youngsters, and called by name. Mention of a child in a column pleases parents and interests friends. Many such items go into scrapbooks. Some columnists regularly run pictures of children in or beside the column space. Pictures of dogs and other pets are not uncommon.

97. *Odors.*  Columnists report what they see, hear, and smell. Their nose reports the news as they pass trees and flowers in bloom, alleys which offend, and business firms and factories with characteristic odors.

98. *First Names.* In small towns, people are Bill and Joe and Mary to their friends. Some columnists refer to Bill Jones; second reference is to Bill, and third is to Mary (everyone knows the Mary referred to is Bill's wife) . Such intimate references also imply the people are well known to the columnist. It would be incongruous to err in mentioning a first name. It might be awkward to so refer to a dignified professional man, a consistent critic of the paper, or an elderly person.

Now is the time for all good men to come to the aid of both parties. — A. B. Jordan, Dillon (S. C.) **Herald.**

99. *Exaggeration.* Some columnists would gag on such adjectives, but it is a fact that some very popular writers attend picnics and then report on them like this: "The most delicious basket lunches in the world are served by those wonderful, wonderful women of the Blank community." It does not seem to matter that similar superlatives are handed another group a week later, or were used a week earlier. But the writer's appreciation must be regarded as genuine.

100. *Candor.* People constantly delude themselves. When a man says "the people of this country believe" something he may actually mean that he, his wife, and a few friends believe it. In thinking aloud, so to speak, with and for his readers, a columnist has a chance to show good reasoning and to analyze poor reasoning. He can distinguish between spoken reasons and real reasons, spoken motives and real ones, and between opinions and facts. Better, he can ask questions which enable readers to derive truths and attitudes for themselves, by themselves. Implicit in the writing of a column is the obligation of the columnist to constantly examine his own thoughts, motives, and information in order that he more nearly find and present the essential truth behind the more or less objective stories in the news columns.

**Candor.**

The columnist, in using techniques and subjects similar to many mentioned in this chapter, has purposes no less serious than those of the reporter or editorial writer. But he drops his serious phrases with a casual subtlety which catches the reader unawares, but nonetheless effectively. And the columnist would add that before you can hand a reader an idea you must first catch him.

## 14.

# *Developing a Column Personality*

THE LOCAL COLUMN is the most revealingly personal thing in today's newspaper. It is more flexible than a by-lined news story. It achieves a more intimate relationship with readers than do the editorials. It has a higher acceptability than most advertisements. It has the strength and weaknesses of its conductor. In newspapers which stress objective reporting and largely non-controversial editorial writing, the personal column stands out as an unpredictable and potentially influential and popular department. Its conductor can be loved or hated, respected or disdained, admired or ardently disliked because readers think and talk of the writer as *him* and not *it*. And, if the column is handled with skill and planning, it will be exceedingly well read.

Columnists seem instinctively to create personalities, but ·not always their own. Sometimes they project caricatures of themselves, perhaps out of a feeling of false modesty, or because — since they face many readers on every publication day — they hesitate to own the humor or philosophy devised in a moment of inspiration. Away from their typewriters, they would not speak with such grandeur of phrase. But out of its continuity, selection of topics, manner of writing, and warmly local spirit the personal column casts the shadow of the man behind the typewriter. Investigations have revealed that those columns are palest which present facts, humor, and opinion in an impersonal fashion. Even good jokes are dull stuff compared to the same material humanized by a popular local personality.

Hallam Walker Davis made this comment:

It is necessary for the column conductor to create a well-defined personality for himself before people will follow him regularly. Quite often he poses as being at least wicked enough to be interesting. Sometimes he assumes the role of woman-hater or of generally disconcerting and uncomfortable cynic. The best of columnists do not do this too much, but all of them do it in some degree. There is a bit of clownishness in the business, and the tendency to play the devil is strong. With this tendency to play-act, column writers often lost sight of their real selves and either do not know just what they are trying to do or else misrepresent it—quite like the modest scholars and gentlemen they are.[1]

**The mere thought . . . is an expression of ego.**

The mere thought of starting a column is an expression of ego. One must believe he has something to say. He must have confidence in the soundness of his philosophy of life, believe he can find time to assemble column material, and think his writing style is passably interesting. He proposes to plan and execute columns for his readers' mental stimulation and nourishment. He assumes that his reading and contacts will permit him to know his people's current interests. And he must think of all or most of his readers — not of his business, club, and church intimates only. His attitude toward columning will partially determine his style, pace, and subject matter.

---

[1] *The Column*, p. 35. Used by permission of Alfred A. Knopf, Inc. Copyright, 1936.

If a columnist stands out in a crowd, physically or in print, he will likely be in some degree a "character." John Gould, author and columnist of the Wichita Falls (Tex.) *Record-News,* discussed this subject in a letter to the authors:

The initial requirement of a columnist, I think, is vanity. All the good columnists I know think well of themselves. Another is raspinarity.

A columnist must have a well-developed streak of meanness in him. I have known men of the shrinking violet type who have tried to write columns and I have also seen the job undertaken by sweet, gentle individuals in whom the milk of human kindness surged strong and plentiful. But none of these ever succeeded at the job. . . . A columnist should have a sense of humor plus ability to keep it in restraint. He should have an observing eye, a listening ear, a good memory. If he has public spirit and moral purpose, they can be helpful at times, but he should indulge them sparingly.

It is well for a columnist to have the courage of his convictions, but he is better off not to have convictions; just notions, and whimsies, and foibles. He should never get in the habit of taking himself seriously. This is even worse for columnists than for editorial writers.

There is just one reason for a columnist. It is to make the paper more interesting. He will do better at it if his offering follows no set pattern. There can be no routine, such as there is for bookkeepers, policemen, and bus drivers. The man most likely to succeed as a columnist is an erratic person, with a somewhat disorderly mind and a good supply of what is politely called temperament. He should not love anybody but his wife, and her in moderation. . . . The fact that he may be ignorant of a subject should not trouble him; most of his readers are as ignorant as he is, and some of them, unpleasant as the thought is to contemplate, even more so. And there is no profit in being agreed with by this multitude.

The columnist must be able to reconcile himself to the fact that it is hard to be clever every day or every week and there are times when he will be corny. Yet he must maintain a certain dignity and a sense of the fitness of things so he will not blast at trivial things seriously.

And, so saying, Mr. Gould demonstrates that he practices his preachments. His saltiness is illustrative of the kind of personality which succeeds without

---

**NOT SO FAST!**

This advice may be given newcomers and new columnists in a small town: Take it easy; don't start pushing ideas and reforms too quickly. Columnists, no less than business and professional men, are likely to get cool receptions for a few months. This is native caution, and will pass. Even columnists of mellow experience usually pretend to be as beset by timidity, bad luck, and other ills as their readers. Minor forms of hard luck seem to draw reader affection, whether real or feigned. Big-shot roles suit few column personalities. Drastic ideas can be attributed to anonymous local readers and trial balloons to more distant correspondents.

"pull"; that is, without owning the paper or holding the top editorial position. It is axiomatic, of course, that a columnist's ideas do not conflict violently with those of the paper, institutionally. But most editors permit columnists to hold individual opinions in most fields.

If the publisher is also the columnist, he and the paper will be mutually identified and merged in readers' thinking. This is perhaps the happiest situation. If, on the other hand, the columnist is to be another staff member, he will be thought of either for himself and possibly by his column name, or as "Jones of the *Herald*." But if the guest conductor or regular columnist is not a member of the paper's staff, the column may be considered a thing apart. An example is the county agricultural agent's column.

While editors today select their columnists carefully in recognition of their potential influence, the variety of persons granted such privileges is amazing. We see columns by educators, ministers, and other professional men. We read politicians' reports to their constituents. Sheriffs, who like to lecture evildoers, write columns of startling frankness. Professional bakers burn the rolls but perfect a paragraph. In California, a rural peddler gathers his items on his rounds. In Maine, a librarian rates new books for her patrons. And in Georgia an amateur poet does his column in rhyme. Summer tourists send letters back from interesting lands. Farm wives do Ernie Pyle-like reports on day-to-day happenings. And farmers think up cracks at the big-city folks while riding their cultivators down row on row.

The popularity of an outsider-columnist sometimes proves embarrassing to a less colorful publisher. But, on the other hand, a column done by an editor has fundamental strong points. A strong personality, projected through a column, implies possession of authority, resources, and prerogatives. Good colum-

**DOTTED LINES**

The appeal of printed forms has not been overlooked by columnists. Types include opinion polls, pre-election surveys, calls for ideas on civic improvements, informal referendums on local propositions, and completion of slogans and verse. Also, this is a convenient way to hand out literature which is too expensive for general distribution. Many persons who would not write a letter will fill in a form.

nists make strong talk. They take chances. They underwrite projects. Of course columns which merely entertain, or are literary or specialized, do not necessarily require strong editorial sanction. But the column which reflects a strong personality and exerts an influence on public affairs needs the editor in the role of conductor or the known backing of the paper. The paper's policy is involved.

Writing skills and mental tools cannot be separated from the effectiveness of a whole, independent personality. That is to say, a good writer must be, in many ways, an outstanding person. His qualities include not only sanction of his paper, but also honesty, sincerity, a deep respect for the human personality, generosity, kindness when kindness is indicated, a quick alertness to man's inhumanities — all these flavored with a certain acidity of speech, coupled with an ability to react quickly in print without screaming, scolding, or preaching. These qualities are not as stuffy as they may sound. Put it this way: Columnists ought to have some maturity and experience in living before they start making over their friends and community, and they need some authority of position and stability of backing.

We do not mean to imply that a column is the most important thing in a newspaper, nor that a strong column personality is going to lead every community to prosperity and fame. But a word in time saves many situations. A laugh may do it, or a tear. A "light" column is not necessarily light in its influence.

People get ideas about the personality of a columnist from seeing and hearing him. However, his column personality may seem a thing apart until readers come to associate with him the qualities he writes into his topics each week. By his attitude and through the printed items he indicates the material he desires for his column. Meeting him mood for

**CRUSADING**

Nothing will project a column personality more quickly than engaging in rough-and-tumble reform. Occasionally a local clean-up is engineered by a columnist with notable results. However, many columnists believe serious campaigns should be an institutional project, not a personal one. C r u s a d i n g makes enemies as well as friends. Once started in a column, it is difficult to drop. Probably a better idea would be to limit the columnist's personally-led drives to popular causes which can have quick, successful results.

mood, cooperative readers will supply humor, gossip, oddities, biting criticism, and town news.

Some columnists who could develop positive personalities take their work too lightly and write too carelessly. They fail to realize the flexibility of the medium — how it permits full revelation of their ideas, their sense of humor, their breadth of interests, human insight, sturdiness of character, tolerance, understanding, and capacity for indignation.

Inevitably, columnists create literary tones which readers will classify as highbrow, lowbrow, blatant, fainthearted, etc. And just as good reporters are known by their news sense, columnists show their ability to recognize a feature, implant an idea, and coax a chuckle. Over a period of months or years, they come to be regarded as cherished friends by hundreds of readers. Certain roving reporter-columnists have had followings of almost unbelievable size and warmth of affection. The stabilizing effect of such columns on circulation is obvious.

In noncompetitive fields, columnists may develop their personalities in print as leisurely as they wish. Then comes a competitor, or a radio newscaster. It suddenly becomes desirable that the columnist not be outranked by a commentator. The column is seen as an instrument more important than previously imagined. It can "talk out loud" on local matters not easy subjects for editorials but of importance in keeping public officials in line, apologizing for newspaper errors, explaining delicate circumstances, and consolidating business gains.

Readers appreciate consistency in the role a columnist elects for himself. If he poses as a "fine" writer, they expect him to turn out a steady flow of eloquent prose or verse. If he tries to be funny, he must not disappoint his fans. If he wants to stand as a strong personality, fearing no man, his readers will suggest many opponents and turn to his department

**PROOF OF RESULTS**

A columnist has "arrived" when his faithful following will respond quickly to a local promotion. At some risk, he may say "Meet me at the ball park Monday night and bring a teen-age person with you — the latter admitted free." If the difference in attendance caused by the column's appeal is noticeable and impressive, there can be no doubt of the public's response. But rather than put it on a personal basis, the columnist stresses the appeal of the occasion and why he will be there. He won't press his luck too far.

Columns in the smaller press have attained quite a metropolitan sophistication, but they don't yet call the town drunk a man-about-town. — Deep River (Conn.) **New Era.**

in expectation of impressive talk. If he is a promoter, a record of successes will help him. Only the hack, saying the obvious things and avoiding controversy, can safely forget the character he has become.

Column personality is indicated also by a writer's vocabulary, his style, evidences of enthusiasm, and basic points of view. Small-town readers do not demand high-sounding language and a flow of literary allusions. But since they read more each year, and listen to movie and radio wits and humorists, it is not safe to assume that their tastes are lowbrow and their discrimination negligible. It should be added, of course, that a writer in a predominantly agricultural community would not try to be the same kind of personality he would attempt to be in a factory district, a mountain country, or a suburban area.

But whatever the environment, the personal columnist conducts a sort of public bull session, in which he wields the gavel in a local Information Please. No burning local issue is without his attention. No local hero fails to get his praise. No public cause flounders for want of his support.

The building of a popular column personality brings many rewards. One of the greatest of these is public acceptance as an individual, coupled with respect for and appreciation of the newspaper concerned. Such assets are as good as money in the bank. They also bring responsibilities. And invitations. If a columnist does a bit of clowning — and clowns are supposed to have great human sympathy beneath the grease paint — he is likely to have invitations to serve as Santa Claus, to auction pies, and be an emcee at civic club minstrel shows. If he is known to have moments of profundity, communities round about will invite him to deliver commencement addresses.

Like all things, columnists mellow with age. Some mature mentally, become Rotary district governors, and take roles as elder statesmen. Others remain salty humorists and sharp writers to the end of their columning. The projection of a successful man's personality through his column can be a wholesome thing — if he works at it and if his style is not boresome. He can give a community much needed guidance. A column by the local editor-leader is a typewriter chat with his readers.

The older columnists often prefer the news item-comment style without humor, without paragraphs, without flights of fancy. Their readership may be large among the older citizens and small among the young. The nature of their work leaves a place for a variety column.

Even the smallest paper may find room for more than one personality. Editorials may be written by one staff member — short, challenging, highly localized. A personal column will dramatize another partner or key employee. Sports and women's columns are standard offerings. Contributing columnists may exploit special interests. Even teen-age opinion is becoming valued column material.

Newspapers thought of as people seem more strongly entrenched than those thought of as corporations, street addresses, or wire service franchises. The humanizing of the press to an even greater degree may be advisable to offset the popularity of nationally famous personalities serving rival channels of communication. Freedom of the press becomes a dangerously abstract term when the public fails to understand that it involves the right of people to be represented in news gathering by *persons* connected with newspapers. Unless Reporter Joe Doakes and Columnist John Doe have the right to print and discuss what's going on at the City Hall, freedom of the press is meaningless.

As a column personality, John Doe may step on sensitive official toes and perhaps get his news-sensitive nose punched. One small newspaper reach-

You go up in life, and you come down. And it's a toss-up on which trip you meet the nicer people. — Ada (Okla.) **Times-Democrat.**

A spendthrift is a mighty nice person to be around. — Merrill Chilcote, Maryville (Mo.) **Tribune.**

ing this author's desk recently carried unusually detailed accounts of city council meetings. Inside was a column which just as thoroughly digested the issues and commented on the roles of persons involved. Soon tempers flared over whether meetings should be so fully reported. Official acts were questioned. Officials issued heated statements. Libel actions were threatened. In a moment of pique, the columnist said he would like to see the mayor "end up in the clink." Later he explained that he was thinking figuratively but writing literally. In such controversies, both public officials and the newspaper people involved try to emerge without loss of face. A clever columnist will achieve reasonable ends without stretching his triumph too far. But one of the penalties of standing out as an advocate of the people is that some resulting enmities may outlast the incident involved.

Of all the small-city columnists who have a permanent place in the history of American journalism, none has a more distinct place than the late Ed Howe, brilliant cynic of the Atchison (Kans.) *Globe.* Not formally educated, he nevertheless attracted world-wide attention with his writing, received honorary degrees, and left valuable newspaper properties. He was painfully serious and just as painfully sensitive. Yet his genius was unmistakable, his insight into human motives almost uncanny. He knew the plain people of the country towns of Kansas and took a suppressed delight in making the best look less than righteous and the sinners look better than their reputations.

Many editors who share few reflections with their readers plead that they "have no time to think." Howe could have so pleaded. No detail of his paper was ignored by him; at various times he was editor, business manager, printer, advertising solicitor, circulation manager, and reporter — often holding several of these jobs simultaneously. Yet he found time to think and to write.

Howe commented, however:

I did my best work on the dullest days; a circus day, or one offering some other excitement, made me entirely worthless. I'm that way now; if anyone is coming to dinner, the day is ruined for me. I cannot help it; I was born that way, and no amount of effort on my part will change it.

In Howe's lifetime it was customary for editors to write paragraphs. He wrote many which were widely reprinted. Typical of his incisive style were these:[2]

A good scare is worth more to a man than good advice.
A panic is a whipping administered by nature to bring us to a realization of our limitations and absurdities.
The greatest punishment is to be despised by your neighbors, the world, and members of your family.
Men hustling to do better than competitors they hate have done more for the world than the souls who dream of universal love.
The nearest approach to the beautiful thing, an angel, is a little girl of ten or twelve.

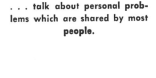

. . . talk about personal problems which are shared by most people.

Although a man of Ed Howe's great loneliness would seem to be shut out from his world, he overcame this lack by being a good newspaperman, a hard worker, and a prolific writer. His faults, often confessed, drew to him those who felt similar worldly urges. This is a familiar column technique. Many columnists say they get the best reader reactions when they talk about intimate personal problems which are shared by most people.

[2] Selected from *Plain People*. Reprinted by permission of Dodd, Mead & Company. Copyright, 1929, by Edgar Watson Howe.

Ed Howe died in 1937. He is remembered as the Sage of Potato Hill. His sometimes scathing wit vividly describes his section and his era.

But while the elder Howe projected a personality which was by nature salty, in a column which was too sparkling to be ignored, it is to a son, Gene Howe of Amarillo, Texas, that we turn for a good example of a deliberately planned newspaper presence. With more genius than he admits, Gene has kept readers alert and often flabbergasted for more than two decades. His column is the "Tactless Texan" department of the Amarillo *News* and *Globe*. Howe went to Amarillo in the early 1920's and made good despite his Kansas taint. He did it by outbragging the Panhandle residents and by championing even the howling dust storms as somehow beneficial to health — crediting what he called Vitamin "K."

Publisher Gene Howe's screwball column, which has mellowed only slightly through the years, carries in the heading an outline cut of cross-eyed old Ben Turpin. Howe calls himself Erasmus Rookus Tack, but readers affectionately refer to him as Old Tack. His capacity for clowning has declined somewhat because of his extensive travels, but his columns are mailed back from whatever resort, hunting ground, or city he happens to visit.

A lot of people are late for church because they have to change attire; and a lot of others because they have to change a dollar. — Fredericksburg (Tex.) **Standard**.

"Gene Howe's column is as carefully calculated as the arch of a lady's eyebrow," wrote Jack Alexander in a *Saturday Evening Post* article, "Panhandle Puck." He declared that Howe fishes for reader reactions, favorable or unfavorable, and is a master of the extravagant apology. Howe feuded with Charles A. Lindbergh and Mary Garden, dabbled in local politics when it pleased him, and staged lavish Mother-in-Law Club conventions.

Anything capable of lifting an eyebrow is likely to be written up in Old Tack's column, including sex, both human and animal. To be in fashion, he established his Big Bull ranch and declared for monogamy in Hereford breeding. To be helpful, he found wives for bashful cowboys and offered rewards to find lost dogs for frantic housewives. He posts big rewards to help solve disgusting crimes. He predicts the weather and brags about it shamelessly when he is right. What his reporters find difficult to include in their stories, Howe frankly unveils in his column. He delights in printing scoops on big wedding announcements and on political maneuvers. His gestures are never ordinary. When he helps people, which is often, he is generous and resourceful. When he asks readers to help him, an outpouring of checks large and small is not unusual.

Many people have sworn to quit reading Gene Howe's column, but most of them have failed. Too many people quote him, swear at him, laugh with him. He is disarmingly subtle when he chooses, but more often is apologetically frank. His pose grows expansive with trouble; in times of drought or disaster his pride of region knows no bounds.

Gene Howe, like his father largely unschooled at public expense, tunes his column on a fairly lowbrow tone but personally he seeks the company of younger, successful friends. In this way he appeals to average citizens but maintains contacts and influence at official levels and in financial circles befitting a successful publisher.

The results? Researchers have reported in amazement that "nearly everyone reads Old Tack." The 95 per cent readership recorded in one survey was no surprise to Panhandle people. The Amarillo columnist, unlike old Ed Howe in many ways, has demonstrated the success of his own formula for making his personality known and felt throughout the circulation area of his paper. His methods might be resented in some regions, but in his own he is perhaps the best-known resident. He manages, at surprisingly

A pessimist is a guy who sizes himself up and gets sore about it. — Ronald Furse, Plattsmouth (Neb.) **Journal**.

regular intervals, to start readers' tongues talking and arguing about Old Tack. Many of his promotions and antics have been worth space on press wire reports.

On the solid side of his personality, Mr. Howe is known as a shrewd judge of people, a sound business executive, and an effective worker in game conservation. In Amarillo, long known as a "newspaper graveyard" because so many papers have bucked the *News* unsuccessfully, his personality is fused with that of his newspapers. Like the A. P. franchise, his column is a valued asset.

But Howe's newspaper policy exploits even further the idea that newspapermen should be talked about. His paper has developed a local columnist on almost every page. He talks about his writers, backs them in their own promotions, and at the drop of a suggestion sends one to Europe and another to Korea to report battle experiences of native sons. Such localization and personalizing of his paper and its news is a formula he believes is applicable in any small and region-conscious community.

Of course many smaller papers have prominent editors who do not write columns. The distinction we have noted is that there are a great many who either deliberately seek to be known as column personalities or who, through much writing under a column heading, become identified as much with their columning as with the paper generally.

When a column personality is planned and projected, the writer usually recognizes his unique ability to dramatize not only himself but promotions to which he gives his support. He backs projects confidently because he knows the high readership of his column and the capacity he has developed, as a columnist, to rally support for his ideas. Some outstanding successes are reported in the next chapter.

There's a simple way to keep up with the Joneses. Just slow down and in a few years you'll meet them coming back. — R. M. Westerfield, West Union (Iowa) **Union.**

## 15.

# Drawing Reader Responses

READER PARTICIPATION in column promotions offers possibilities still to be discovered by many writers who have not tried this two-way pattern. It is partly a matter of personality; some columnists wish to work undisturbed by reader enthusiasm and demands. And possibly many others have lacked an appreciation of the possibilities.

The extent of reader participation can be controlled, but at the expense of some disappointment of contributors. However, in addition to coaxing contributions from local writers, columnists can think up promotions which either appeal because of their novelty or because of the public service rendered. The reader responses have a direct relation to circulation, advertising effectiveness, and newspaper influence.

Sometimes publishers' wives assist in handling communications from readers. Again, columnists have given extra hours of their time. Most writers worry not over the extra work, but for fear of not having the work-making responses.

Elaborate campaigns and devices are not needed.

There are all sorts of inspiring "three little words." For the "two-word" class we nominate "Hi, Dad!" — Wickenburg, (Ariz.) **Sun.**

Personal columns are able to touch the heart-strings of a community. Regular readers grow sensitive to the moods and emotions of the columnist. In time they come to think of themselves as an entity. Not infrequently a columnist forms a club which enlists many or all of the readers. The 75-Year Club, for example, was sponsored by Mrs. C. E. Greef's "Over the Back Fence" column in the Eldora (Iowa) *Herald-Ledger* for more than fifteen years. Civic clubs have joined in giving annual dinners for such groups. The idea has been used successfully in other states, with minor variations.

The high readership of a column enables it to carry appeals to most of the people in a warm, informal way. Many columnists, in letters to these authors, have reported instant and generous responses. A request that readers send picture-cards to a sick child brought more than 700 and quickened recovery. A farm family which lost everything in a fire soon had more wordly possessions than it had before. An appeal for residents to cut tree limbs hanging over sidewalks and to trim shrubbery obstructing views at street corners was unusually effective because the columnist announced the exact hour and minute he would cut his own. The mayor did likewise, and city trucks were sent out to pick up the trimmings.

If columns have wide readership, even minor dramatic touches may have stirring responses. Facts speak louder than preachments; columnists learn the deft stroke of the typewriter which expresses just the right amount of sentiment.

The objection is sometimes made that good citizenship is a duty, not a game. Right; but some things won't be done if appeals are not dramatized or brought alive in some new way. A columnist should be a first-rate idea man. Ideas sell advertising which moves goods. And news men of the editorial side, now in competition with radio, television, demonstrations, give-away promotions, and many other forms of dramatics, cannot afford to do business in the same old way. Readers who enjoy their newspapers are . . . joyful. And the joyous respond.

But reactions to columns may develop slowly. People need time to become conditioned to a writer's personality and style. A writer may turn out passable stuff for years before he and the readers suddenly discover that they are capable of responses on a higher emotional and intellectual level. Then he and they form a team which feels power surging in its promotions.

Success in one column may give an assist to others. Soon the home-grown columns are outpulling any syndicate matter carried in the paper.

Some columnists get mail by the sack. They are mentioned often wherever circulation men meet readers. It is sometimes enough just to sell a column.

As might be assumed, Amarillo, Tex., is a columnists' town, both as repects the *News-Globe* and the rival *Times*. There people were likely to be heard talking about Lewis Nordyke, political writer for the *News,* whose "Random Thoughts" column has had unusual success. In a modest position on the editorial page, this column in three years caused Nordyke to open 16,000 letters. He received 4,000 telephone calls. He was invited to make more than 200 talks. The column gave away 60,000 buckeyes as good-luck charms. A Christmas Birthday Club attracted more than 3,000 members, and several hundred persons joined a Golden Wedding Club. These groups held annual mid-year picnics and members came from several states to attend. The paper served refreshments and presented fav o r s.
The Chr i s t m a s

. . . newsmen cannot afford to do business the same old way.

club was open to all persons who were born between December 15 and January 3. Obviously, birthdays in this period are lost in the year-end festivities and one gift is likely to serve for both birthday and Christmas. The success of the promotion comes, in part, from the fact that a ready-made unit of the population is singled out for attention.

The demand for buckeyes grew out of a chance remark, but soon the columnist was filling his pockets before making any round for news, was carrying a bushel of buckeyes in his car, and the paper was helping mail out thousands in small sacks. Even with this success, however, Nordyke did not hesitate to prime the pump. He sent dollar bills to readers who reported somebody's good deed — if the story was worth printing.

Such a columnist is soon in debt to hundreds of readers. Nordyke occasionally had a "thanking day" in his department. Here is an example:

THANKS—to more than 16,000 persons who have written letters and cards to this column in the last three years. . . . To those who have sent thousands of letters and gifts in response to notices of shut-ins and ailing children, such as little Zoe at Dimmitt and Little Joe at McLeans. . . . To the many who have telephoned in items. . . . To those who sent trinkets and things to the Corncrib, my home workshop. . . . To Mrs. Vida Jansen of Amarillo for a wonderful pecan pie. . . . To Amarillo music teachers for a western-decorated feed trough. . . . To all who helped this column bring a mother and son from distressing circumstances in faraway Brooklyn. . . . To the more than 3,000 members of the Christmas Birthday Club . . . To the scores of members of the Golden Wedding Club . . . To Bob Stone for a guest register in the Corncrib, which now contains the names of thousands of guests. . . . To Mason King for helping put on the big Christmas parties in the middle of the year. . . . To the hundreds and hundreds who sent Christmas cards and Valentines. . . . To Mrs. Sears, Mrs. Warren, Nosey Joe, and a host of others who have contributed verse and anecdotes. . . . To Lindsay Nunn of Lexington, Ky., for growing buckeyes, and to Charles Fisk, who has had more than 20,000 buckeyes delivered

With some persons, no matter what you try works.—Springer (N. M.) Tribune.

to me for giving away. . . . To the scores who have sent selections from their scrapbooks. . . . To hundreds who have responded with information sought through the column's Service Department. . . . To all who have said good and bad things about the column or who have in any way helped with it or have read it regularly, occasionally, or just once. . . . To Wales Madden, Sr., for helping in the crusade against publication of wedding cake pictures. . . . To former Rep. Eugene Worley for trying to pass a law requiring ramps on federally-controlled public buildings for the good of those who find steps and stairs difficult. . . . With so much help, a column is an extremely pleasant and satisfying chore.

Nordyke later became co-publisher of the Stephenville *Empire-Tribune* and transferred his "Random Thoughts" column to that paper.

Such columnists belong to the class which we might refer to as "calculating." They think it helpful to father a brand new idea about once a month. This may be a Plump and Pretty Club for the stout, a One-Cup Club in protest against ten-cent coffee, or a personal campaign for dog-catcher. The resulting mail is likely to fill half the column, saving much time. But the main consideration is that readers are pleased. Indeed, if readers are not amused, promotions must be changed, or dropped. A good columnist knows his people.

Some reader responses are partly in the imagination of the columnist. He may create fictitious characters and make-believe situations which give him great freedom of expression. But there are real Alibi Clubs and Monday Morning Quarterbacks, some of which hold banquets and give coaches opportunities to explain victories and losses. There are societies for the prevention or promotion of this and that. There are Sidewalk Farmers Associations which have citified members who talk good agriculture but practice it little, or none. Consider the possibilities for fun and philosophy in a make-believe Society for the Suppression of After-Dinner Speaking. Debatable issues grow out of the name itself:

The first seat-covers were triangular. — Casper Nohner, Hayti (S. D.) **Herald-Enterprise.**

1. Are there too many societies already?

2. Is suppression worse than the thing suppressed?

3. Is speaking after dinner worse for speaker or hearer?

4. Should dinners also, perhaps, be suppressed?

5. Should after-dinner speaking be replaced by other forms of communication, such as music, dancing, or sign language?

Marriage might be described as an institution that entitles women to the protection of strong men who steady the stepladder for them while they wash the kitchen windows. — Holdredge (Neb.) **Citizen.**

Readers like to comment on a common topic. This may be a timely subject or an invitation to nominate a Good Neighbor, Best-Dressed Man, Good Deed of the Week, or Most Courteous Boy Scout. One sees mention of absurd weeks, such as Be Kind to Stray Penguins Week and Hang-nail Prevention Week.

It should be stressed, of course, that the columnist is only part prankster. Mixed in with his hare-brained stunts are subtle suggestions and obvious morals which have a powerful influence on readers' responses. Give a columnist room for a joke, anecdote, or light essay and he will find space to promote a blood bank or build a fire under peace officers who think people have lost interest in their laws.

Some consistency in column conducting is as worthwhile as dreaming up innovations. One columnist, who neglected to ask children of his town to send in Santa Claus letters, got a few anyway and realized, too late, that he had broken a long-standing newspaper custom in his town. He apologized and asked for letters to Santa for the following year — in advance.

Opinions of newspaper philosophers differ on whether columns should take note of public issues usually treated in editorials. But if the columnist is also the editor — or even if he isn't — some attention to local affairs is inevitable. Citizens appreciate the wide readership of the column and therefore call the writer when storm sewers won't drain, when a railroad proposes to diminish train service, when a national figure slurs a region in a radio talk, and when they have trouble reading a road map or timetable. When permitted, the column becomes a sounding board for readers, especially on matters resulting in minor irritations. Weighty matters require background articles for full discussion, of course. But when a columnist sounds off and gets results his following realizes his influence and remembers him when the next civic corns begin to ache.

When responses slow down, a columnist usually can stir up readers by denouncing himself in faked letters or telephone calls. Or he may make a deliberate error, knowing he will be corrected. To err is so human that his errors, if minor, will add to his popularity in some circles. The mail always spurts when a rival town is complimented for being clean, having courteous policemen, pretty girls, getting more rain, etc. When a new bride writes in for recipes, readers can be asked for proved recipes, advice, or even household gadgets. Whether to take gift offers from advertisers can be decided only by the columnist — and the advertising manager.

. . . they call the writer when storm sewers won't drain . . .

An old column device is to present some perplexing personal problem or dilemma. Readers like to work problems for a dumb columnist, figure his income tax, and think up comebacks he should have thought of when insulted by a visiting celebrity. One columnist feigned great hesitation about speaking before a state university audience, but was assured by readers that "you are as smart as they are," and given pep talks in scores of telegrams designed to cure his stage fright. Another columnist known for his flabbergasting stunts offered a $100 reward for proof that a prairie fire can be started with a lighted cigaret tossed from a car. Win or lose, he gains reader interest and creates interest in a problem on which he has taken a somewhat dubious position.

Column techniques also have other applications. Columnists in growing numbers have radio programs. Some of these read excerpts from their own writing or from newspapers in nearby towns. Some become famed as speakers for special occasions. A few have assembled shows which they take into other communities for benefit performances.

Promotions through a column are a natural outgrowth of the writer's interest in and contacts with people. He reacts quickly to readers' stories. Poisoning of dogs brings him snorting to defense of people's pets, but a month later he may be found agreeing with irate gardeners that pets should be penned.

With an approving nod from his publisher — if he is not the publisher — he will next begin trumpeting for a county hospital or a road bond issue. Regular news columns can lay down the facts, and editorials can analyze the tax structure involved, but the columnist talks about the joys of smooth roads, the terrors of having a sick child when roads are impassable, of children boredly home-bound when they would like to be spending money in town. He sees and reacts sharply to what others grow accustomed to — mosquito breeding grounds in vacant lots, children running wild for want of planned recreation, men idle for lack of small industries. These things are presented not with heavy didactics, but in quotes from children, mating calls from mosquitoes, and descriptions of how it feels to be a father, out of work, and gnawed by pains of futility which hurt worse than hunger.

Columns which carry the weight of newspaper authority may take the form of one-subject essays which are really editorials in 12-em form under a heading. The open-letter type, addressed to re-

Shading "gimme" over to "lemme" would be progress.— Brookline (Mass.) Chronicle.

sponsible officials, is fairly rare. It carries a heavy wallop. The following example, addressed to a state highway department, is by Harry O'Brien in the Park River (N. D.) *Walsh County Press*:

This is to inform you, if you do not already know, that the condition of highway 17 between Park River and Adams is such that it is a definite menace to life and property. It has many holes that create hazards for everyone that travels the road. The damage was done during the spring and winter. Similar holes are to be found on other highways, including our main east-west highways, Nos. 2 and 10. Damages to these roads have long since been repaired. Are not the necks of those who use highway No. 17 as important as the necks of those who travel on Nos. 2 and 10?

Do unto others as though you were the others. — Ted Burges, Clear Lake (S. D.) **Courier.**

A column conducted with imagination and resourcefulness needs little promotion. If printed on the editorial page, however, it may be boosted by occasionally running the heading and an anecdote on Page 1. Promotion of a poor column is worse than futile, but anything which will add to its intrinsic worth and interest is defensible. Like the newspaper of which it is a part, the specialized department rests chiefly upon its current interest. About the only immortality it can hope for is inclusion of bits in readers' scrapbooks and possible fame through printing of excerpts by magazines and other newspapers. By inference it suggests its own worth by reprinting clever bits from other columns, with proper credits.

In general, it may be said that columns which merely entertain, or merely discuss an issue in a routine way, are not as effective, or as well read, as those which encourage readers to participate in activities. Genius is the greater gift, but ability to plan can be acquired. Moreover, the column is peculiarly adapted to promotion of community activities. Cumulative good will is an important result of helping people sell benefit tickets, obtain better public services, and rehabilitate stricken neighbors.

Say it with brakes and save
the flowers. — Webster (S. D.)
Reporter and Farmer.

Yet the columnist must not promote too much, and too often. He must not become a bothersome busybody. He must strike a balance by selecting projects which have some popular and emotional appeals. Occasionally he may back a movement which, without him, has no chance for success. Always he remembers that nothing is better for his column than a record of successes; once committed, he goes all out for a cause or a project.

# 16.

# Women as Columnists

ANY REMAINING DOUBT about the ability of women to handle most newspaper jobs disappeared during World War II. Because of the manpower shortage, they were called in from the fringes of journalism to work as reporters, political writers, copyreaders, wire editors, photographers, advertising saleswomen and copy writers, and columnists. Many moved up, in their opinions, from the society desks to general assignments. After the war some of these never returned to their former jobs.

In the small-town field, many wives kept newspaper plants running while their husbands were in military service. The man-wife partnership has long been common in small towns and cities, but women's emergence as columnists has been and is rather slow. Perhaps one reason for this has been an inclination of women to leave expressing of opinions to men; to gravitate to counter sales, bookkeeping, society news writing, and even to mechanical work.

Yet women have qualities well adapted to columning. Among these are enthusiasm, fluency of expression, keen observation, a ready sympathy and

**REFERENCE**

For many practical suggestions on writing directed to women, consult **How To Write for Homemakers,** by Lou Richardson and Genevieve Callahan. (The Iowa State College Press, Ames, Iowa. Copyright, 1949.)

appreciation of emotional values, convictions on moral issues, ability to describe things vividly, acute human insight, interest in problems of child rearing, and knowledge of household management and the women's world. Not all these qualities are found in all women, of course, but they are associated in general with the sex.

As women's educational training has become similar to men's, the "new woman" has come to insist on an equal footing in business, politics, and in the professions. Less is heard of women's intuition. The women's angle exists, but of far more importance is the range of female interests. In fact, college counselors have even come to deplore the tendency of co-eds to ignore courses — home economics, art, music, etc. — which would make them more proficient in the women's world and in writing about homes, gardens, fashions, children, health, and welfare. Fortunately, this trend appears to be weakening somewhat as journalism sequences are combined with sequences leading to careers in fields which stress women's interests. Opportunities in advertising, industrial editing, retailing, manufacturing, public relations, and radio are being called to the attention of young women by vocational counselors. Writing to and about women, who do so much of the nation's

. . . lovelorn columns did not raise women in the eyes of newspaper men.

buying, is a field which can support considerable expansion.

The term "sob-sister," originally given in recognition of women's quick sympathy and keen human-interest sense, was for years one carrying a taint of opprobrium. Writing advice to the love-lorn did not raise women in the eyes of newspaper men. Working at the society desk with the monotony of births, engagements, marriages, and parties was not attractive to young women of ambition and imagination. Nevertheless, increasing numbers of college-trained women journalists are excelling in feature writing courses and going on to earn their way on newspapers. Some of them are writing columns of various types. Even now, however, many of them are not well trained or informed on matters of primary interest to women.

There's one place where inflation has not set in. A good mother still is worth a dozen youth reform groups. — Pineville (W. Va.) **Independent-Journal.**

What are women's interests? Far from complete, here is a list of some of the most important, which can be treated in a newspaper column:

1. Engagements and marriages.
2. Household management.
3. Beauty care.
4. Fashions.
5. Rearing of children.
6. Health and safety.
7. Clean government and good moral conditions.
8. Women's clubs and organizations.
9. Entertainment and recreation.
10. Public welfare.
11. Religion.
12. Education.

Today's woman says she wishes to be a whole personality. She talks of equality and opportunity and fair remuneration. She points to a new leisure given her by inventions which save her time. Her new interests include hobbies, crafts, adult education, politics, and foreign affairs.

The personal column has a strong appeal to women who have discovered that its flexibility covers the breadth of these new interests. But appeal is not enough. Columning demands a certain maturity, a basic philosophy, a style, and an ability to analyze life situations. It is not surprising, therefore, that among the women columnists of the smaller cities and towns are not only girl reporters and editors' wives, but also school teachers, farm wives, and professional women.

Their columns do not follow definite patterns, but these are among the types which may be recognized:

1. Society editor's comments and news roundups.
2. Household hints.
3. Beauty hints.
4. Fashion notes and advice.
5. Feature columns.
6. Farm household hints.
7. A women's day.
8. Women's club activities.
9. Semi-editorial columns, sometimes by society editors who discuss community problems.
10. General columns, both of one-subject and variety types.
11. About-town columns of news and short features.
12. Amusements.
13. Specialized columns, such as those of the home demonstration agents.
14. Shopping-around columns, which combine advertising and news items, fashion hints, and household guidance.

On the average small paper, society editors are kept busy writing up engagements, weddings, club news,

---

**WRITE TO PERSONS**

Many years ago a well-known newspaper woman in San Francisco wrote a human-interest column under the name of Annie Laurie. . . . She worked hard to make her copy really good, but for some reason the feature fell flat. . . . Her editor studied her pages for a few minutes, then made this suggestion: "Tonight when you go home, pick out some woman on the street car. Watch her face, try to feel what she is thinking about. Then, tomorrow, when you write your column, think about that woman. Write your copy directly to her. Get a mental picture of her reading what you have written. Next day, pick out another woman, or a man." . . . From then on the young newspaper woman wrote to **persons** rather than **about things**. From then on, she could write. — Lou Richardson and Genevieve Callahan in **How To Write for Homemakers.**

personal mentions, and church activities. As space permits, and to provide copy beside the ads, they may also print recipes, fashion hints, information on gardening, and other syndicate or locally written material. Examination of weeklies shows that there is not much localization of this material, although it is about the subjects of women's conversation. One does not find, in news items, the animated spirit and enthusiasm common in female conversation. The personal column seems, therefore, well suited to women's abilities, manner of expression, and variety of interests.

"People like to read about things within their own realm of experience, so keep it human and folksy," said Madeline A. Chaffee, editor of the Cranston (R. I.) *Herald,* as quoted by *Publishers' Auxiliary.* "I try to keep each column light and readable, but with a point. There is in general no continuity from column to column — except that an imaginary character called Aunt Kate, along with her favorite niece, Marta, and her big tiger cat Timmy, proved so popular that she appears now and then."

Mrs. Wilma M. Collins of Grimes, Iowa, winner of state and national prizes with her column, "It's Your Town, Too!" got her opportunity in a typical way — by asking for it. She complained to a circulation manager that the paper did not have enough news of returning war veterans. As a result she was invited to gather and write this news. Having reared a family old enough to give her some leisure, she went to work for the Grimes *News.* In that first year she entered her column in the Iowa Press Women's annual contest — and won third place. In the next three years she won nothing but first places, then took the weekly newspaper column division award of the National Federation of Press Women.

"Yes, I love writing my column," said Mrs. Collins.

Nothing prompts the payment of an old dentist bill like a new toothache. — Vivian Shankland, Eureka (S. D.) **Blade.**

**AIR FARE** *by Peg White*

 **OVER the BACK FENCE**

 **Yes, BUT**
*By Vera C. White*

**NAN** ◢
About Town

 **For Women Only**
*by Mrs. W. E. Barnes*

**'Round about Mead**
Observations of a
City Gal in the Country
By Louise M. Mowry

**ERMA** ●● *the Girl of the Gumbo*

 *Let's Eat*
BY
IDA BAILEY ALLEN

 **HILL**

**SNAPS**
*by*
*Eleanor Jette*

 *-- annegrams* — by ann england —

**GIRL SCOUT CHRONICLE**
Mrs. Jake Trice, Editor

**THE CLOTHESLINE**
Unusual Sources Provide Interesting
Gifts for Last Flurry of Xmas Shopping
● By MURIEL W. SHONNARD

**Typical headings of women's columns.**

"It has grown to be so much a part of me that I would be lost not to be able to write it. Even during vacations I send back a column to the paper. I have missed writing only one column in the four years since it started. I have added to my work of raising a family, but when they are away at college and on to lives of their own I will still have a full life."

Mrs. Collins has many other activities, including offices in the Red Cross, Sunday School, Parent-Teacher Association, Press Columnists of Iowa and Iowa Press Women. These give her many subjects for columns. She writes on such a variety of things that readers never know what to expect. For example, she writes about her children, her sick dog, a day in a hospital, trips to press meetings, interviews with celebrities (Harry Truman, Tom Dewey, Gloria Swanson, etc.), spring, juvenile delinquency, band concerts, and men's ties. A column on ties won her the national prize.

Another national prize winner is Mrs. Gene V. Davis, feature editor of the Boonville (Mo.) *Daily News,* whose "Topics in Type" column also won her first place honors at a University of Missouri Journalism Week contest. She is a member of many women's press groups, has sold articles to *Good Housekeeping,* and has won other top awards in feature writing. She began her column in 1944.

"I have no particular pattern or formula," Mrs. Davis wrote these authors, "I just depict home life, joys, sorrows, and perplexities in a small mid-western town as seen by one who has lived in such a place 53 years and finds the life full and inspiring.

"I have had no formal training in journalism. My appearance in print began about seven years ago. I am a housewife, mother, and am handicapped by deafness. I write because I love to, because I see drama, pathos, and romance all about me, and be-

A survey shows that there are 595,179 movie seats in the theaters in the Chicago area. That's a lot of gum. — Hazel Keith, Windom (Minn.) **Citizen.**

cause when I picture these things my readers seem to feel that I have expressed their own thoughts. If something that I write may give importance to routine work or add charm to drab days that is my reward."

Here are excerpts from a column titled "The Friendly Hour:"

It is entertaining to look down from an upstairs window upon the main street pattern of the town in mid-afternoon. The people move to and fro like uncertain ants. They meet and pass, or stop to put out hands — antenna like — in greeting. They bunch up in groups and then thin out. The flow is continual, pleasantly indolent, and aimless. For this is the let-down hour. It is the pause before the evening rush, it is the sauntering, friendly, visiting hour.

The judge comes down his office steps, stands with one hand thrust in his trousers pocket, and leisurely surveys the street. An acquaintance strolls by and stops for a chat. The two fall into comradely step, headed for the coffee shop.

A young man and his sweetheart swing along, halt at a corner for prolonged goodbyes. He lifts his hands to draw her coat collar tight, pulls her to him slightly, pushes her away with a little shake.

A widower idles at the curb. Well-dressed and suave, he looks out at the crowd from under a snappy hat brim, yet there is a touch of pathos beneath the suavity, a searching, lonely look. . . .

Here comes Grandfather and Grandson. A very little son, clumsy in his warm snowsuit, whose hand can scarcely reach Granddad's hand, whose little white-shod feet stumble now and then. How carefully and proudly Grandfather slows his step! . . .

An elderly married man leans upon a parking meter in front of the soda fountain-drugstore, and sends a guarded look up the street, then down the street. Rendezvous?

Children race through the crowd, bumping into adults, careening around groups of men that have gathered to talk about the weather, the price of crops, the outlook on the farms. . . .

Salesmen in shining new automobiles pace their cars like gaited show horses. A huge trailer truck grinds by with its uneasy load of stock. . . .

The doors of the refreshment shops swing open, shut,

Join the navy, son, and see what's left of the world. — Bertha Shore, Augusta (Kan.) Gazette.

open, shut. It is the let-down hour, the friendly, visiting hour in Small Town.

Columning seems to have an especial appeal for women whose children have grown up. Mrs. C. E. Greef of Eldora, Iowa, started her column, "Over the Back Fence," fifteen years ago after her four boys left home. Like most other columnists in her state, she is an enthusiastic member of the Press Columnists of Iowa.

"I have never done what I thought ought to be done in the column, but have just gone along and commented on what was uppermost in my mind at the time, "Mrs. Greef told these authors. "I do make notations from time to time, and, if I were a more systematic person, I would keep files of suggestive topics and material for same. I do keep a copy of all my columns and hope some day to make up a thin book out of the best, particularly those that have the flavor of old days in rural Iowa.

"I have had no writing courses, but I do like people best of anything in the world. I have few reticenses in revealing my innermost thoughts and, having lived in this town for nearly fifty years, I know most everybody and try to avoid items which have a sting in them. I crusade sometimes for local projects — with more or less success."

Mrs. Greef wrote for the *Herald-Ledger* under the by-line of Cynthia Gray for years and now is with the *H. L.*'s sister paper, *The Index*. In a single column she may tell of a visit of an old friend, acknowledge postcards from vacationing friends, thank readers for gifts of fruit, record the success of a former resident, report the bright sayings of a friend's child, extend good wishes to a new Kiwanis club, and reveal the remarkable story of a young couple at college who eat on one meal ticket — each eating every other day.

"The Woman in the Shoe" is an appropriate title

No one can convince me that there are the same number of minutes in an hour spent playing bridge and waiting for a youngster to come home from a date. — Laura M. Klinefelter, Adams (Wis.) **Times.**

for Mrs. Gracye Dodge White, wife of the publisher of the Lancaster (N. H.) *Coos County Democrat.* She is the mother of seven children, all of whom get frequent mention in her column under special names she has given them.

Mrs. White, a columnist for five years, told Publishers' Auxiliary that fan mail gives her the greatest satisfaction. Readers' responses show that they like simplicity and humor. They like to identify themselves in what she writes. She received letters expressing delight that she, too, likes to go barefoot. She gets much advice about how to raise her family. When she reported a mouse in her kitchen, readers hastened to tell her ways to catch it.

Mrs. White has won honors both in column writing and for her juvenile stories. Much of her writing has a touch of humor. Here are some excerpts:

I know a woman who, each spring, sets her mind in order. She says she doesn't do so much housecleaning as some folks, but she does spring clean her soul. She throws out what malice she has been hoarding. She sweeps out any gossip she may have been thinking about. She mops up envy. And she shines her soul with a special cleaner called kind thoughts. Then her outlook is just fine and she can be tolerant of everything and everybody. . . .

At last I had Joy's hair grown out to a pretty length. I had it trimmed at the barber's and I do say so, she was one cunning little girl when she stepped out of the chair. I was proud of her. But pride goeth before a fall. I wasn't so proud next day when we discovered her under the dining table right after she had given herself a special Joy haircut. We have gone into seclusion for a few weeks, Joy and I.

If you want to be absolutely certain that that path will be beaten, start a little scandal about your better mouse trap. —Hardwick (Vt.) **Gazette.**

"Farmer Peck's Wife" is the earthy title of a column in the Lapeer (Mich.) *Lapeer County Press.* The author, Mrs. Ray W. Peck, is pictured with wide grin and twinkling eyes in the column heading. Her column is as sprightly as her picture as she tells about joys and tribulations of life on the farm. She talks of children's pets, farm hands, home extension club work, visiting neighbors, canning fruit, haying time, raising turkeys, setting out plants, and thinning zinnias. Mostly her column is light and personal, but she warns against accidents, such as having paraffin burst into flames during canning. Few things are hotter than boiling paraffin.

A long-standing urge to write caused Mrs. C. A. Wimberly to take an idea to the editor of the Amarillo (Tex.) *News*. She proposed to write homely anecdotes from the viewpoint of a farm wife. She had lived on a farm and felt she knew the language. The editor challenged her to submit about fifty columns, probably thinking this request would end the negotiations. But when she delivered more than the quota set, the editor agreed to give the column, titled "Mrs. Poke Bonnett," a trial run. Now, several years later, it is still running. Mrs. Wimberly writes of her husband, Poke, the children, and farm life in general. Often there is a short-short twist in a column. Example:

It is true, the astronomer who knows exactly where any given star will be at 11:30 tonight, cannot be certain about his teen-age daughter. And he can do about as much about one as the other. — Wickenburg (Ariz.) Sun.

When we have callers, Poke usually stations himself in front of his purple chair to guard against someone else's sitting in it. Though I can't see why anybody would be foolish enough to trust themselves in that maze of bumps, pushed-out springs, baggy skirt, and whooshing excelsior.

Tonight the Vanters dropped by and Poke got maneuvered half-way across the room. Mr. Vanters sat down in the purple chair while Poke perched in anguish at his desk.

"Are you comfortable?" he asked anxiously.

"Fine, fine," said Mr. Vanters heartily, and the chair scooted him down into a semi-reclining position in which we gradually lost him to a drowsy spell.

Finally, Poke said in a loud voice, "Well our boy is getting along in a nice way with the mumps."

"What? Mumps?" Mr. Vanters popped upright and rushed Mrs. Vanters to the door.

Poke scurried over to home base in front of his purple chair and said kindly, "Now don't worry. Sit down and stay a while longer."

Smooth prose, sometimes beautifully descriptive and occasionally acid with scorn (against landlords who ban children, for instance), fills "The Park Bench" column written by Irene M. Gogerty in the Des Moines *Highland Park News.* She writes of "autumn days marked for loveliness," of people distressed by small fears and frustrations, of wild roses on a roadside, and "the gentle goodness of winter rain pattering its eternal song." But mostly she writes of people. Example:

He sat across from me on the bus, an aged little Chinese man. His face was covered with a network of fine lines. He wore old but neat clothing and carried a small parcel. I wondered what those Oriental eyes had seen, besides the view from the windows of the bus. . . . Not far away sat another "study," an ancient colored lady, tiny and wrinkled and sad, holding an immense cluster of luscious red roses. . . . Two small boys, their faces contorted by two huge masses of dirty pink bubble gum. . . . A seedy, pale-eyed, dusty drunk, shuffling along in a rusty coat and a shapeless, battered hat, unmindful of the summer sun. . . . A noisy girl, too much peroxide, too much make-up, too little soap and too little work. . . . A thin girl with a pinched, old look, carrying a fat, laughing baby. . . . Three little Negro girls in immaculate starched pinafores, their tiny braids tied with brightly checked ribbons. . . . A heavy-set, middle-aged matron, looking complacently well fed, popping soft chocolates into her round, painted mouth. . . . A business girl in a chic green suit, her left arm encircled with twelve small bracelets. . . . The rude giggles of two 'teen agers, both of them looking like something out of a side show with their artless application of lip stick. . . . A beautiful Chinese girl, her dark loveliness accented by a white suit and a large hat. . . . A small boy polishing windows with an air that easily suggests he'd rather be fishing. . . . There are some of the people I see, and I am sure that in the group you will recognize some of them, too.

Mildred P. Keeshan of Manhattan, Kan. classifies as a free-lance columnist. She writes a "This 'n That" column for several weeklies and it is used over a radio station also. Hers is a variety column, with

What this country needs is a machine that does the work of one man and takes 15 men to operate it. — DePere (Wis.) Journal-Democrat.

paragraphs on the beauties of Kansas, the taste of berry pie and whipped cream, preparations for welcoming a visiting teacher, children's pert remarks, adult education, innerspring mattresses made too soft, black walnuts on the ground, walnut divinity on a plate, legends of Christmas, keeping up with the Joneses, beating a rug to release an anger, and that milestone reached when children start helping women across a street. *Cosmopolitan* printed this paragraph from her column: "Funny how a family can bear up under a tragedy and go to pieces when the water has to be turned off a few hours."

"Girl of the Gumbo" is the title of a column by Erma Freesman in the Manhattan (Kan.) *Republic, Daily Mercury,* and several other papers. It is a down-on-the-farm recital of pigs and ducks and never-ending routine; of visiting relatives and neighbors and their effect on work schedules, of little excitements on Gumbo Hill. Brief biographies of interesting neighbors are carried frequently. Like most columnists, she seldom reports outstanding success in anything of her own. Her neighbors always have better gardens, lovelier flowers. Here are some of her remarks on gardening:

> My neighbor, Mrs. Oscar Fritz, dons a large hat and her dress is spotless as she wends her way up and down the rows of that lovely garden of hers, with that ever-busy hoe. Her garden is so pretty some folks could write a song about it. All I can do is write things in my column about the beauty of her garden. What does she do? Ah, she gives me garden sass — so you see it pays off.
>
> How do I look when I go to our garden for a good hoeing spree? I don my oldest overalls, or slacks, put on a shirt that matches the age and appearance of the slacks, and as for a hat, the hatless vogue is definitely my style. But I do wear sun glasses so that my face, or I should say the skin on my face, resembles a piece of brown shoe leather or else a broiled lobster, if it is my first time out, and my arms have mountains of muscles and look like shoe leather. My hands, they never were very pretty — even in the winter when I take good care

I saw again the other day a great and beloved editor whom I have known through the years. He carried sadness in his face, old from remembering a son killed in the war. But he said to me, "I have a new grandbaby." — Bernice McCullar, Lumpkin (Ga.) **Journal.**

of them — become rough as sandpaper, with fingernails broken and jagged and all crevasses decorated with Mother Earth. On my feet I wear any shoes I can get on; every pair will be stiff as a board from too frequent watering, and they are usually flecked with white paint, double-soled with gumbo and down at the heels, Time marches on and if you want to get all the garden clean at one whack, like I do, forget the time, dump your clocks and watches in the rubbish heap, and let your hubby wield a can opener. Still, after all that, my garden isn't pretty. The rows are crooked and half the beans never came up and the moles upset my cabbage plants. But I keep trying to raise a little garden sass. I do enjoy digging in the gumbo.

You can't hurry in an attic. Too many years of living are stored there and once you've entered its dusty domain time seems unimportant. — Mildred Keeshan, Manhattan (Kan.) Tribune-News.

Women columnists, in whom the desire to point out moral and emotional values is strong, like to sum up a situation in terms of values before telling the story. The following incident was reported by Mrs. Alma Turnbull, "About Folks," in the Cedar Falls (Iowa) *Record*:

The true Christmas spirit is often lost in an orgy of gift buying and gift exchanges, so when one of the really heart-warming episodes comes, it makes for happiness all over. Everyone knows how impossible it was to buy tree lights before Christmas and many trees were unlighted as a result. Such was the condition of Mrs. Shepard Philpot's tree at 1321 Washington, where she lives with her daughter. Mrs. Philpot is 99 years old and the neighbors knew how much she would like to have tree lights for her ninety-ninth Christmas celebration. Last Saturday one of these neighbors brought her own tree lights and said, "I have enjoyed these lights all this week. Now I want you to put them on Mother Philpot's tree so that she may enjoy them over this Christmas period."

The lights went on, not only on the tree but also in the hearts of all who heard the story.

Unusual typography is used in the "Pencil Patter" column of the La Jolla (Calif.) *Light*. Dannette Evens, the writer, emphasizes many words, and names, by putting them in light caps. She flits gaily from descriptions of "buff colored hills shadowed by violet ravines" to light gossip, and from national politics to once-popular croquet. It has a ring of gayety and youth.

We have been writing of the more quotable columns and have mentioned a few taken at random. There are scores of others, some quotable and some highly localized. Some are given to summaries of social events, problems of the home, activities of farm women, or about-town personalities. Women write as they are and where they are: society editors, housewives, hobbyists, book lovers, gardeners. Their ideals are stressed.

"My purpose is to entertain, and to instruct in the simple things of the home," said Mrs. J. J. Spikes ("As a Farm Woman Thinks" in Floydada, (Tex.) *Hesperian*) in a letter to these authors. "I believe in Christmas, Santa Claus, God, friends, redemption, and the good earth."

In general, it may be said that women are increasing their stature as columnists. Their comments are sharper and their scope wider. They travel more and report what they see. Margaret Turner, women's editor of the Lubbock (Tex.) *Journal* went to Europe for her paper. Now her "Woman's Angle" column has an international ring which it probably will never lose. She has had dozens of invitations to speak before women's clubs.

Other women have improved their columning by serving as officers in clubs, political organizations, and sports groups. And once a legislator, always a commentator.

The effectiveness of women's columns is, of course, directly proportional to their cleverness, their understand-

. . . columnists would do well to consult a good book on the subject.

ing of people, their aptitude for making phrases, and their use of techniques and devices. Some seem instinctively to do the right thing; others show less imagination and resourcefulness. They seem to excel in lively one-subject columns.

In writing about the home, columnists would do well to consult a good book on the subject. Such a book is *How To Write for Homemakers,* by Lou Richardson and Genevieve Callahan (Iowa State College Press, Ames, Iowa). Their formula for writing good copy about the home can be adapted to the column:

1. Visualize your audience.
2. Analyze your problem.
3. Organize your thinking and your material.
4. Dramatize your presentation.

By visualizing an audience they mean that a columnist should think of *people* primarily, rather than *things,* when writing. It is helpful to imagine a certain reader and her reaction to your words. The columnist's problem is simpler than that of a person writing a booklet or some other printed matter. But there are problems of choosing the best literary form and of amusing the reader, or instructing her, or goading her to action. Column material may be endless chatter unless thinking and material are organized. Once taken, a point of view should not be changed without notification to the reader. A first-person narrative should not be indiscriminately allowed to change to second-person writing. Of course, a personal reaction to facts may be given in the first person, then the writer may change to second person or third person. But the reader should see the change clearly and it should seem a natural transition from "I" to "you" or "he."

A person never really knows how many friends he has until they come to his funeral. — Pauline Wagner, Walnut (Iowa) **Bureau.**

Dramatization in a column sense means breathing life into copy by use of lively verbs, interesting nouns, colorful adjectives, and novel points of view. Quotations suggest life. Short sentences, mixed with longer ones, suggest movement. Illustrations give reality. Mild exaggeration may be needed to produce a certain effect in the reader.

Women readers are said instinctively to look for clues to the personality of writers. Creators of life, they look for evidences of its myriad moods and facets. Too much "I" may seem affected, but women's magazines are filled with "you's." Friendliness and helpfulness are expected.

But some women think with more impersonal insight and prefer not to write as women, but as thinkers and commentators. Some of these turn out quotable paragraphs and other material quite as adeptly as male contemporaries.

Many newspaper publishers, especially of the smaller papers, have not fully sensed the importance and value of women readers. Magazines make strong appeals to women, but many small papers are weak in reader interest for them. Some have very good sports pages, farm pages, etc., but little appeal outside the social news for women, who spend 85 per cent of the family income.

Probably there is a potential women's columnist in every publisher's territory. Why shouldn't a newspaper which needs a women's column call for volunteer would-be columnists, run a series by different writers, and let readers elect one to write regularly? If this plan is too bold, there are others. And there undoubtedly are many fine, undiscovered women columnists.

There's little that will spoil a child like living next door. — Elizabeth Ann, Lakeville (Conn.) Journal.

*17.*

# Handling Specialized Columns

THE PERSONAL COLUMNIST is versatile in method and resourceful in finding appeals to many reader interests. In many cases he carries the weight of highest authority and takes a Page One position. He may at the same time share space, however, with a few or several other columnists.

On small papers, most of these contributors are local; some may be syndicate writers, regional or national. Local columnists are not always staff members. Both in number and reader interest, these specialized columns have grown to a point meriting the close attention of publishers.

Specialized columns commonly found in the non-metropolitan press include:

| | |
|---|---|
| Sports. | Labor. |
| Business. | Oil. |
| Organizations. | Religion. |
| Gardening. | Teen-agers. |
| Health. | Farming. |
| Hobbies. | |
| Agricultural extension services. | |

**READER COLUMNS**

Diane Mecham of Santa Rosa, Calif., says the most popular column in the town's paper is one written by the readers themselves. They are invited to write such columns and are paid three dollars for each one accepted. — **The Press Woman.**

Methods and devices of writing are so similar in all columns that these will not be discussed again here. Rather, brief mention will be made of factors peculiar to the fields from which subject matter is drawn.

A factor common to most one-interest columns is that they have ready-made audiences. These fans ask little more than that their enthusiasm be shared and that the column be up-to-date and accurate. They eagerly share their knowledge. They enjoy contests and exhibits. Their subscriptions are not likely to lapse.

#### SPORTS APPEAL UNIVERSAL

The most uniting single interest shared by the average reader family is sports. This is true despite the fact that sports is a collection of many diverse activities. Usually one or several local schools have teams in which fans are intensely interested. To the "home teams" must be added the participant sports, such as golf, tennis, and softball; the promotional sports, such as wrestling and boxing; and various minor sports such as playground activities, swimming meets, and community baseball.

*. . . fans eagerly share their knowledge.*

Major reader interest in small towns and cities is found to rest on the teams in which community pride is felt. But the sports columnist's subjects come from a much wider field, perhaps including rodeos, weight-lifting, croquet, marbles, chess, and any other sports activity involving tests of skill. While his division of column space may roughly approximate presumed reader interest, he does not overlook intensive concentration by small groups and participation by large groups. He seeks balance. And because the news columns bend under loads of words on major sports, he can afford to divide space with minor sports in his column. He avoids repetition of news story facts.

A sports writer often finds ability to conduct a column is a requirement in his job. Perhaps a two-column space must be filled daily or weekly. If there are two sports writers, there likely will be two sports columns. The senior columnist may not be a second edition of Grantland Rice or Bill Corum, but if he is loyal to the home teams, easy to know, and reasonably analytical and accurate, he will in time become a popular character. He will speak at year-end sports banquets and a playing field may be named for him. His responsibility to be honest, well-balanced, and fair is no small one. He sets the tone of fan thinking.

Sports columnists share the paper's obligation to speak for the community when its team wins or loses; to maintain sanity so rival towns won't suspend business relations; to be fair to coaches as educators and to players as readers' sons; to work for good sportsman ship; to combat bribery and gambling; to cooperate with the coaches by refraining from giving away strategy in advance and by resisting the temptation to overplay the ball carriers; and to help management keep sports control in proper hands. A sense of independence is demanded, lest sports writers become fawning publicists rather than reporters with discrimination and critical judgments.

The sports columnist speaks and writes English; that is, he strives for fresh style but avoids the jargon which is the mark of the hack. As a phrase-maker he has few equals. His literary freedom and the fact that he deals with colorful narrative combine to make him a stylist in prose. He may even write some verse. That he should know sports and write in the vocabu-

## HOMETOWN CRITICS

High-voltage criticism is out of place in most towns and cities. Yet the small-town columnist is expected to voice his opinions — the conclusions of the people's "taster" of the lively arts and literature. As such, he writes as an average man or at least as a small-town man. He remembers to report local performances in terms of participants' ability, time, and intentions. But he does not spare visiting celebrities who do less than their best before the home folks.

lary of each is axiomatic. But as a writing man he may develop the skills which lead him into humor, or fiction, or feature writing.

Only a writer conversant with his subject is likely to develop the verve and confidence needed in writing for fans. But some modesty is a necessity and a safety factor. A linotype operator may know more baseball history than the columnist. A bookkeeper may excel at chess. An ad man may have a superior knowledge of golf, or horse racing, or polo. A good sports library is the best recourse when the sports writer is asked to settle a wager or explain a rule.

The column is a flexible instrument in dealing with fans, explaining bonehead plays, stopping rumors, awarding compliments, promoting attendance, and editorializing on sports problems. But unhappy days come to columnists sensitive to crank letters and other fan outbursts. Usually these letters are written in the after-heat of a contest. Replies can be calmer recitals of rules, facts, and principles. It may be sobering, also, to divert attention to other worthwhile sports.

Predicting winners is an evidence of a columnist's proficiency in sports analysis — or the lack of it if he is unlucky. Few sports prophets have had better succuss than Herman Phelps, the "Demon Dopester" of the Lexington (Ky.) *Herald*. The "Dopester" began forecasting football results in 1927 and has an all-time winning prediction average of .800. Lacking this access to a crystal ball, a columnist can set up boards of predictions, interview a few fans each week, or engage in substitute promotions.

We now have an expert taxy service running from Washington to all forty-eight states. — R. B. Lockhart, Pittsburg (Tex.) Gazette.

### BUSINESS

Merchandising is much more of an adventure than one would surmise from reading the advertisements. Some merchants have begun to make column-like comment in their ads, and the practice probably will spread. Business men long have been inarticulate in the face of shortages, inflation, style changes, and other vexing conditions. And newspapers of the smaller communities have carried little news or comment on theories and practices in retailing, reports on trips to markets, success of advertising, etc. This field is open to columnists with a vision for what might be done to serve merchants and interest readers.

### ORGANIZATIONS

Columns on 4-H clubs, Scouting, and veterans organizations are among the most numerous in small papers. School news columns, which sometimes grow into entire pages, also abound. Editors also sometimes grant space to persons who write columns on civic club happenings and personnel, country club activities, and Parent-Teacher programs. While not columns in the sense used here, collections of calendar announcements, church news, and club briefs are assembled in vertical form under standing heads. The test of any of these contributed columns is whether readers are served or entertained. Writers need periodical renewals of enthusiasm and guidance on column content and style.

Dresses that make women look slim make men look 'round. — Charles A. Knouse, Perry (Kan.) Mirror.

### GARDENING

Columns on gardening are available in syndicated form, with or without illustrations. Interest usually is higher when columnists are local. A column may grow into a page with other gardening features and considerable advertising. Garden clubs often cooperate, sometimes by holding flower shows, distributing bulbs, cuttings, etc., and furnishing testimony on the success of certain methods. Localization is essential to maximum reader interest, and timeliness is almost as essential.

Unusual columns have been written on local wild flowers and legends on them.

Illustrations increase readership. These may be taken from cut services as line cuts, but local news-photos financed by garden clubs, advertisers, or the papers are common at the height of the flowering season. Some papers have given away thousands of roses and shrubs as subscription premiums or in co-operation with civic clubs and chambers of commerce.

### HEALTH

More often than not these are syndicated columns. Professional men and nurses find it difficult to write about health without appearing to be advertising themselves unethically. State health associations and departments of public health issue much material through publicity departments, and the federal government presses turn out a steady flow of pamphlet material. Syndicates serving newspapers also have health columns.

Here, as always, localized health news would have more readership and influence than the impersonal articles so often seen.

### HOBBIES

These have smaller but intense readership and are best written by a competent hobbyist. The heading should suggest the subject, and content should appeal to readers at whom the column is directed. While intrinsically interesting, column material should be given the usual tests of timeliness, accuracy and readable style. It is easy to offend with inaccuracy or failure to present latest developments.

### LABOR

Large local groups, such as railroad or factory employes, may be given regular space. But because of the controversial nature of labor issues, column content is likely to be restricted to news and personal mention. Usually the column is written by a mem-

Charles Washburn said, "A short term on a newspaper is better than a long term in school." That statement, however, is subject to some modification. Much would depend upon what newspaper and what school. — Palo Alto (Calif.) **Times.**

ber of the labor group who is well liked. The space is given in recognition of the importance of the group economically and because of similar interests and concentrated readership. If management-employee relations are good, the columns regularly carry items complimentary to each. If labor relations become strained, the columns may become more stiffly objective, leaving any comment to the editor's column or editorials.

A news item says the wife is the boss of the Esquimo family. So there's no use going north, either. — Jim Chism, Pelham (Ga.) **Journal.**

### OIL

Columnists in this field are not numerous but are important in areas fortunate enough to have deposits of oil and gas. Full-time oil writers usually write for week-end editions a column which might be called a hodge-podge of the oil world. Included in its content are personal mentions, editorials, analyses of trends, predictions, and reports on trips into the field. Also seen are thank-you's and apologies.

Other industries similarly covered also are productive of column material.

### RELIGION

The growing number of radio broadcasts on human relations and "your life" problems appears to be one cause of renewed attention to religion in the news. The column angle is that there are trends and shifts of thought in religion. There are building plans and financial drives.

The number of columns on religion in small papers is not large. Retired ministers capable of avoiding denominational clashes are among the commentators. Some editors, especially the older ones, like to write about religion. A few write Sunday School lessons in a journalistic manner.

Column material includes local items, comment on news service releases, book reviews, and excerpts from magazine articles and sermons. A few papers carry a "Sermon of the Week."

### TEEN-AGE COMMENT

Categorizing of the adolescent mind at 17 years of age is traceable in part to advertising promotion, but some newspapers see a relationship between reducing juvenile crime and giving adolescents a chance to be heard. Also, printing opinions of youth seems a logical follow-up of civic club and American Legion programs in which boys and girls become public officials for a day. Junior citizenship may be expressed in columns of surprising poise and commendable constructiveness.

At their worst, teen-age columns become frivolous with boy-girl gossip — usually in school pages. Unjournalistic and sometimes libelous, they seldom last long despite the fact that they have all the reader interest of a dog fight or family row.

### FARMING

Considering how much small towns rest on agriculture and how much interest small-town papers profess in the subject, a surprisingly small amount of competent writing is done on farming as a business and a science. The explanation is, in part, that most newspaper men are not farmers and also do not have time to gather news afield. Also, farmers as a class are intolerant of error in matters which concern them.

However, some small papers put columnists on the road with conspicuous success. Or they free a reporter to give some time to getting up a farm page, assisted by farm agents, farm leaders, and agriculture teachers. A few dirt farmers write columns.

A folksy column with a touch of humor, many quotes, and rich in personal mention cannot be excelled in reader interest. Finding someone who can do it well is not easy. Serious column comment on farm problems involves as many problems as writing on the stock market or government. And both of

A small town is where the telephone operator gives you the right number when you ask for the wrong one. — Maumee (Ohio) **News.**

these are properly included in any study of farming today.

The best substitute for specialized knowledge usually is a good reporting job. The reactions of the columnist are sufficient to give personality to the column when combined with quotes and excerpts.

### AGRICULTURAL EXTENSION

Farm extension agents appreciate the column as a bulletin board for announcements, requests, and brief reports. The certainty that it will appear with regularity makes possible reduction of other efforts to communicate with farm people.

However, such columns also reflect the personalities of the writers. Some include bits of philosophy and humor. But mostly they briefly review crop conditions and carry news of extension activities. Townspeople, especially merchants, are interested in crop conditions, farm sales, and marketing.

Here are some typical Farm Bureau column excerpts from Iowa farm agents:

I was over to Allison Township's resolution meeting Thursday evening and we had a rip-roaring discussion. I always like a person who comes right out and says what he thinks — as long as he agrees with me.

I wonder why people call money dough. Dough sticks to your fingers.

— Osceola County

As corn picking approaches, it's well to check over the machinery involved to make sure it is ready to go. Just got a new bulletin on "Corn Picker Adjustment" that may help you. Get yours.

— Sawyer Sez.

World understanding begins at mother's knee; so does prejudice.

— Boone County

I had a short but very interesting visit Wednesday at the test plots being carried on by the folks at the Central Popcorn Company at Schaller. In this test area more than a hundred popcorn inbreds together with

It's about time for some society to award a plaque to the citizen who hasn't got one. — J. E. Sterling, Hugo (Colo.) **Plainsman.**

many popcorn crosses are being compared. Some nice advances have been made in popcorn breeding in recent years and of course the only way to continue these gains is through additional research and plant breeding.

— Sac County

Next week we'll be at Ak-Sar-ben. Some of the best beef calves in the county will be shown there. Some other good ones won't make it. Dick and Sue Ann Clark are both heading off for college, Dick to Iowa State and Sue Ann to State Teachers, so they won't be showing their champion Hereford. The champion Angus and grand champion Shorthorn will be there, though.

— Shelby County

The outlook for dairying remains steady; no radical changes are seen and the typical high demand for dairy products should continue. Hogs look like good property and fall breedings can find justification for increases. Sheep are scarce and the increase in numbers will be most apparent in the form of farm flocks. In both the sheep and cattle picture the rancher is no longer in a position of having to sell she-stock but rather is making replacements.

— Clay County

Feeder cattle and lambs arriving from the West are heavier than usual. Lambs are running 80 pounds or more. Current prices seem to be 27-28 cents a pound, or 22-24 cents for lambs contracted earlier. I was told that one Nebraska farmer had his cattle contracted for October, yet they have changed hands seven times already before leaving the farm.

— Mills County

Limestone should be applied about six months before seeding legumes. This means it should be applied as soon as the corn has been harvested. Don't put it off — put it on! Finely ground limestone is best, but be sure of the needs. Have your soil tested.

— Page County

Putting by-lines and possibly telephone numbers or mail addresses on specialized columns channels reader responses to the writers and tends to place responsibility. Some publishers take the position, however, that they should know what responses, complaints, and bouquets are reaching staff members.

Old Dobbin may have had his faults, but he never scattered you all over the road just because he met a one-eyed horse at night. — Ronald Furse, Plattsmouth (Neb.) **Journal.**

Small papers must limit the number of columns carried. Furthermore, editors dislike to drop departments, once they are started. Every column, however poor, has a following. And columns are inflexible in that readers expect to find them every week, and in the same place.

As one publisher stated it, he almost had to beat off with hoe-handles the persons who wished to write columns of humor, poetry, health, and other specialized matter. He recognized the value of good columns but was mindful that poor ones use space needed for news.

But when the right person develops a good column idea, he may in time get a chance to see it in print. The doubt in the editor's mind usually concerns the writer, not the idea.

**The doubt in the editor's mind usually concerns the writer, not the idea.**

## 18.

# Guidance—Control of an Environment

**M**EN OF FREE SPIRIT cherish their opportunity to control, at least in some degree, the environment in which they live. The desire to do so motivates most editors in the formulation of their policies. The realization that press freedoms might be lost if newspapers should fail to supply facts, analyses, and leadership has stiffened support of self-government, but historically the editor has not been like other men, and the newspaper business has not been like other private firms. These facts are not palatable to some critics of the press, but they are demonstrably true.

There are differences in editors, in newspapers, in towns, and in people. Theoretically voters are equal at the ballot box. The ballot stands as a symbol of citizens' right to have a part in the decisions which affect them and in selection of men who represent them. That they do not always exercise this right because their votes seem lost in the mass of similar votes does not diminish the fundamental importance of their franchise. However, as voters they may neither know the candidates nor understand the

There are differences in editors . . .

issues which are so variously explained to them. In large cities, parties and machines may reduce to the vanishing point the ability of unorganized citizens to influence public policies.

It is one of the satisfactions of small-town living that people know each other and that local issues are small and near enough to be understood. And it is the privilege of editors and columnists in these towns and small cities to know conditions as they are, people as they are, and problems as they are; to exert a personal leadership both in thought and action; to bolster their written word with the spoken plea; to see their ideas develop not only in material ways but in the lives of people born, married, and sometimes buried within their own lifetimes.

These editors speak out in various ways. In some states the traditional editorial is preferred by the better papers; in others, fewer than half the small papers carry editorials under their mastheads. Pontificating in pious tones no longer seems the thing to do. Excesses in writing style have tended to disappear with tightening of libel laws and development of newspaper work as a business. The editorial essay is not dead, but many of its masters are. Yet guidance of community thought and action is an editorial function. No serious student of journalism can fail to regret any weakening of the editorial voice.

We have noted that the friendly personal column, often found on Page 1, is supplementing — in some cases supplanting — the formal editorial. A small paper may have one column that is the voice of the editor — or may not be — or it may have two columns, or three, or even more. The column's rise in number and popularity may be a concession to the fact that an editor today is not necessarily the best read, most traveled man in town. News is no longer a commodity exclusive to a newspaper. College degrees are no longer rare. Local readers, from housewives to farmers, endeavor to understand issues which affect them. With these the editor shares viewpoints. It is a wholesome condition on which both editors and readers differ in detail while agreeing on fundamentals.

As columnists, editors seldom make any claim to infallibility. Theirs is a more relaxed approach to life than that of editorial writers. What they lack in profundity they make up in terms of broad tolerance, good humor, and a reception of divergent viewpoints for purposes of illustration and education. Columnists can use all the arts of the editorial writer, then add others. They furnish some entertainment as the price they pay to get good audiences. They can be as big in the community as they are able. They may be less than brilliant and still be influential; the one greatest demand is that they not be dull.

An outsider is not a good judge of a column's effectiveness. What may seem to him trivial and clownish may have overtones which subtly affect reader attitudes. A writer's influence accumulates so that his stature is the totality of his work. As a teacher, he can afford to let readers sense the moral values in his theme. As a preacher, he can remain largely a teacher. As a leader, he can save his heavy verbal artillery for critical community issues. As a citizen, he can take rank with the school superintendent, the bank president, and the county judge.

Columnists who have combated provincialism have had strong allies in public education, good roads, libraries, radio, advertising, and civic clubs. There are no apologies for small-town and rural life in their writing, although constructive suggestions come naturally from their thinking, study, and contacts. But because column material usually is collected throughout a day or a week, instead of being composed in isolation or on the fairway of the Country Club, it often has the flavor and earthy quality of the

**DISTURBING**

A thought recurring in editorial comment on newspaper leadership is this: Some readers are certain to be disturbed when an editor speaks out on a public issue. Many more will be disturbed when he **fails to speak out**. Which shall he fear?

streets and offices. The number of viewpoints expressed in columns runs high.

The popularity of columns is traceable, at least in part, to the growth of towns and the larger size of newspaper staffs. Newspaper men now have more time to write. But it also is true that we have better educated writers, a fact with which we associate a lively desire to know and to speak and to write. Whether this education is formal or acquired with experience, it removes inhibitions and inculcates a desire to develop as a personality.

Some resistance to columning is not only prevalent, but probably wholesome as well, with regard to the desire of journalism graduates to have a personal soapbox before they have gained the necessary wisdom and understanding. Some columns can be written without the mellowing of experience, but even here a young writer usually is advised to first prove his ability to write superior news stories and features about his special interests.

Even a casual study of trends will show that successful columning may be started at any mature age. Many oldsters, fortified by rich memories and an undertanding of the little things which people think and do, are writing superior columns. Some very salty characters have been amusing and guiding readers for a quarter of a century or more.

In every state, columnists are answering the questions: "What is the meaning of this?" and "How is it going to affect us?" No local crisis is without the sobering comment of editors who write with some detachment, as trained observers, yet with the warmth of a worried friend. In one town, during an epidemic of burglaries, some high school boys were caught.

"But for the grace of God," wrote a columnist, "these boys might have been your own."

He pointed out that the boys were from "good

## EDITORIAL PAGES

In any discussion of editorials, it is necessary to consider the case for the editorial page — not editorials alone. Even small papers can, by grouping features, produce a page of opinion, background information, and local feature items. The editor's column can be prominent on this page, or just as appropriately can be run on Page One.

families" and had no real need for the goods stolen. Their search for a thrill showed a definite lack in their lives. Damning the younger generation for such outbreaks, he wrote, isn't scientific. A columnist probes deeper. He seeks expert advice. In talks to peace officers, truant officers, school officials, Scout leaders, and others he traces the development of anti-social traits.

He connects these with misused leisure time, lack of parental supervision, failure of the community to provide planned recreation, lack of understanding on the part of peace officers, and similar shortcomings. He seeks a positive program, including education of all the community.

Such a columnist does not seek to excuse young offenders, but he does not thoughtlessly condemn. His attitude will vary, however, according to his age. In moments of candor, the older writers may confess to worse sins of their own generation. Some scolds, however, never fail to point out the misdeeds of the youth of other nearby communities — as a warning to local youngsters. A community is fortunate if it has an editor who trusts the young and is not ashamed to ask the advice of teen-agers. He who champions boys and girls will not be forgotten when they are men and women.

Readers are people, and especially they are parents. Mention of their young arouses emotional responses. And since most columnists are parents, too, their attempted guidance in matters affecting youth is without pretense. So it was when William Allen White was moved to anger by reports from parents that Emporia, Kan., police, in the presence of children, were shooting some of the dogs which "waited patiently about" the school grounds. White wrote, in part:

It's all right to be a cop; even to be a dog killer is a public service. But even a cop, even a dog killer, ought

**LEADERSHIP**

Columnists, backed by nearly unanimous readership, have an opportunity to nominate civic leaders and to reward them with appreciation. By their attitude, they can make public service palatable. The smear word "politics" then will not drive good men from local leadership. Similarly, a columnist can vigorously defend a leader who is under the fire of some self-seeking group or person.

to be able to use just a little brains, just a mite of intelligence, and if not that, just a little heart.[1]

Columnists may raise cain as a professional duty, but in general they stand for domestic and civic peace. They hear gossip with regret, not elation. Here is pertinent comment by Sara Roberta Getty in the "Looking and Listening" column of the Somerset (Pa.) *American*:

"I thought you should know" is a comment one hears many times. Once in a while it is the remark of a kindly, even though mistaken friend; more often it is done because some one wants to make a disturbance between friends, out of jealousy or envy, and perhaps partly because the person himself is unhappy, unstable, and worn by seeing others happy. . . . If we ever feel like passing on something disagreeable, let's think instead of something pleasant and pass that on; it will make us feel better and make others happy at the same time.

Guidance usually is on an impersonal basis in small-town columns when critical, except where public officials are concerned. Then advice may be more pointed. "The Plainsman" in the Lubbock (Tex.) *Journal* wrote this "Memo to the City Commission:"

There seems to be considerable dissatisfaction with the way misdemeanor charges are handled down at the police station. At least, such dissatisfaction is indicated in mail, phone calls, and through personal visits to us from time to time. The principal kick seems to be that an individual hauled in for allegedly violating some city ordinance is deemed to be guilty simply because he got pinched; that if he's given a chance to fight the charge — which some claim they are not — he hasn't got a Chinaman's chance, anyway. The feeling seems to be pretty general that there's too much cooperation between the police department, which is a law enforcement agency, and the corporation court, which is a judicial agency . . . .

**Then advice may be more pointed.**

---

[1] *Forty Years on Main Street*, pp. 376–77.

If this condition actually exists, and our guess is that it must exist to some extent, you gentlemen of the commission doubtless want to get it straightened out, not only in a spirit of fair play, but also to safeguard the City of Lubbock. The City might get a whacking big damage suit sometime, growing out of failure to give the citizen the opportunity of a fair and impartial trial.

Not having been born yesterday, we realize that few people admit their guilt when arrested, and that fewer still admit guilt after they've paid off. Our experience has been that 99.44 per cent of the people arrested will swear until they're blue in the face that they've been mistreated, etc., and of course we long ago stopped believing fairy stories.

However, under the American code, a citizen charged with law violation is presumed to be innocent until proved guilty, rather than vice versa; and every person charged with law violation has a right to a fair trial in case he wants one.

It would be good business for the commission to make certain that everything is as it should be in the matter of arrests, fines, and rights of citizens.

**HIRED HELP**

"This is being set by John Brown, our new Linotype operator," wrote a columnist-editor who probably will have less labor supply trouble than some publishers who think printers should be seen but not heard — of.

This face-saving criticism is in distinct contrast to the way a frontier editor probaby would have handled the situation, and a far cry from the tempo of a big-city daily tearing into a city commission it does not favor. In smaller cities and towns most critical comment is softened, at least in opening chapters. Editors remember that they have to live with hometown officers and officials, whether these are re-elected or not. Moreover, personal guidance may take the form of attending city commission meetings regularly. At least one columnist boasts that he has missed few commission meetings in 22 years.

In these parlous days, things often reverse themselves. In the Southwest, for instance, two-gun editors have passed but today two-gun sheriffs include typewriters as standard equipment. They write columns. A Dallas *News* staff writer reported that Orear Watson, high sheriff of Upshur County, Tex., was one of the most widely read newspaper writers in that area. Ex-football star and army flier, Watson makes no pretense of being a journalist. But his chatty weekly column in the Gilmer *Mirror* is regarded as a potent factor in reducing crime.

"A lot of folks," said Russell Laschinger, his publisher, "turn to the sheriff's column before they read anything else."

Starting the column was one of Watson's first acts after taking office.

"I wanted to break down the idea that peace officers are a hard-boiled, heartless lot who delight in punishment," he explained. "I wanted to take Upshur Countians behind the scenes to show that the men who wear a badge can be friendly and sympathetic."

The writing sheriff seeks to unite his county against reckless driving, juvenile delinquency, and drunkenness. He rarely uses names and he speaks of locking up prisoners by saying, "He is now visiting with us." At Christmas he was able to make this unusual report:

> Our business has been very good during these holidays. I mean that we have only locked up one person. This man just got a little too much Christmas spirits and he didn't seem satisfied until he spent the night with me. Next day about noon I went in and talked with him. After a bit he told me he would like to spend the rest of Christmas day at home. He told me he would report back any time I asked him to. I let the man go, as he told me it was the first time he had been drunk in the last six months.

In other instances, peace officers have their weekly reports ghosted by reporters. But not so is the case of T. W. "Buckshot" Lane, sheriff of Wharton County, Tex.; he writes the longest and frankest reports the authors have seen. He also reports to the people by radio.

"I find by warning and educating the people through radio and newspapers you can do plenty

---

They were talking about my turning 40 years of age, and how it is that one is young only once. But, take it from me, once is enough if you work it right. — Billy Arthur, Jacksonville (N. C.) **News and Views.**

good," Sheriff Lane wrote the authors. "I hardly know how in the world I could contend with the criminal situation in this county if it were not for the interest taken by the people, brought on and encouraged by the aid of newspapers and radio talks. All I have to do is run a column regarding the danger of driving with no tail light and name a specific instance where a life was lost or considerable damage done, then ask all people to check tail lights at once. That tale is picked up by service stations and by the people, then for quite some time we have no tail light trouble.

"I once had a certain bridge in the county where several wrecks and deaths occurred; in fact there were lots of wrecks there. I wrote a tale on the bridge and an oil derrick there, saying the derrick stood as a monument to the dead and as a warning to people using the bridge. For months there were no more wrecks there."

The sheriff's column, which appears in several newspapers in the area, is titled "Buckshot Lane, Sheriff, Wharton County, His Writin's and Musin's." It is an uninhibited, ungrammatical report printed just as he writes it. Editors using the column say its readership is virtually equal to the literate population. And Lane, like the other writing sheriffs studied, won re-election at the polls. They believe a column is a powerful political instrument.

The following are excerpts from one of Sheriff Lane's weekly columns: as printed in the Bay City (Tex.) *Daily Tribune*:

Folks the past week was to me a very high temperature week, for it was the week of elections, rumors were flying high against me, I was unable to answer all of them and I was unable to get out and among the people, for I was more than buisy.

We began the week by having Criminal District Court the first day, Monday, we did not so much as call a jury still we tried six persons and as follows   first was an

A gentleman will not tire out a lady by making her chase him. — Petersburg (Va.) **Journal.**

auto thief and he was glad to take 4 year in the Pen for it was his second offense, the second was glad to get off with four years, for he had 14 marihuana cigaretts on him when I caught him right here in the jail trying to peddle it, he was a trusty, third was more than glad and very thankful to get off with five years suspended, he was a burglar and was caught in the building, but he had never before been in any serious trouble, the fourth took four years for forgery, and I am sure that had he fought the case he would have gotten at least ten years, fifth was a woman and she was glad to get off with two years down the river for she had cashed many forged checks but only one in this County and the last was muchly surprised to find that Judge gave him four years in pen for he actually was entitled to be sent as a habitual criminal, having been in the Penitentiary four different times.

Tuesday came along and on that date we called up a Jury, we had six cases to try, the first didn't show so we forfeited his bond, the second who had the day before demanded a Jury took one look at those grim faces and said I don't think I want a Jury, so he asked the Judge for mercy and was glad to get off with 5 years in pen, he was a three time looser and a fast burglar. . . . I personally want to thank you good men that laid by their businesses of one kind or another and reported for Jury service. I realize it is a great bother and burden on you men to have to come into the Court room and sit idly by and wait to be called on to listen to some tiresome criminal case, and I realize each and every one of you men loose money by coming and you neglect your private business, but fellows trial by Jury is one of the AMERICAN ways of doing business, it is one privilege the American citizen has and certainly we do not want that American privilege and right to break down, and unless you good men do volunteer your services as Jurors it will in time be a breakdown, and when that time comes I hate to think what may be the outcome. . . .

During the week in Wharton, the Aldag addition, I had a call from a good lady and she was in some sort of a stew, she and all the kids were out there within the street  they had two small magnets tied together with a piece of wire to pull them with  it was hot and so was the lady, she was pulling that thing back and forth, and it was getting results, for ever so often she would pick it up and a dozen or more tacks would be stuck to it, she said Buck I have had nine flat tires in just the last few days, I don't know if some body is mad at us or what has happened, but look in this can, she had a big tomato

Back in the good old days the dishwasher, the mixmaster and the sweeper came equipped with sex instead of an electric motor. — Edwin F. Abels, Lawrence (Kan.) **Outlook.**

can over half full of tacks, she said we have been dragging this thing up and down and we have been down on our knees, looks like some one has it in for us. . . . I believe that some persons riding by accidently dropped a sack of tacks, for I know the Man and Lady and so help me never in my life did I ever hear any person say any thing but good about them, I just wonder how many more people have picked up tacks on this spot there is many cars going by there during a day and night, and in each occasion a flat was had some body cussed some body else, but all and all no body knows just who to cuss, and if those tacks were put there on purpose it was a mighty sorry thing to do.

Jail report for the week: 1 investigation, gen., 2 drunks, 1 Statutory Rape, 1 Insane, 1 Assault with Knife, 1 Threat to take life with shotgun "It was not loaded" 1 Disturb Peace, 1 Drunk Driver, 3 Federal Prisoners, we have in Jail 22 County and 11 Federal Prisoners.

> Your friends may lie to you, your mirror deceive you, but a flight of stairs will be brutally frank. — Helper (Utah) **Journal**.

Such columns are being imitated not only by sheriffs but by other officeholders. Peace officers have the advantage that their activities are close to the people and involve many of the factors which make news. Such columns are not beyond criticism, of course. In them it is possible to pre-try the accused, to show bias toward races, and by unfortunate remarks do the opposite of what this chapter is concerned with — control of an environment in some degree.

However, a sheriff-columnist gives voters and taxpayers an insight not only into his activities but into his policies and thought patterns. On the other side of this picture is the newspaper which carries only the merest summaries of court and crime news, and gets these from the records and indirect sources. A better balance would be normal reporting of public affairs, giving the people a check against their peace officers' versions, and an editor's column, which from time to time might evaluate the findings of both reporter and sheriff.

## 19.

# Press Columnist Organizations

*[Because the columnists of Iowa are active and well organized, and because their activity might be used as a model in other states, this chapter is given to a description of their program.]*

THE COLUMNISTS OF IOWA, through their organization, the Press Columnists of Iowa, have become pretty well acquainted and have found, to their delight, that "columnists are people." With rare exceptions, the columnists of the Hawkeye state do not run to literary pretensions, to journalistic all-wisdom, to upper-strata intellectualism. They are just run-of-the-crib Iowans. And, since Iowa is fairly representative of other states, probably it's fair to assume that columnists anywhere in the United States are not given to literary, journalistic, or other pretensions.

The obvious explanation is that any such pretensions are knocked out of the small-town writer, within weeks after manifestation, by the readers with whom he cannot escape daily contact. That, plus the fact

*. . . any pretensions are knocked out of the small-town writer . . .*

# SING BROTHERS, SING!

The Ding Darling cartoon on Iowa press columnists.

that often the columnist was pitched into the writing business, willy nilly, without much preparation, and therefore continues to be humble.

The Press Columnists of Iowa have made a study of the "columnists are people" aspects of themselves. They did this through their organization office, and the oft-disturbing but tried-and-true device of a questionnaire. They asked themselves how they happened to be columnists anyway, then countered with a query about hobbies, possibly with the thought that a hobby might offset tendencies toward column phobias. From these questionnaires, thumbnail personality sketches have been prepared, and are the basis for a "Who's Who Among Iowa Columnists" on the weekly programs quoting the columnists on the university and college radio stations.

Later in the questionnaire, because the prominence and influence of the columnists in their communities are very real, they are asked what organizations they had served as officials and whether they had served on city councils or in the legislature.

Iowa columnists, organized for five years, were well prepared to make the survey. Elections of the Press Columnists of Iowa are carried on by mail. The secretary's office in Des Moines handles records and edits and distributes a clip-sheet. The secretary and the board of directors establish policies.

Every columnist in the state is a member of PCI by virtue of his column. Money for the small expense involved is raised by a registration fee at the three or four meetings held each year. Members may, if they wish, have a copy of the membership certificate, a large affair bearing a cartoon by the famous Iowa cartoonist, Ding (J. N. Darling).

A Ding carton also appears on the "kernelship" awards made by the columnists. Indirectly, these awards signify the leadership and importance of columnists in their own communities. Only colum-

Don't learn the traffic rules by accident!—Calhoun (Ky.) **News.**

nists can present the awards, and these are made to such persons and in such ways as the individual columnist determines. He gives them, of course, for outstanding community work by persons in his home area — the school superintendent, the retiring head of an important business, a faithful Sunday school official. The columnist decides to give an award to some person; writes the secretary for a "kernel" award; receives it; and presents it as he wishes. That's all there is to it. The award has gone to some five hundred Iowa community leaders, to a former Iowan, Herbert Hoover, and to dignitaries whom Iowa editors have visited, including the president of Mexico.

The phrase, "Kernel of the Iowa Tall Corn," seems to carry the connotation that the person receiving the award is an essential part of all Iowa— a local leader whose accomplishments help make a great state. And the pun on "kernel" and "colonel" has many uses.

Each year the PCI sponsors some activity not entirely "columnar." One year, it was the choosing of a "Queen of the Lands" — an Iowa farm girl who represented Iowa in out-of-state affairs. In a previous year it selected five "Master Iowans." In another, PCI officials gave a series of lectures on column writing at Iowa colleges.

Since woman's life is four years longer than man's, you'd think she could wait about having the last word. — DePere (Wis.) Journal-Democrat.

\* \* \*

#### THE PCI COLUMN SCORE CARD

Iowa columnists have developed a score card for columns which the PCI calls the "double T" or "T-T," because of its two divisions, "topic" and "treatment." This card runs:

Topic:
  Actual interest of readers   )
  Potential interest of readers)  . . . . . . . .   45 points
Treatment:
  Writing of column . . . . . . . . . . . . . . . .   40 points
  Appearance of column . . . . . . . . . . . . . .   15 points
                                                   ———
                                                    100

The column that would get 100 points, the perfect score, would be on a topic, or topics, in which 100 percent of the readers actually already were interested, or could reasonably be expected to become interested by the column if written and printed perfectly. To be written perfectly, the choice of words and arrangements of phrases would be such that no one would reasonably conceive a better expression; printing would satisfy a similar standard.

Mathematicians may deny it, but it is possible for certain well-arranged sets of curves to make a triangle. — North Canaan (Conn.) **Western News.**

This score card can be tricky. Its intelligent use demands independent consideration of each factor and its suitability for readers of the paper in which the column appeared.

This score is primarily for grading a column against its own possibilities, in its own paper and for its own readers or possible readers. But by comparing totals, judges can use the scores for comparing columns in different papers and in different areas.

The score obviously is not complete enough for grading columns as to their fitness for being quoted in (1) other papers of the area, (2) the metroplitan press, or (3) magazines. For that, the elements of timeliness (or timelessness), of brevity, and of universality of interest have to be added. But if those are added, the Iowa "TT" score is adequate for judging columns as to quotation possibilities.

### REASONS FOR WRITING COLUMN

Response to the questionnaire sent by the secretary to all PCI members throws some light on the origin and nature of the species, *humanus columnist*:

The replies to the query on *Why did you begin writing a column?* support the conclusion that columnists got into their sprightly business for many reasons. Here are some of the answers to the questionnaire:

• Substituted on father's column in 1928 • wanted to get rid of canned stuff • by accident • wanted column for news that wouldn't fit other columns • Dad was away and

I tried his column • best way to get across editorial ideas • natural thing for a newspaper man • outlet for interest in public activities • I blame it on evil companions of teen age days • wrote column in high school • heard of columns' popularity in other papers • lends individuality to paper • began columning in fourth grade • bought a newspaper • needed a galley more to fill front page.

Just had to . . . the urge was wearing me down • to satisfy readers • my family grew up and I sighed for other worlds to conquer • seemed a good place to express one's self • it was an impulse during vacation • writing to boys in World War II • only thing in newspapering I hadn't done by 1931 • just wanted to write • orders of editor • propositioned by editor.

Effort to segregate personality from other departments of paper • editor said needed column and looked at me • my ambition since early childhood • following anonymous letters to editor • birth of late baby made me ill, started column to kill time • because I don't go for editorials • for five years enclosed private column in weekly letter to shut-in father; it became newspaper column • substitute for profound editorial stuff • because of heart trouble, which made me quit sheriffing • as substitute for long-winded editorials • as hobby • public demands a column, so I write it.

### COLUMNISTS ARE PEOPLE

To support the declaration that *columnists are people,* here are some of the replies to the query, *What are your hobbies?*

Making doll clothes • gardening • really good music • a certain kind of housekeeping • modernizing newspaper office • African violets • athletics • porch-sitting • flower arranging • planning trips I never can afford • photography • ventriloquism • barbershop quartet singing • making doll cradles • sing in gospel quartet.

Collecting cook books • doing good deed each day • helping three children to voting age • sewing • flowers • folks • North and South American history • organizing new groups • American Indians in my counties • piano by ear • some arithmetic • sitting by streams • handwork decorating • jazz music and cooking.

### HOW IOWA'S COLUMNS ARE EVALUATED

A continuing study of columns is being made by the Press Columnists of Iowa. This is being done by a weekly reading of the columns of the state at the

Mother knows her little boy is growing up when she finds the Charles Atlas coupon torn from his comic book. — Mona E. Kissinger, Junction City (Kan.) Republic.

office of John M. Henry, secretary of the association, at Des Moines. From this study a clip-sheet is made up, including thirty excerpts from as many columns, as a part of the Monthly Bulletin sent to all Iowa columnists. Three times a year further studies are made at forums. The spring forum is at Iowa State College; a second is at the State University of Iowa; the third is at Drake University in Des Moines.

All forums are the essence of simplicity. At each meeting there are two discussions, one on materials and the other on methods. A past president of the association presides at each, with at least ten columnists on the panels. Audience participation is emphasized. By a session's end each columnist has had an opportunity to speak.

The materials used in Iowa columns and the methods of presentation probably differ little from materials and methods of columnists in other states, so the continuing study in Iowa is in effect an examination of columns of all the states. As a matter of fact, spot checks made by the author of this chapter, in his reading and editing of column material for his "Main Street" column in *Cosmopolitan,* showed the materials and methods of the country's columns parallel those of Iowa closely.

. . . subjects extend from philosophy to upkeep of farm-to-market roads.

The Iowa materials, naturally, are of a range as wide as the writers' interests. This means, of course, that subjects extend from those topics which are of universal interest, such as the home, personal philosophy, kids, man-and-woman, and friends, to those areas of state or local significance, such as corn-affecting weather, upkeep of farm-to-market roads, and the school situation.

The clip-sheet from the sec-

retary's office has been issued for the last four years, and is edited by his secretary, Miss Betty Adelman. It is intentionally made a cross-section of the columns — the excellent, the fair; the serious, the frivolous; the humorous, the few pessimistic; the pleasant, the sarcastic. What it does not contain is material of an entirely local interest — the plea for paving of Cross Street, the whoopla for the high school athletic teams. It might well contain this, because what it would clip from any one paper would be representative in this field for all the others. But the clip-sheet tries to include only those quotes which logically can be reprinted by other columns in the state, and to this end it does not use excerpts of local interest only.

There are said to be only seven original jokes, and all but one of them go clear back to Adam. They can't blame him for the mother-in-law one. — Everett M. Remsberg, Vista (Calif.) **Press.**

The methods of handling the material also are numerous. They extend from the hortatory in which the reader is urged to drive carefully, to vote at the general election, to support the hospital bond election, on to the incongruous comment, used usually "just to get a laugh" but which can be very effective in putting across an editorial point by ridicule.

Professor L. N. Flint of the University of Kansas, whose booklet, "Paragraphing, The Sprightly Art," written in 1920, has been the bible of most students of columns — especially those earning quotes — developed some twenty classifications of treatment of column material. In Iowa, these twenty types are used nearly every week, as they are in other states.

But in Iowa, as in other states, some styles of writing have developed which defy classification. A typical columnist, questioned about his style and method, will laugh and say, "Oh, it seemed a good idea at the time to write it that way."

Perhaps it should be emphasized parenthetically that Iowa columnists, for all their organized study of their weekly output, pretend to be casual about their writing. They insist that they just sit down and spread their elbows and write whatever comes to mind. And probably that really is the way they do it. Actually, however, they do give a lot of thought, at odd moments, to what they are going to write, and how they will express it. So, when they do sit down and spread elbows they are pretty well prepared.

. . . they do give thought, at odd moments, to what they are going to write . . .

# 20.

# In Conclusion

Wʀɪᴛɪɴɢ the small newspaper's personal columns has become a serious but pleasant business. The hobby stage of columning has passed. The exceptional readership and unmistakable influence of the medium have been generally recognized. A trend toward column essays of greater literary merit is well defined.

... local columns are not preferred by ALL publishers.

The columnists themselves testify that they derive much entertainment from their efforts to amuse others. They appreciate the greater community stature they attain by becoming popular writers. For some of them columning represents the best minutes they give to their papers at the typewriter.

Many of the small-city and town editors and reporters do not write columns, of course. Some of them prefer the less-demanding brief editorials of opinion. A few of them have a hostile attitude toward all columns, including the home-grown variety, for various reasons. In some regional and state press associations the subject has reached the stage of warm debate. It is a timely topic because, as Professor Thomas Barnhart of the University of Minnesota has stressed in recent speeches, "As to whether personal columns may replace editorials eventually, the answer is that it is not just a possibility, nor a probability, but an established trend."

The growing popularity of the column is not universal, of course. Some editors feel a distaste for it. These include some who do not like to write editorials, either, but do, and others who do not like to be spotlighted by an actual or implied by-line. Other criticisms of the column are (1) that it is too light to express institutional policy, (2) that it lowers the dignity of an editor and impairs his community standing, (3) that it is either too easy to write or, if well done, too consuming of time, (4) that it requires a literary rather than a journalistic style, and (5) that columns by non-staff members weaken editorial authority. Also, the critics damn the column as a device because so many poor ones are seen.

The sometimes unstated fear is, also, that the traditional editorial essay will seem pallid in comparison with the lively personal column.

Column enthusiasts point out that good columns and good editorials do exist in the same — good — papers; and certainly editorials are not improved by omitting columns. The two departments can be complementary. And use of column techniques in signed editorials might enliven a page which also can be converted into a device for backgrounding the news with not only opinion, but features, cartoons, etc. One thing is clear: editorial responsibility must be somehow bolstered. The editorial writer now finds himself rivalled not only by the local and national columnists, but also by the by-lined interpretative reporter.

Every editor must choose the literary forms which he thinks can best do the whole job and also merit

A good wife can do most anything for a man except put his hat on just right.—Loyd Burns, Toledo (Iowa) Chronicle.

the press freedom he exercises. As an editor he recognizes his responsibility to weigh facts, interpret the news, and express opinions on what events mean to his community. Small papers are demonstrating that the editor's personal column can do the whole task or, supplementing the editorials, can amuse, promote, and serve. It is not our purpose here to debate the position of the editorial, but to record and examine the evolving patterns of the newspaper columns.

The case for the personal column includes the following points:

1. High readership — rarely exceeded.

2. Strong influence; effective in results.

3. Well suited to use by a writer of many contacts and a variety of duties.

4. The column humanizes an editor and restores personal journalism.

5. It is pleasing and flexible in typography and position, although as a continuing feature it should run on the same page each week.

6. It carries material not usable elsewhere.

7. It supplies a change-of-pace and entertainment as an antidote to dullness.

8. It is a good instrument in combating competition.

9. It encourages reader responses and contributions.

10. It has the strongest emotional appeal possible in a continuing feature.

11. It can set the tone of community thinking and so become an instrument of leadership in thought and action.

12. It develops creative ability in thinking and writing.

13. It combats Afghanistanism — that tendency to pontificate on remote subjects — and gobbledygook, that habit of obscuring thought in vague and "fine" writing.

14. It builds the popularity of the columnist as a person and thereby opens new avenues of usefulness and influence.

Let's profit by the mistakes of others. We may not live long enough to make them ourselves. — Mason City (Ill.) **Banner Times.**

15. It improves community attitudes and conditions the people for the reception of new ideas and for reactions in crises by using the twin tools, high readership and a man-to-man frankness in discussing local problems. Other points might be mentioned, but the above list includes most of them in a general way.

The personal column imposes two important imperatives: (1) the necessity for writing it every day or every week, and (2) individual responsibility as its conductor. The first of these may not seem important, but the fact is that many town and small-city editors do not write editorials, others write them only occasionally, and some merely reprint editorials from exchanges. The second imperative may be considered in connection with the relative anonymity of the editorial "we." Men who would shrink from writing an indifferent column do not hesitate to turn out inadequate editorials of opinion — with few facts or evidences of reasoning. While a brilliant essay can stand on its merits, the use of "we" and "this newspaper" and other non-individual terms by small newspapers offers few challenges.

The small boy's lament: "If I'm noisy they spank me. If I'm quiet they take my temperature!" — Jim Cornwall, Stanton (Neb.) **Register.**

On this subject Carl R. Kesler wrote as follows in *The Quill*:

It is easy to dismiss the editorial "we" as a convention which offers no real handicap to the thinker behind it. But it can be a handicap, not to thought itself, but to communication of thought. It can rule out use of the personal experience, of the hopes and fears and tastes of the individual human being that do so much to translate his thought into words and phrases that will reach the minds and hearts of other men.

The first person writer, if he chooses to use it, has complete flexibility of expression. If a special bit of knowledge or a personal anecdote or even a frankly admitted prejudice or dislike will help point up his theme, he has "I" and "me" to convey it to his readers. If he is worth his salt, the anonymous editorial writer also thinks as an individual, but too often he can avail himself of his individual experiences only by circuitous rhetoric. . . . The impersonal, institutional approach forces the editorial writer to write didactically. It permits him few "ifs" or "buts" about an issue. Senator Jones is right . . . How this piece of legislation is wrong . . . we cannot allow this or condone that. This type of argument is not effective between individuals and I sometimes wonder how effective it is between newspaper and reader. When you try to make a point in ordinary conversation, you are likely to make allowance for the other fellow's ideas while advancing your own.

The personal column is of course conversational in method. And in small communities its conductor is so generally known that the "I" prevails in essence even when the writer avoids it. But the columnist has such a flexible instrument that he can fill the space without scolding, quarreling, or explaining events already detailed in news stories. And most any editor, worried with shortages and costs, is likely to be saner for having to spend a little time each week philosophizing and pondering on the smaller satisfactions of life. Otherwise, he may take his role much too seriously. And an editor who regularly attempts to create something amusing or stimulating will have the help and advice of others of like mind in his community. Such a meeting of minds at several levels of wit, humor, and seriousness is readily possible through the personal column.

In his attempts to influence public opinion the columnist may be blunt, moderate, or subtle. Some writings which seem mainly to provide light entertainment include well-directed policy statements which reach more people than would a serious essay. For, like modern educators in general, the columnist tries to interest as well as to inform, to inspire as well as to instruct. It is important that a serious subject be presented by an interesting person. And the reader goes to the column in the expectation that it will speak to him, or about him. It is this localization, as well as a light touch, which accounts for high readership.

As we interpret the teen-agers, the perfect match would be between "Whatta Guy!" and "Some gal!"—Pineville (W.Va.) **Independent-Herald.**

A meeting of minds at several levels is readily possible . . .

A letter to the authors from Miss Elinor V. Cogswell, editor of the Palo Alto (Calif.) *Times,* is pertinent:

My column materials fall into four main categories.

1. Matters I get steamed up about, chiefly local.

2. Civic projects, political issues, municipal business which the general reader passes up as dull. These I try to slide into with anecdotes and a light touch, hoping to trap readers who would otherwise not inform themselves. It was to do this sort of thing that I started my "Editor at Bat" column.

3. Palo Alto and area history. Columns dealing with landmarks, picturesque characters of early days, traditions, and backgrounds interest me very much and seem to have good readership.

4. Tripe to fill. Letters, anecdotes, angles. After all, the column must come out.

Some days the news developments make certain discussions almost mandatory. Other times, we work for weeks on angles before something finally jells. When I really have an idea, I brood over my approach and sometimes rewrite the lead a dozen times. After that it goes fast, as a rule. Once I've gotten into a topic I write with some excitement and considerable pleasure. . . . The column is a more congenial medium than the formal editorials, which must be an expression of a group opinion or group policy, and which must be presented with dignity. Dignity is often stuffy. In my own column I can often send up trial balloons, strike a glancing blow, smoke something out.

Miss Cogwell's letter keynotes many of the principles and practices which the authors believe form the basic pattern of small-newspaper columning. She is an editor. When the writers are staff members or contributors, the materials are likely to be more specialized, or written in such a manner that institutional policy is not contradicted. The personal column maintains its appeal regardless of whether the writer is editor, preacher, teacher, farmer, or housewife.

To summarize: the future of the editor's personal column and other local columns looks bright, indeed.

Well, you still can use a dime for a screw-driver. — L. S. McCandless, Craig (Colo.) **Empire-Courier.**

The hometown column has proved its ability to get and to hold circulation. On many papers it has brought a resurgence of editorial influence. It offers much promise in the field of creative writing. It promises a sharing experience in that editors can in it regularly report their brightest thoughts and experiences, while permitting readers to enrich the space with theirs.

In small towns and cities, people live more through their emotions — loves, hates, enthusiasms, sympathies — than through abstract ideas. Daily, as they move out upon the community scene, they find nature alive, folks alive, business alive, young people abubble with energy and interests. It is a scene in which people are cheerful and full of laughing; and some grieve. Death is not a statistic when the dead is a friend.

It must follow, then, that local newspapers, which best mirror these scenes, should be similarly alive and throbbing with the spirit of people. Names make news, surely, but names pick up personality, movement, glamour, and excitement when clothed in the column techniques of suspense, quotation, anecdote, biography, light essay, verse, and witty paragraphs.

The personal column carries a high-voltage impact when well used. And more and more small-newspaper writers are learning to use it effectively. Both they and their readers are enjoying the experience of thinking and laughing and acting together. In some states the columnists are organizing to meet and study their art and methods.

Meanwhile, the difference between the unplanned and unimaginative columns and the better ones is startlingly great.

That is the challenge.

*Appendix*

# Selected Columns

## Pregnancy Contest

**By Nelson Brown**
**Mason (Mich.) Ingham County News**

Final returns in the Presbyterian pregnancy contest came in last Wednesday. The score was 7-0 in favor of the girls. Four months ago the Rev. and Mrs. Marshall Simpson invited six deacons and their wives to a party at the manse. All six of the wives, seven including the preacher's, were expecting. The Rollin Darts, the Ed Murrays, the Marvin Lotts, the Harold Hosleys, the Bob Inghrams, and the Simpsons, all six couples, had girls. Odds then climbed to six to one that the Dick Browns would have a boy. But they didn't. Nancy Joan arrived to make it seven girls from the seven sets of parents at the party.

The demand is growing that all seven girls be baptized at one time. It's a good idea, I think, and as one of Nancy's grandfathers I have given my consent.

Those who have seen the seven little girls are hoping that the deacons' party at the manse will be made an annual event.

There were six, not seven, vestal virgins. Vesta was the Roman goddess of the hearth. The Romans kept a sacred fire burning on her altar at the foot of the Palatine Hill. Four priestesses of Vesta, later six, were known as vestals or vestal virgins. They had charge of the sacred fire. Daughters of noble families sought the positions, which carried the perquisites of the choicest seats at the games in the arena. The virgins served for thirty years — ten to learn the duties of the temple, ten to perform them, and ten more to teach them to others. At the end of thirty years a vestal was free to return to her father's house, or even to marry. The fall of a vestal from virtue was regarded as the most shocking of crimes and was punished with death by stoning, or burial alive.

Although the signs read that only fathers and grandmothers are permitted to visit the nursery at St.

Lawrence hospital, I had a look at the new granddaughter there. The guardian of the portals let me in as a grandmother. It was a great sight — row upon row of little baskets containing newborn of all sizes, shapes, and colors. It's a mystery how the nurses keep the youngsters and their mothers straight — if they do.

A hospital door is an ideal vantage point for viewing human nature. For a half-hour while waiting for others in the party to come down I stood outside the exit. Some people would come out bubbling over with joy and high spirits. Probably they had been on the third floor to see the new mother and the new grandchild. Others would come dragging out the door, their faces showing gloom and worry. They hadn't been welcoming new members of the family. They had been watching some loved one getting ready to depart.

The saddest sight of all was that of a young couple who came out the door, the woman sobbing and the husband carrying a pair of baby shoes — about the size of a two-year-old boy. Was the youngster sick with some dread disease? Had he been run down in an accident? If the occurrence had been in a small town I could have learned of the tragedy. I could have shared in the grief. But in a big city like Lansing is getting to be, sharing of burdens is hard to handle.

*    *    *

Saturday afternoon I stopped at Palmer's orchard down towards Leslie to buy muskmelons. I parked behind a car with an Alabama license. Two young men from Alabama were stopping to see sights that Michigan tourist literature seldom mentions. The Alabama youths were walking through the orchard, marveling at the trees borne down with gorgeous fruit. They had never seen a sight so pretty, they said. They rated the unexpected view of the apple orchard as high on Michigan's lure list as the sight of the Great Lakes, the Soo locks, and Greenfield Village.

*    *    *

Girls away from army and navy installations have to get their men between wars. The way young men are being shifted around in World War Two-and-a-half is going to make for another crop of out-of-state sons-in-law and daughters-in-law.

It was just getting so that local couples were once again reaching the altar when the new emergency arose. There's a flurry right now to those strictly local weddings; but it won't last. Soon boy will meet girl in San Antonio, New York, or San Francisco, and she'll remind him so much of a girl back home that he won't be able to wait to get home.

War romances work out just about as well as the others. Maybe because one set of in-laws, at least, is a long ways off.

*    *    *

Thanks to Richard Whitmyer of Okemos for selling a sound Kalamazoo wood and coal range so cheap and for helping load it. And thanks to Al Rice for the loan of his truck, Frank Rathburn for the loan of his stove trucks, and to Russ Huntington, Claude Cady and Dick Brown for helping unload the range, and then to Russ again, along with Jack Shaffer and Ted Hall for moving out the old range and getting the new one in and set up. Finally, to Bert Royston for his carpenter work and getting the stovepipe in place. That appeal in the *Ingham County News* last week resulted in four offers of ranges for the Mason widow.

# *The* 5:15

**By Gene V. Davis**
**Boonville (Mo.)** *News*

The 5:15 bus lumbers to a stop at the Main Street corner, and its doors jerk open. The group waiting huddled against the wind turn eagerly and clamber aboard. Friendly greetings are exchanged with those already seated. The doors bang shut. The driver shifts into low and the bus moves off. The downtown gang is going home to supper.

The bus has seen its best days. It is drab and gray with the winter's grime. The windows need washing. Here and there in the cracked leather of the seats are gaping holes where little fingers have pried and turned and twisted. The floor is littered with cigaret stubs, chewing gum, and candy wrappers. But it is a homey place.

The girl clerk settles back in her seat with a sigh and wriggles her feet out of her slippers. A busy day and a long one. She wonders what Mother will have to eat. Lucky she caught the 5:15; this way she'll have time for a bath before supper.

The old man leans forward to rest his chin upon clasped hands grasping his cane. Everyone on the bus knows him, but the old man knows no one. His sight is failing and his memory is tricky. The years have been so many. How can he guess that the chic young woman across the aisle is the little tomboy who used to climb his apple trees? Faces come and go, familiar, strange, blurred. He stares at the floor. Once he would have scorned riding this short distance home. He would have taken the blocks in quick, free stride, his carpenter's tool-box light on his shoulder, his bright saw swinging from his hand, his lips pursed in a whistle. Ah, me. Time.

The professional man, expensively coated, hatted, gloved, smiling and urbane, sits a little stiffly in the midst of this easy-going crowd of small-town neighbors. He left his automobile at home today for his wife to use.

The little girl has been to take her music lesson. Not too crazy about it, either. Same old piece again next time, and she is tired to death of all this "one-and, two-and, three-a-a-nd, four" stuff. But this is fun, looking through the big windows at the familiar streets, riding in a great room where one may walk about, where one sways thrillingly at street corners, and like as not sits down on the floor unexpectedly at stops and starts.

The little boy is concerned with the mechanism of the bus. He has made friends with the driver and watches enviously as the long-handled lever is shifted back and forth. His bright eyes observe the ways the doors swing open and shut at a touch. The grinding of the engine on the hills is music to his ears. His small hands tremble as the steering wheel is whirled to bring the big bus laboriously around a sharp curve. When he grows up, he'll be a bus driver — yes sir, that's what he'll be.

The merchant is glad that the day is done and he is returning to his home and family. He chats with his seatmate, a long-time customer and friend. Both like the bus. No strain of driving, no parking problems, they agree; relaxation for a dime.

The woman shopper props her bundles on the seat beside her and goes over in her mind a quick menu for the evening meal. She had to hurry to make the 5:15 but she will be home in time to bake biscuits for supper if she doesn't stop to change her dress.

The bus rattles along. The driver, with accommodating informality, lets the children out right at their homes so that they need not cross an intersection, and stops in the middle of the block for the old man to back slowly down the steps and out. Chatter flares and dies. A little child laughs. Now and then the sides of the bus quiver as if in appreciation of a passenger's joke, or in amusement at the little girl's latest tumble into the aisle. It rumbles to a stop to let a mother out and stands patiently, vibrating with interest, while she greets a teen-ager who has come up to board the bus.

"Darling, where are you going?" . . . "Play practice, school, Mom. Left note on kitchen table. Back on 9:20. Havetohurry. Don't worry. Bye!"

The bus gathers the youngsters in and waddles off like an old mother hen, clucking contentedly. Part of the life of the town is in it. Busily binding the people, the homes together — the 5:15 p.m. bus.

## Indian Summer

### By Duane Dewel
### Algona (Iowa) *Advance*

It's grand just to be alive in Iowa in autumn, when the trees turn to glory colors, and the dry corn whispers in the wind.

— Where the trees are content with their summer's work — and stretch branches high to meet the oncoming snows and the cold winter wind — where the brown and black earth turned by the plow waits peacefully for the work of the weather to prepare it again for fruitfulness.

— Where the sky is a soft blue, haze filled, as soft-looking as a featherbed — and as deep as the ocean — pleading perhaps for man to look into its depths and dream a bit — to build air castles — to contemplate — and to find again a sense of well-being.

Brown leaves covering the hillsides along the rivers and ponds, returning to the earth to supply the roots with food with which new leaves will spread forth when the springtime comes again.

Sheltered trees here and there proudly bearing a riot of color in the midst of neighbors who have shed the summer's coat — shrubs, still green in the low spots, flamboyant against the dull browns and russets of those who went before — perhaps unnoticeable in summer, yet standing out brilliantly against otherwise drab surroundings.

Busy squirrels scampering among the leaves, planting walnuts against the winter's need, their bushy tails waving as they race for a tree, there to scold whomever halts their important work.

The blueness that spreads over the land from the burning of leaves and cornstalks, and the fall smells that gain tang and zest from the tinge of smoke in the air.

White chickens, startling in contrast against the dull grasses, spreading in ripples from the barnyards to the fields — cattle and horses in the fields searching quietly and purposely for the last remaining food of summer.

The placidly flowing river, bearing leaves tenderly downstream, here and there laughingly racing them over the rapids — then settling soberly to work again in steady progress toward a greater river, there to lend its mite toward the tide that ceaselessly flows to the sea.

The sun, warmer by contrast in the fall — its rays feeling antiseptic as mankind turns as if on a spit to bask in effortless comfort and gaze moodily into the distance as Nature waits for a moment in contemplation of a summer well done before plunging into the fury of winter's retort to be born again.

Cottony silver fluff floating high in the air — thin strands of spiderwebs glistening in the sunlight — letting the wind bear them where it will — secure in the knowledge that in this happy land few seeds fall on barren soil.

Jackrabbits loping easily across the plowing, ears up and nose questing the breeze — occasionally bounding high from sheer happiness.

The noisy tractor, seemingly subdued, as it pulls the pickers through the cornfields, rustling the stalks into yielding wagon-loads of golden corn to bulge the bins — and the harvesters roll through the rows of soybeans rattling the seed in a rippling flow of yellow and brown into wagons and bins.

Ducks anxiously and warily circling and circling a slough in distrust of hidden dangers — or streaming dark streaks in the brilliant sky in the mornings and evenings as they leave their shelter for food or to take off again in their instinctive flight to the Southland.

Noisy sparrows and starlings taking nature's spotlight as their more beautiful cousins have departed — busily dry-bathing in the dust, chirping carelessly — flying races with each other — impudent in their contempt for feeble earth-bound men.

Dogs sleeping relaxed in the sun or busily nose-down practicing for ecstacy when they too can mark the fall of a bird to be borne back proudly, meltingly brown eyes shining, for a pat on the head.

The tans of the corn against the black plowed earth — the shocked corn in stately rows marching up and down the rolling fields — the green where the ungleaned seeds performed their duty and sprang to life — smoke rising straight up from the chimneys — white houses and red barns left naked and unashamed — glistening through the groves.

The ruddy moon turning to brilliant silvery white as it rises — dimming the stars around it — turning shadows into havens of friendly mystery.

It's grand to be alive in such a world — to be content — to let the troubles of mankind slip away for but a short time — to give balm to the mind troubled with man-made worries.

For it seems in the fall Nature turns with reassurance of a coming Spring, the ageless promise that "God's in His heaven, all's right with the world."

## *Father's Day*

### By Giles L. French
### Moro (Ore.) *Sherman County Journal*

It is not appropriate that a father should remark on the day set aside by enterprising necktie salesmen for his benefit, nor make statements regarding the cost thereof. Father's day is a pleasant notion, intended, aside from the commercial aspects thereof, to pay respect for the so-called head of the family. We are sure that in most cases the sergeant who was officer for a day behaved in a manner that did not bring down the ire of the real family ruler. He was appreciative of the kiss on his bald spot, the decorated necktie, and the cake he knew he shouldn't eat. Fathers, by the time they have become available for family celebrations, should know how to accept attention for a day.

* * *

Cattle over the counties of Oregon look fine this spring and fears that the cold weather might have hampered the growth of grass were useless.

This is the time of year when Americans in great droves pack up their old clothes, their credit cards, their year's savings, their children and with the family auto keyed to a high speed take off across the continent to see how many miles they can drive in a day.

There's lots to see in America, even in Oregon, which is but one state. Oregon is perhaps as diversified as to scenery as any state and the traveler can find mountains, seacoast, range land, wheat fields, row crops, irrigated lands, forests, and cities all in a day's travel. Oregon pays little attention to all this moving population. Its inhabitants sell few colored post cards, erect few cabins, have few entertainment places designed to snare the vagrant dollar. We take 'em in stride and are not much given to commercializing on them.

\* \* \*

It seems odd that a nation can produce so much and still work but a few hours per week. Would it be possible to pay off the national debt if we put in forty hours per week instead of the thirty-five or so that is average for many workers.

\* \* \*

This column can't help but feel sorry for those who have to go to the government for their living. This doesn't only include those who work for the government; it takes in the groups that must rely on some government bureau for their rate structure, and may take in the farmers. Sometimes they have asked for the protection (years ago) but it always pinches in the long run.

\* \* \*

A fine degree of citizenship was demonstrated at the school meeting in Moro Monday night when representatives from Moro, Wasco, Kent, and Grass Valley talked over their common problems and arrived at a decision without bitterness, heated argument, or rancor. School meetings in which no one raises his voice or waves his arms are few. That is, if there are real problems to decide, which there were.

\* \* \*

If those striking bakers stay out until the lady of the house learns to bake real bread the strike will be lost. We'll bet there're some happy husbands over it already.

\* \* \*

Doctors are getting pretty good at taking the good working parts of the human anatomy and using them in a different chassis. It may get to be quite a business and we can all get funeral expenses out of our spare parts when the end of coordinated operation comes. The insurance companies will probably chisel in and demand their share, however.

# Getting Along With a Wife

### By Justin Hammond
### Corona (Calif.) *Daily Independent*

How to get along with your wife! That's what we are going to write about today. Ahem!

First of all, to get along with your wife, you must give up any ideas you may have about living your own life. It makes it easier that way. Always be cheerful. When she says, "On your way to the grocery store pick up a spool of red thread for me and then mow the lawn, clip the hedge, put the patio furniture away, burn the papers, empty the garbage, bring the clothes in off the line, and dry the dishes" — smile! And get busy.

\* \* \*

Always be considerate. If you both like white meat, learn to eat the drumsticks. If she likes to sit in the back row at the movies and you can't see unless you are in the fourth, sit in the back row. You can still enjoy the popcorn.

\* \* \*

In the car, don't open the windows. You know how it blows her hair. You may feel as though you're suffocating, but you won't. I don't think.

\* \* \*

Don't bother her with details. She'll never finish that dress if you keep asking her to sew on buttons. It doesn't take more than half an hour for a handy man to thread a needle.

\* \* \*

If you want more gravy, get up and get it, you dope. She's been on her feet all day and they're killing her. Never bother a woman whose feet are killing her. And for heaven's sake don't make any crack about wearing more sensible shoes.

\* \* \*

Be attentive. A woman appreciates little things like your giving her your pay check.

\* \* \*

Be generous. Let her have the car. It won't kill you to walk to work or to the grocery or to the post office. And be sure you keep it filled with gas. You know how she hates to waste time around a smelly old filling station.

\* \* \*

Don't grumble when she has the girls in for bridge. It's her house after all, isn't it! You can always go back to the office or sit in the bedroom. If you're lucky there may even be a piece of cake left for you.

\* \* \*

Don't laugh at her hats. If she wears a postage stamp and a feather, tell her it's *tres chic.*

\* \* \*

Under this system, don't expect to have any time of your own — or any fun. But that's how to get along with your wife.

# H-Bomb

**By Mrs. Leslie K. Hull**
**Waukon (Iowa) *Republican-Standard***

Every time I sit down to this faithful old word-machine and try to write something about the H-bomb, the trusty old thing balks. . . . It doesn't clatter cheerfully, willingly, or at all. . . . It seems to sulk.

\* \* \*

I look into its Royal face, not long since polished and renewed after a long stretch of disrepair and hard use. I try to find the answer there, as I have found so many answers in the past. Because I often sit down to the typewriter with my problems, and find them solving themselves as I put them into words, phrases, sentences, orderly paragraphs.

\* \* \*

"I've served you faithfully," the old key-and-ribbon device says placidly. "I've seen you through sickness and health, trouble, bereavement, unhappiness, and suffering. Your tears have often fallen on me, and I have set down your inmost, secret thoughts. I have recorded your most joyful news and your happiest moments. I have seen you through a depression and a war, uncertainty and security. I have written down your letters to those you love most dearly, and I have recorded your business transactions. I have dealt with a volume of correspondence, some of it destined for far-off places.

\* \* \*

"Remember the letters you wrote to your father? Don't you recall the ones that went to Oak Ridge during the war? Have you forgotten the notes that went to training camps in many places and finally followed a certain lad to Europe? I've been a faithful servant, but now I don't know how to serve you."

\* \* \*

(Remember, it's my typewriter that's soliloquizing like this. I didn't know she had in her to be so grandiose, so searching, so dramatic. I thought she laughed at me sometimes for my flights of fancy, my tears, my sudden delights. I thought she'd never, never let me down.)

\* \* \*

Oak Ridge. . . . Hanford. . . . Bikini Atoll . . . Hiroshima . . . New Mexico . . . "Show your pass." . . . "Get along, please; where's your identification paper?" . . . Confidential papers; burn all contents of this wastebasket. . . . Wonder what's doing in that laboratory? . . . Where did Officer X go? We never see him any more. Heard he was on some secret mission. . . . Wonder if Russia has the bomb?

\* \* \*

Smythe report. . . . Lilienthal. . . . Hickenlooper. . . . Heavy water. . . . Hydrogen. . . . Uranium. . . . How much do you know about physics, anyway? What's an atom? . . . How can anything be split if it can't be seen? . . . Who's got the biggest rock to throw now? Wonder if it's safe to offend Mr. Neanderthal today; looks like he has run out of jagged stones by this time.

\* \* \*

Peace, it's wonderful. . . . All men are brothers and the world is one union. . . . Tommy won't eat his five-dollar vitamin pills. . . . My child is dead because it starved to death; starved, I tell you, because it never had enough to eat, never, never, never. And I'm dying too, because I'm hungry and I'll never be fed. . . .

United Nations. . . . Peace parleys. . . . Cold war. . . . Shooting war. . . . War by innuendo. . . . Hands-around-the-world. . . . Send your old shoes to the suffering. . . . Give Grandpa's old underwear to the underprivileged. . . . This man is your brother and you are his keeper. . . . (But does Russia have a bigger bomb than we do?)

\* \* \*

Back to normal. . . . Buy a new washing machine. . . . Build a new house. . . . Help Europe recover by touring over her scars in the deluxe wagon-lits. . . . Wear a dress from Paris. . . . Sprinkle the essence of the Riviera in your hair. . . . Dream among the lilacs when spring comes to Shakespeare's Avon. . . . (But wouldn't hydrogen atoms split into deadlier fissions than uranium's?)

\* \* \*

So this is what it is like to die. . . . This is the end of time and space and the coherence of atoms that were my body and my personality. . . . This is what it is like to be one of the 50 thousand, or was it 50 million, that could die under one bomb's blow. . . . The stars are reeling in their courses. The world is off its track. . . . The sun has exploded. . . . The universe has come to an end, a scientist's end, born of hate and bred of governments, suspicions of each other.

\* \* \*

Perhaps this is a thousand Hiroshimas in one blast. . . . The end of hate and the fiction called peace. . . . But whose bomb did it? Was ours the biggest? Were we first? . . . There isn't time to figure that out now because time is over and space is finished. . . . And the houses of government. . . . And the palaces dedicated to peace palavers. . . . This is all. This is an atom's work. . . . Well done.

\* \* \*

"I didn't mean to put it down," says the old typewriter. "Those words are ugly. They are frightening. They are the most daring words you've ever put through a ribbon of mine, and I wish they were unsaid. I wish they had never had to be set down in black and white. They should have been written in flames. . . . Or fissionable atoms, perhaps.

\* \* \*

"But what do you, or I, know about atoms, for all your reading the Smythe report and all those complicated new physics books? You shouldn't try to tell people about such matters; you're too uninformed. After all, you've never seen an atom bomb explode. . . . You've had nothing to do with the whole business; your hands are clean. I guess. . . Of course you always go and vote. . . . You help put people in office. . . . You have opinions. . . . You voice them (although you couldn't, so well, without me) . . . .

\* \* \*

"I'm afraid. . . . And, unlike a human being, who often thinks he must be proud and hide his feelings, I, your faithful old typewriter, don't mind saying so. . . . There's no place to hide any more. . . . No place at all. . . . And the stars in their courses, the universe in its place, at hazard — all . . . . You did say that, didn't you? I wish I didn't remember. . . . I wish I could forget. . . ."

# Melancholy Mood

**By Barney Marshall**
**Webster Groves (Mo.) *News-Times***

This week you will pardon me, please, if I don't sound like I had just come out of the carnival funhouse. This has been one of those weeks when everything goes wrong; and I just don't feel good. It isn't anything I can put my finger on, or anything that has happened to me alone.

Why, tonight's paper alone carried more stories of thwarted plans, disillusionment, and inconvenience than you would normally read about in a week. A burglar shot himself while staging a robbery, a man got caught stealing benches to provide seating facilities for watchers of his TV set, another had to shoot at some recalcitrant rogues who parked their car in front of him and cut off the breeze, one city's entire police force got fired simply because they had looted the city's parking meters, and one poor fellow had to give up his false teeth to his wife in a divorce action.

See what I mean? It's something big, and it's all over the place.

\* \* \*

Then there's that poor Mr. Erickson, up in New York. Three nasty old judges have gone and sentenced him to two years in prison and fined him $30,000. Why, the poor fellow will probably have to go through a couple of his desk drawers to raise that kind of dough. And what'll his vast gambling empire do while he is salted away in the city penitentiary? He can't direct operations from there. (Wanna bet?)

Closer to home, a Senate investigating committee is bothering the bejeebers out of an innocent and well-meaning little gangster-political group, stepping on toes all over the place and no apologies offered. This sort of thing can't go on. Why, it's getting so a guy can't conduct a legitimate bookie business, or take political bribes from gangsters, or tamper with ballot boxes anymore. There is one ray of hope, however. In Kansas City a guy can always commit a juicy little murder.

\* \* \*

Another thing is that peace movement Russia is trying to conduct in Korea; and the rest of the world won't leave her alone. Uncle Joe sends his little delegation down there to enlighten the poor people in that cultural and economic outpost, and what happens? Bingo, a big bully way over there in the United States starts limbering up his slingshot and making a batch of threats. What kind of a world is this, anyway?

Ya can't steal benches, ya can't loot parking meters, ya can't take bribes, ya can't conduct book, ya can't wage a little war, without somebody's gotta be buttin' in all the time. I don't feel good. I'm gonna leave the typewriter uncovered tonight and pull the cover over me, instead. Maybe when I finish this column tomorrow I'll feel better.

Yep, two psychiatrists, two sleeping pills, and a couple of alka seltzers later, and with my medals polished and my Eisenhower jacket freshly pressed, I feel better. All this talk about the Webster Groves cavalcade has helped, too.

Boy, that thing's getting big. It started off as just a germ of an idea, and now it's snowballing into the biggest thing ever pulled off in Webster Groves. It begins to look like everybody in town is going to take part in it, and there is more enthusiasm being shown by sponsoring groups than this town has seen in a long time.

I saw a project like this pulled off up in Iowa a few years back, in a town about the size of Webster Groves, and its over-all effect made it the biggest thing that town had ever done. It not only packed about 80,000 people into a stadium the four nights it went on and provided a whopping good show, but it proved to the merchants, the service clubs, civic groups, social organizations — everyone in town — what could be done when everyone worked together.

It looks to me like Webster's pageant ought to be even better than the one those Iowans put on. There are more organized and active groups here than that town had, and I believe there is more interesting history behind the birth and growth of Webster Groves.

I know from experience that by the time you have spent a couple of months in the preparation for a thing of that sort — catching up on the written history of your community, riding up and down the street in an old buggy or auto for publicity, and wearing old-fashioned cloths to create atmosphere — the first thing you know, you've got a project on your hands you're proud to have a part in. And a stunt like that never hurts business, either.

## *It's Great To Be 8*

### By Opal Hollomon Melton
### Boonville (Mo.) Cooper County Record

The librarian reminded our 8-year-old visitor that she could keep the four books she selected two weeks, but the young lady sat Indian fashion and read two that evening. It was no trick to finish off the others the next day and go back for more. She has been a patron of the library during brief summer visits here since she was 2½, and is at home there, a good friend of Mrs. G. A. Russell and Miss Jessie Dedrick. Were she not a bookworm I would know she could be no relative of mine. It is easy to forget the progress children make, and I waved a hand at a bookcase filled with Junior Literary Guild books belonging to our daughter and said, "I'll read them to you." "No, I'll read them to you," she corrected, and she has.

* * *

Oh, to be 8 again, with enthusiasm for everything excepting afternoon naps, having the tangles brushed or combed out of curls, ordering anything but a sandwich when the family eats at a restaurant, and trying on dresses that need altering.

* * *

To be 8 is to be an eager helper when green beans are to be strung. She sorts out all the yellowish ones that have to be hulled, and evolves a method and trics to sell it to an adult. The first bean is firmly ejected by squeezing and then the pod is pulled apart by a small thumb jammed into the space formerly occupied by the bean. "It works most of the time," the 8-year-old observes.

* * *

To be 8 is to have unlimited patience with the cocker pup even when she plants a wet kiss on a snub nose, and carries off small sox and shoes. The 8-year-old thinks to string an empty spool on a heavy cord and make the puppy a new toy. She says, "Oh, give her a little something," whenever the dog begs for food, as if the rest of the family were not too inclined to take the same attitude. She tirelessly parades the pup on a leash, and takes the blame when she pulls loose and goes across the street. She keeps her head, however, and does not dart after her but comes for help, as instructed.

* * *

To be 8 is to yearn to go swimming every day, but to accept gracefully being talked out of it after a reasonable explanation. To insist on wearing favorite dresses and sox, and when refused a request to put on new

white slippers for a morning of play, to have a quick retort, "Well, I'm the dressy type."

* * *

To be 8 is to think most 4-year-olds are pests. It is to want to do whatever the other children are doing, such as going to the matinee or the carnival at the park. It is to be able to eat cotton candy, and peanuts, drink soda pop after a whirl on a ride, then sleep like a cherub and have no serious after-effects.

* * *

To be 8 is to moan and groan one minute over mosquito bites and the next to display them with pride to a child next door.

* * *

To be 8 is to keep promises by compromising. The letter to Mommy and Daddy isn't written on the stationery bought for that purpose, but on a post card borrowed from Uncle. It states, "Hope you are fine. I am fine." The signature and X's for kisses take up the rest of the space with an added group of X's "for Daddy."

* * *

To be 8 is to love grandparents and other relatives enough to help talk Mommy and Daddy into letting you fly alone on the airplane to St. Louis to visit them, and when the person who happens to meet the plane happens to be engrossed in a magazine story and fails to see you arrive, to have the information desk page her over the loud speaker. Then to be bored when well-meaning friends ask about the trip.

* * *

To be 8 is to be an expert with bubble gum, a reader of comic books, a listener to soap operas, a wise shopper for color books and paper doll cutouts. It is being adept at thinking up scrapbook ideas, and a tireless addict of the pastepot. It is being so well behaved in church that grown-ups are hard-pressed to be as quiet.

\* \* \*

To be 8 is to whistle constantly, to tell riddles and jokes, and an endless number of moron stories, such as: "The moron tiptoed past the medicine chest so as not to wake up the sleeping pills." And one cockroach said, "I was in the cleanest house today," and the other exclaimed, "Please, not at the table!"

\* \* \*

To be 8 is to learn the words of all types of songs, and sing them. It is to laugh out loud often and have few troubles. In fact, to 8 is wonderful!

## *Looking at Life*

**By Bernice Brown McCullar**
**Lumpkin (Ga.)** *Stewart-Webster*
*Journal*

LITTLE LIGHTS: I was sitting on the bus, and a man in overalls came in and sat down in the seat in front of me, beside a very well-dressed girl. He tried to talk, but she replied so briefly and discouragingly that he stopped. And I thought of how the words that he offered must have come out of his loneliness, and of how all of us, like him, are lonely, and of how we strike little matches of companionship to light up the loneliness and the dark . . . of how they flare and flicker for a little while, and then go out, leaving the darkness again, and the loneliness still there like an old pain.

\* \* \*

SHORTEST POEM EVER WRITTEN:

Troubles . . .
Adam
Had 'em.

THE AWFUL TRUTH: The trouble with my friends, the dirty dogs, is that they are always telling the truth. Especially my Yankee friends. I would advise you to have nothing to do with Yankees, as Sir Roger de Coverly would advise you to have nothing to do with widows. Yankees have a way of sneaking into your heart when you are not looking, and first thing you know you are fond of them, and there's not much you can do about it. One of them — a newspaper man who stops by my small cottage and eats my dark Rosa's chicken pie and cakes, was here last week. And he said to me, "Why don't you Southerners say what you mean? When you say 'All men are created equal' you ought to change it to 'All white, Protestant, Democratic men are created equal.' " I thought of old George Orwell's devastating remark, "All men are created equal but some are more equal than others." Also, I looked around and saw a lot of signs saying "Colored Entrance." And it moved me to wonder if I and my fellow Southerners would be surprised to see a sign on the celestial habitations reading, "Heaven. Colored Entrance." (That is, of course, providing we get close enough there to read the signs.)

\* \* \*

SUNDAY MORNING SYMPHONY: Didn't have to teach Sunday School Sunday. So I spent the morning in my back yard. Took my coffee and typewriter and the Sunday papers out in the sunshine, and sat under my silver poplar tree. I had just had a new birdhouse built in it, and I thought that would be a good time to interview prospective tenants. (Rent: songs.) But I didn't get much of a chance at it. A sassy-looking red bird, knowing he was beautiful, and arrogant about it, was perched on its porch. He eyed me reflectively, as if considering whether he was going to let me live in the cottage attached to the birdhouse. I got so intimidated that now I am paying *him* rent: crumbs every other day, and a worm a week.

\* \* \*

MEMORY OF A GREAT MAN: I stopped the other day to see again the Little White House where Franklin Roosevelt sometimes got away as a great president could, from the cares of the world, and lived with simplicity. I looked again at the 130 walking sticks there, at the ship models which he built and which people built for him, at the old battered cooking utensils, and the ice box, and the breakfast tray on which he ate a few hours before death struck. And then I went over to spend the night with my friend who runs the hotel there, and who was getting a barbecue ready for him the hour that he died. "We were never really concerned about him as a great President," she said to me. "He was a sick man, and our friend, and we loved him. That was all." And that may have been what he found that was best at Warm Springs.

\* \* \*

MAGIC MOMENT: Have y o u ever noticed the quality of expectancy and wonder and breathlessness that life takes on just that second before you open the mail box? Of course the contents turn out to be prosaic bills and circulars, often. But it could be just anything: news of a new job, a legacy, the engagement of people you love. I come homeward through the dusk at evening to the things I love, and in the box there are letters, sometimes from a little boy grown tall, now in the Air Forces in Alaska, and a sweet-faced girl now a nurse in New York. My children. And beyond the

lonesomeness is the memory of our laughter together in the old far-off years, and of our shared sorrow when the gray shadows of death fell about us, and the fourth one of us went away into the silences. And in their letters are the bright adventures they are having in far places across the earth. . . . I walk into the quiet and empty house. I see the picture of my daughter on the wall. My boy's dog comes to nuzzle me. The loneliness for them envelops me. But I lean upon a great staff of pride that they are doing work they love and do well, and make a contribution to a world that needs it sorely.

\* \* \*

COFFEE: If there is anything on this earth better than a good cup of coffee, I have not found it. I am going to speak to God, when I get to heaven, about swapping some of that milk and honey I am always reading about in the Scriptures, for a good cup of hot coffee.

\* \* \*

THE TALE OF THE MISPRONOUNCED WORD: Did you know that in the 12th chapter of Judges in the Bible there is a story of 42,000 men who were killed because of the way they pronounced a word?

\* \* \*

My favorite trait in human beings: kindness. My unfavorite trait in them: pretense.

\* \* \*

NOTEBOOK STUFF: I like old Thomas Hardy's saying, "Make two lists: one of the things that everybody says and nobody believes, and the other of the things that everybody believes and nobody says."

\* \* \*

WHO ARE YOURS? If you could talk for an hour each to any six people who ever lived, which six would you choose? Mine would be

Socrates, Horace, Sir Thomas More, Sappho, Dante, and Christ.

\* \* \*

MISTAKES: I heard somebody say that the reason we start the history of the novel with old Samuel Richardson, who wrote Pamela, instead of with Defoe, who wrote Robinson Crusoe, is that Defoe made the mistake of not knowing that a novel should be boy-meets-girl. "It was silly of him to have invented Crusoe's Man Friday instead of Woman Wednesday." Yet, as I asked, what about Melville's Moby Dick? Great novel, and no woman.

\* \* \*

MOUNTAIN TOP: Spent a whole year in New York working on a doctorate (don't know whether I want it since I heard somebody say that you could be a p.h.d. and a p.i.l.l. all at the same time) and although I saw cathedrals and heard brilliant lectures on world affairs, and sunburned my tonsils looking at skyscrapers, the high moment of the whole year to me was sitting in a darkened theater listening to Ethel Waters, in the play "The Member of the Wedding," sing an old, old hymn of my childhood, "His eye is on the sparrow, and I know He watches me."

# *In Defense of Attics*

**By Hazel Murphy Sullivan**
**Sun Prairie (Wis.)** *Star-Countryman*

There ought to be a law! About attics, I mean! No house should be without one. I'm not thinking of a stingy cubby-hole under the eaves from which one needs a shoehorn to extricate himself intact, but a gen-

erous allotment of what modern builders call "waste space" with a window from which one can look down on the world and feel superior to the folk who don't have attics. A real attic should have the kind of roof on which the rain plays a pleasant tattoo of needle pricks, and corners dark enough to hide an elf or a fairy, a pirate or an Indian, or even the little girl you used to be.

Sure, it's dusty and cobwebby and musty. These are as much the prerogatives of an honest to goodness attic as the mold on roquefort cheese or the whiskers on a T-bone steak.

No amount of rumpus rooms in the basement will take the place of an attic. You have to descend to a basement. Attics are something to aspire to, to climb for, and should be worth the effort involved.

You can have your i m i t a t i o n k n o t t y - p i n e paneling, and your orange-crate bookcases, and your ruffled curtains. Put them in the rumpus room if you must put them somewhere. As soon as you get them installed, you'll want to show off the transformation, and that means company, and company means order and neatness with the care of one more room in the house added to your chores.

But an attic! Did you ever hear of anyone trying to show off an attic? It's a place of escape. Nobody but a bosom friend ever gets to set foot among the miscellaneous treasures it houses.

There's something fixed and stable and permanent about an attic and its contents that modern apartment-living takes no cognizance of. Persons with attics are likely to be substantial folk. Anchored to an attic, one thinks first and carefully before moving about from place to place.

Attics have time for traditions and

spiritual and physical growth, and accommodate each step in the family development from the first doll and the broken cart right up through the pennants and dance programs to the love letters and wedding picture which so quickly becomes old-fashioned. Where else can the family set up the easel with Uncle Will and his walrus moustache, or properly store the Christmas tree ornaments, or the mail order camera equipment which never worked, or the sea shells and Chinese lanterns, or the first May basket?

Like a brooding hen, the attic puts a protecting wing around the family's follies and foibles. It's also a place to go with discards of the spirit when the heart's too full for comfort. Here one can hide the hurt of a fancied slight or relive last night's dance. It affords an opportunity to read the first love letter in peace and away from prying eyes.

It accommodates itself to changing circumstances. What if you are married and have a home of your own in a swanky, two-by-four apartment where everything folds up and shuts up except the children, and utility is camouflaged to look ornamental? You can try on the costume you played Ariel in and find in the old trunk the prom dress you wore when you were a size 12. The manuscript for the Great American Novel, the diary with its sweet and foolish confidences, the stamp collection, and a half dozen other evidences of outgrown hobbies which captured an adolescent's fancy! They are all here.

Truly, an attic is the one place in an era of cramped living where one can take off the face he meets the world with, and laugh, or cry or dream to his heart's content.

No wonder it takes so long to clean an attic!

# Trip to the City

**By Mrs. Walter C. Stone**
**Camden (N.Y.) *Advance-Journal***

As I have remarked here before, I think a series of good meals would make the Russians into different people in short order. This has been in my mind very strongly since I went to the city to attend a luncheon with Walt, not long ago. Up a little later than usual the night before, preparing the larder for the family during my absence, and then going in heavily for hormone cream, I got up a little earlier than usual to get away in time, and skimped on breakfast, as one often does in such circumstances.

Then, clad in firmly geared nylons, a closely fitted suit, hat, fur scarf, and earrings (and other things that go with them) I said I was ready, and we started off. The morning was lovely; just right for a trip.

But we hadn't gone far when the slight weight of the hat, the pressure of the earrings, hairpins, snugness of the coat, and those nylons, soon became torture. I felt the slight weight of the fur around my neck like the anchor chain of a trans-Atlantic liner. My left eye felt as if a spear had been run through it and left hanging there. Home seemed so dear, and so far off.

I eased all the tight things that I could without taking myself completely apart, and tried to think of summer gardens in bloom.

Arrived in town, we made our way to the hotel where the luncheon was to take place. I wondered how I could live out the rest of the day. I took deep breaths. "I'm getting better and better," I murmured, and wished I felt that way.

In the lobby were the evilest, ugliest, most unattractive people I have ever seen. "That man would murder his own grandmother for the price of a beer," I thought, looking at a gray-haired gentleman reading a paper on a couch.

"As for her," I muttered, watching a pretty young woman, "She thinks she's just it. I wouldn't wear such clothes if you paid me. She must have stolen them off a bargain counter. You couldn't give me her hat."

Oh, my head, and now my tummy. It was all tied in knots, I realized dismally. I felt ill and irritable. Maybe the awful sensation would go away after eating. So I welcomed the call to luncheon. But it seemed we were not to eat for a while yet, not until a certain amount of preliminary greeting and conversing had been taken care of. I gazed across the room at the crisp French rolls on the tables, the inviting glasses of ice water. And now I had to fight off faintness. Through the cold weakness which crept upon me I smiled stiffly, nodded and laughed, and wondered why the pale, dull-looking woman in the mirror across the room from me had my hat on.

I was determined, however, not to give in to the faint which threatened. If you admit you feel faint, there is such a sympathetic flurry of "Here, drink this. Let me take your hat off, take your hair down, undo your skirt, take off your shoes, fan you, etc." that I didn't want to make the announcement if I could avoid it. I still remember the rag-bag that a crowd of sympathetic people turned another fainting victim into. A scare-crow was a mannequin compared to her, she was so disheveled.

The people around me swam in a haze of dullness. I couldn't see why they were laughing at each other's remarks.

Seated at the table at last, I supped tiny sips of ice water, took tiny bits of roll, and tiny spoonfuls of soup. I couldn't take big ones. I was like the famine victims who have to be underfed on decent food, at first, until they can be overfed. The people were still dull.

Suddenly, as the soup and roll hit their mark, I laughed outright at somebody's wisecrack. I was still shaky, but the spear was being withdrawn from my left eye and my clothes didn't hurt any more. After the meat course and a cup of sugar with a little coffee in it (I read that sugar gives you energy) I decided the party was probably one of the best I had ever attended, the people so witty and cordial, and after I had downed the blueberry pie and cheese, and more sugar and coffee, I knew it. Their conversations were intelligent and humorous; they were so well-wishing, and everybody liked everybody else. Most of them had, it seemed, children at home, too, and it was fun discussing them together. I'd love to see all those agreeable, friendly people again, just as soon as possible.

(I ought to send a copy of this to somebody who would see to it that there was a chicken in every Russian pot on Sunday. In no time we'd have Uncle Joe's boys and girls so contented that they'd start being our pen-pals and playing canasta with us by mail.)

## Honest Confession

### By Earl L. Tucker
### Thomasville (Ala.) *Times*

A professor of pediatrics at the University of Minnesota has come up with the discovery that a child isn't a delinquent simply because he throws a single fit or steals a single candy bar. He says a delinquent child is one who keeps on having tantrums or steals a whole flock of candy bars.

Somehow, I can't get startled at the professor's announcement, because I've been knowing it all the time. If petty larceny constitutes delinquency, then I was reared with a bunch of hoodlums and held high office in the ranks of a gang. I wasn't the general, but certainly no general had a more eager lieutenant when a peach orchard or a watermelon or cane patch had to be captured around midnight. Of course, I did all of those things when I was just a mere lad. After I got 21 years old I quit all that foolishness. I got where I didn't care for watermelons.

Perhaps the richest haul ever made by my gang came when I wasn't along and to this day I deplore the fact that I refused to join the expedition. Douglas Pritchett, Billy Tucker, and Eddie Tucker invited me to go to a big Fifth Sunday meeting back in the summer of 1922. The fact that I didn't go has caused me much worry in my declining years.

Fifth Sunday meetings back in those days were something. People carried wagon loads of food and spent the day. They sang and worshipped and talked and ate, after which they talked some more. They hadn't heard about Communism then, so I suppose they just talked about the people who weren't there.

Well, everybody was in the church when the above trio got to the meeting. They began to scout around among the various boxes and baskets of food and finally they came upon the biggest, brownest, and juiciest looking chicken pie they had ever laid their eyes on. Brother, it was one out of the book. Will power is a fine thing, but chicken pie is a fine thing, too. Will power lost out and the chicken pie was carried under the hill and et.

Twenty-eight years passed and a few days ago Miss Jodie Jackson was having lunch at Mrs. Eddie Tucker's hotel. Miss Jodie had just returned from a meeting at Midway and during the meal, she began to go into reminiscences of old days at the church. She recalled how, twenty-eight years ago, somebody had stolen her chicken pie. Eddie gulped and swallowed and choked. He turned to deep purple from choking and then changed to a scarlet red from embarrassment. He knew then, for the first time, the owner of the pilfered pie. Then he turned white from fear. Other people at the table said he changed color so rapidly that his face resembled a moving picture of Belingrath Gardens in technicolor.

Finally, after a lot of stammering and beating about the bush, he confessed his sin. He feels a lot better about it, and is going to repay Miss Jodie with a chicken pie, based on 8 per cent interest compounded every Fifth Sunday.

This story proves that stealing a single chicken pie doesn't make a delinquent. All three of the criminals have done well and are respected citizens in their communities. Douglas is a successful attorney and Billy holds an important post with the Missouri Highway Department. Eddie Tucker married a very fine lady.

The story also proves that a fine looking chicken pie shouldn't be left lying around in the open. Those same boys, now that they are grown, would not think of stealing a chicken pie. Unless, maybe, they went to a Fifth Sunday meeting at Midway Church and happened to find everybody in church.

# Index